FROST

and the

BOOK OF NATURE

FROST

and the
BOOK OF NATURE

George F. Bagby

The University of Tennessee Press • Knoxville

Grateful acknowledgment is made to Henry Holt and Company, Inc., for permission to quote from *The Poetry of Robert Frost,* edited by Edward Connery Lanthem. Copyright © 1916, 1923, 1928, 1930, 1934, 1939, 1969 by Holt, Rinehart and Winston. Copyright © 1936, 1942, 1944, 1951, 1956, 1958, 1962 by Robert Frost. Copyright © 1964, 1967, 1970 by Lesley Frost Ballantine. Reprinted by permission of Henry Holt and Company, Inc.

Selection from *Collected Poems* by Wallace Stevens copyright © 1954 by Wallace Stevens. Reprinted by permission of Alfred A. Knopf, Inc.

Selection from *Opus Posthumous* by Wallace Stevens copyright © 1957 by Elsie Stevens and Holly Stevens. Reprinted by permission of Alfred A. Knopf, Inc.

Selections from Thoreau, Henry David; *Walden,* edited by J. Lyndon Shanley. Copyright © 1971 by Princeton University Press. Reprinted by permission of Princeton University Press.

Grateful acknowledgment is made to the editors of *Twentieth Century Literature* for permission to reprint "The Promethean Frost," most of which appeared in the Spring 1992 issue of that journal.

Grateful acknowledgment is made to Duke University Press and the editors of *American Literature* to reprint "Frost's Synecdochism," which originally appeared in *American Literature* in October 1986 and was republished in *On Frost: The Best from "American Literature,"* edited by Edwin H. Cady and Louis J. Budd, copyright © 1991 by Duke University Press.

LIBRARY OF CONGRESS CATALOGING IN PUBLICATION DATA

Bagby, George F., 1943 –
    Frost and the book of nature / George F. Bagby.
        p.   cm.
    Includes bibliographical references and index.
    ISBN 0-87049-805-3 (cloth: alk. paper)
    1. Frost, Robert, 1874–1963 — Criticism and interpretation.
2. Frost, Robert, 1874–1963 — Knowledge — Natural history.
3. Modernism (Literature) — United States. 4. Natural history in literature.
5. Nature in literature. 6. Metaphor. I. Title.
PS3511.R94Z547   1993
811'.52—dc20   93-18330
                                                                                    CIP

For
Mildred I. Bagby
and
Susan H. Bagby

Contents

Preface

The protagonist of Frost's sonnet "Time Out," climbing a central mountain of American nature writing, comes to a central realization:

> The mountain he was climbing had the slant
> As of a book held up before his eyes
> (And was a text albeit done in plant).

The metaphor that lies behind this realization—the metaphor of the natural world as a book or a vegetable text—reflects an imaginative outlook that, as the following chapters seek to demonstrate, is thoroughly characteristic of Frost. The metaphor and the perspective that it suggests shed light on almost every element of Frost's nature lyrics: the intellectual tradition that lies behind them; the epistemology in terms of which they may be understood; the structural principles according to which they are put together.

"Reading the book of nature" is an enterprise that obviously involves a number of epistemological assumptions—about the ultimate intelligibility of the nonhuman world, at least in some respects, on some occasions; about the meaning inherent in physical objects and events: a thing is not merely a thing, but a sign or emblem (or symbol or hieroglyphic). Less obviously, it is an enterprise that, at least for Frost, has direct structural implications. The archetypal pattern in Frost's lyrics—what I have labeled the "emblem poem"—begins with the observation or description of a natural emblem (object, scene, or incident) and then "translates" the emblem's significance or lesson, "reads" the natural text. Or, to put it in terms closer to Frost's own "synecdochist" label: the emblem poem first describes the partial, physical vehicle of the synecdoche that constitutes the poem, and then comments on the larger—spiritual, epistemological, psychological, or ethical—tenor of the figure. Students of the romantic poets will recognize in such emblem poems close cousins of what M. H. Abrams has called the "greater Romantic lyric," the "descriptive-meditative" pattern developed by Coleridge, Wordsworth, and the second generation of romantics.

I have chosen to call such poems emblem poems chiefly because Emerson, who defines so many of the intellectual and imaginative assumptions lying behind Frost's poetry, frequently uses the term *emblem,* and because Frost himself, on at least one occasion, suggests that his poetic approach might be called "Emblemism." Emerson, it is true, calls natural objects symbols at least as often as he calls them emblems; but it has seemed preferable to use the latter term both because Frost sometimes objects to being called a symbolist and because any discussion of symbolism in modern poetry unavoidably entails a multiplicity of possible meanings. The term *emblem poem* may also hint at the seventeenth-century roots of the habit of mind that gives rise to emblem passages and poems in nineteenth- and twentieth-century American nature writing.

To read Frost's poems in terms of the "book of nature" or "emblem-reading" metaphor is of course to come at them from a particular critical angle. In temporal terms, this approach is more vertical than horizontal; it seeks to understand Frost primarily as a modern descendant of a poetic tradition, and only secondarily as one member of a collection of twentieth-century poets. I have favored the vertical or historical approach (though I have also offered occasional suggestions along the horizontal axis, especially in chapter 8) not only, or even chiefly, for its usefulness in pursuing intellectual history or in tracing poetic influence, but for its practical value in understanding the poems. To read Frost in terms of Browne and Milton, of Bryant and Emerson and Thoreau, is worthwhile above all because it helps to "open" the meanings of his nature lyrics—without, I trust, reducing them to mere echoes of an earlier tradition. Frost is a modern and modernist poet—but one whose work has its roots in, and one who regularly adapts the imaginative resources of, a particular tradition.

In broad terms of intellectual history, studying Frost's nature lyrics in light of the emblem-reading process helps to show how American romanticism, more than its British progenitor, is shaped by our cultural roots in seventeenth-century habits of thought. More specifically, that approach demonstrates in detail how deeply one central strain of Frost's poetic consciousness is permeated by Emersonian and Thoreauvian assumptions, not only in general intellectual matters but also, with surprising frequency, in many details of language and imagery. Not incidentally, I have also been concerned with the question of how Frost uses the intellectual and poetic resources of the emblem-reading tradition to cope with some of the inescapable difficulties of the life of the mind in the twentieth century.

I have also tried to suggest, in chapters 4 through 7, at least a general correlation between variations of poetic structure and movement in the nature lyrics, on the one hand, and the details of their unfolding vision. In the poems discussed in chapters 4 and 5, certain structural tendencies are associated with an imaginative state in which the mind often finds itself alienated from, even oppressed by, natural fact; it can in most cases only record and perhaps question that situation. Certain other structural tendencies, however, are associated with a more muscular imaginative response to natural fact, as seen in chapters 6 and 7. In the poems examined in chapter 6, the mind rises up to dominate natural fact in a remarkably Blakean or Promethean fashion. Finally, in the poems discussed in chapter 7, Frost arrives at his—and American nature writing's—characteristic balance between imagination and external reality: the mind actively discovers, but now the natural world also actively reveals, meaning. In the balance of this climactic stage of his imaginative seeking, Frost demonstrates not only what Richard Poirier has called "the work of knowing" but also, in Emerson's phrase, "the naturalness of knowing." Fittingly, the lessons discovered in this final group of poems generally involve relationships—not only between the human and the natural, but also, more surprisingly in view of Frost's reputation, between human beings.

Indeed, the Frost who emerges in the poems discussed in chapters 6 and 7 eludes his critical reputation—as a poet who is skeptical, ironic, qualifying, playful, above all defensive—in more than one respect. The Frost who emerges in these poems is in fact a major visionary poet in the tradition of Blake, Wordsworth, Emerson, and Thoreau: a powerful seer who not only pursues but often finds a literal, although secular, revelation in, and with the help of, the natural world. This Frost, and the boldness of some of his natural fictions, are genuinely remarkable; but it is Frost, after all, who is willing to claim that "All revelation has been ours" and to suggest that, in partaking of the sustenance of his vision, we may "Drink and be whole again beyond confusion." In the following chapters I have urged among other things that such lines, though hardly modest, contain a measure of literal truth.

A word, finally, about the whole concept of "nature" as it is used throughout this discussion. Oscar Wilde—as far removed from Frost temperamentally and intellectually as any contemporary is likely to get—asks: "what is Nature? Nature is no great mother who has borne us. She is our creation. It is in our brain that she quickens to life. . . . Art is our spirited protest, our gallant attempt to teach Nature her proper place" (312, 291). Wilde anticipates Derrida's essential point, in his discussion of "nature" and "culture" in Rousseau—that there is no such thing as "nature" outside of or separate from "culture," that culture or "the supplement comes *naturally* to put itself in Nature's place" (149). In other words, without art (Wilde's term) or culture (Derrida's), we cannot even arrive at the idea of "nature." Or, to apply another deconstructionist term, "nature" is thoroughly textualized: particular trees and mountains and streams may exist (without meaning) outside of literary works, but "nature"—that beautiful scenery and potentially meaningful text—exists only in certain traditions of painting and what we call nature writing.

Frost, clearly, is not a "postmodern" writer; yet the sophistication of his thinking about most of the conundrums of modern epistemology may serve him well even from a postmodern perspective. He is well aware, as poems like "The Need of Being Versed in Country Things," "Tree at My Window," and "For Once, Then, Something" make clear, that in some sense the mind actively creates any meaningful reality which it perceives. Following Frost, I have touched on such questions at many points in these chapters; but I don't believe that Wilde's or Derrida's insistence on the artificiality or textuality of "nature" lets the air out of a simpleton's balloon bearing that title. Whatever the literary or extraliterary status of "nature," it remains an active player in Frost's drama, useful to the poet both psychologically and poetically. In terms of Frost's own fictions, "imagination" (a postmodernist might prefer to say "language") struggles to assert itself in the face of "nature," and then, having done so, to win a kind of peace and even kinship with "nature." We need not view either of these terms simplemindedly to believe that that struggle—whether seen in the basically religious terms favored by the nineteenth century, the psychological terms favored by Freudians and others, the linguistic terms favored by Derrida and others, or even the purely utilitarian terms favored by a working dramatist—has its unmistakable uses and benefits.

Acknowledgments

It is a pleasure to be able to thank publicly some of the people who have helped me in making this book. My understanding of Frost owes much to the work of other critics, recognized in notes throughout; my students at Hampden-Sydney College have also contributed to that understanding. I'm grateful to Mid Scanlon and Jane Holland for typing earlier versions of the manuscript; to Gerry Randall of the Hampden-Sydney library for interlibrary loan service above and beyond the call of duty; to the National Endowment for the Humanities for enabling me to participate in a summer seminar for college teachers in 1988, where I drafted the fifth section of chapter 7; and to Hampden-Sydney for summer research grants in 1987, 1988, and 1991, as well as sabbatical leave in the spring of 1991, to work on the manuscript. Special thanks to friends and colleagues who have read and suggested improvements in earlier versions: Marie Borroff, Mary L. Fawcett, Steve Berrien, Harold Bloom, Edgar Dryden, Lowell Frye, and Elizabeth Deis. My greatest debt, finally, is to Susan Hrom Bagby. Without her presence and encouragement over these twenty years and more, this book, like its author's life, would be much less than it is.

CHAPTER 1

"Assorted Characters"

On snow and sand and turf, I see
Where Love has left a printed trace
With straining in the world's embrace. (120)

1.

A characteristic metaphor in "A Lone Striker" suggests several of Frost's basic assumptions about the natural world and its relationship to the human observer. A rather Thoreauvian mill worker feels the impulse to abandon his industrial chores, wander into the woods, and stand on a cliff "among the tops of trees, / Their upper branches round him wreathing, / Their breathing mingled with his breathing." The last line contains the freshness both of biological accuracy (trees produce oxygen, men carbon dioxide) and of metaphor. Nature, by implication, is not merely physical; like humans, it is inspirited. From this assumption comes, among other things, Frost's recurrent animism. Natural presences may be as friendly as the breeze that turns the page of the poet's book "to look / For a poem there used to be on Spring" (342),[1] or the mist and smoke that serve as "guardian wraiths" of a cabin and its pioneer inhabitants (414). Or they may be as threatening as the snowstorm which, like a "beast," roars "with a sort of stifled bark" (9), or the monstrous ocean of "Once by the Pacific." In either case, natural objects tend for Frost to be presences, not merely objects.[2]

The metaphor of "mingled breathing" also suggests a further possibility: that, in favorable circumstances, nature and human being, tree

1

and wanderer, can "con-spire" together. That "conspiracy"—the subject of this study—is designed, as we will see, to enable the human observer to derive meaning from physical objects, scenes, and processes; it functions in a complex but (in its own terms) logical process; and it is rooted, like so many elements of American language and culture, in seventeenth-century England.

The process by which the human observer and nature may conspire to create meaning depends on a number of epistemological assumptions: not only that both partners are inspirited, but that there is an extraordinary, almost mysterious, congruence between certain natural phenomena and certain elements or states of the psyche. A visceral sense of this extraordinary sort of kinship runs deep in American nature writing, of course—not least in two of the nineteenth-century forebears most immediately related to Frost.[3] Emerson, visiting the Jardin des Plantes in July 1833, reacts with the sensibility that will shape the 1836 *Nature:* "Not a form so grotesque, so savage, nor so beautiful," he writes, "but is an expression of some property inherent in man the observer,—an occult relation between the very scorpions and man. I feel the centipede in me—cayman, carp, eagle, & fox. I am moved by strange sympathies" (Emerson, *Journals* 4: 199–200). Thoreau, likewise, considering "sun and wind and rain, . . . summer and winter," is struck by the "sympathy . . . with our race" which they demonstrate. "Shall I not have intelligence with the earth?" he asks. "Am I not partly leaves and vegetable mould myself?" (*Walden* 138).

This is exactly the sort of attitude which lies behind the otherwise curious drama of a poem like "A Leaf-Treader." The poet spends an entire day not merely raking but almost ferociously "treading on" leaves, not for any utilitarian purpose but in a clearly manic response: "Perhaps I have put forth too much strength and been too fierce from fear." What he fears, what motivates his manic treading, is a "threat" from the leaves themselves: "All summer long I thought I heard them threatening under their breath. / And when they came it seemed with a will to carry me with them to death." The "invitation to grief" which

Frost senses in the fall of leaves results, clearly, from his Emersonian sense of "strange sympathies" or "an occult relation" with the foliage, from being "partly leaves" himself. As he explicitly recognizes, "They spoke to the fugitive in my heart as if it were leaf to leaf."

In "Leaves Compared with Flowers," another characteristic poem that might at first glance seem curious, Frost senses not one but two kinds of "strange sympathies" between people and trees: the blossoms of trees reflect the observer's brighter moods, while their foliage and bark again reflect darker states of mind:

> Leaves and bark, leaves and bark,
> To lean against and hear in the dark.
> Petals I may have once pursued.
> Leaves are all my darker mood.

Here Frost appreciates leaves for the same epistemological reason that Thoreau appreciates owls, whose hooting, he tells us, "is a sound admirably suited to swamps and twilight woods which no day illustrates, suggesting a vast and undeveloped nature which men have not recognized. They represent the stark twilight and unsatisfied thoughts which all have" (*Walden* 125).

Like Thoreau's, Frost's sense of "occult relations" between natural phenomena and human moods derives from a venerable intellectual and imaginative tradition. Particularly in view of his youthful exposure, chiefly through his mother's influence, to Emersonian and Swedenborgian ideas,[4] it is not surprising to find throughout Frost's poetry echoes of the doctrine of "correspondences." That doctrine is an important feature of Renaissance thought, especially in the seventeenth-century poets whom Emerson and Thoreau most admire. Herbert, for instance—in a poem which Emerson quotes near the end of the 1836 *Nature*—celebrates the limitless "symmetry" and "proportions" that link man as microcosm with created universe as macrocosm.[5]

Emerson, searching for an epistemological mechanism to solve the fundamental dilemma of Cartesian dualism—"souls never touch their objects," as he puts it in the powerful opening of "Experience" (*Collected Works* 3: 29)[6]—discovers, by the circuitous route of Sampson Reed and Emanuel Swedenborg, the philosophical doctrine which lies behind a poem like Herbert's. Though he soon passes beyond the details of Swedenborg's cumbersome version of correspondences, the general idea remains a linchpin of Emerson's thought. "The fundamental fact in our metaphysic constitution," he regularly assumes, "is the correspondence of man to the world" (*Complete Works* 7: 300–301). And it is a "metaphysic" fact with immediate epistemological consequences: if indeed the mind can be certain that "nature is its correlative" (*Collected Works* 2: 21), if there is in fact "perfect parallelism between the laws of Nature and the laws of thought" (*Complete Works* 8: 8), from such a grand parallelism may come a cognitive bridge between the soul and its objects, and hence "the naturalness of knowing" (*Journals* 5: 168).

In its full development by Emerson, the doctrine of correspondences provides a particularly apt solution to the basic Cartesian dilemma. On the one hand, it preserves the autonomous status of both spirit and things. Mind need not be reduced to substance in the obvious impoverishment of materialism; matter (at least in Emerson's theory, if not his practice) need not be subsumed to mind in the solipsistic dead end of complete idealism. Mind and matter, subject and object, can coexist without being compressed into a single entity. Yet, at the same time, the theory of correspondences or analogies guarantees that there can be commerce between spirit and substance, since each mirrors the other. Sensory perception, even of the most commonplace objects in nature, can lead to more than sensory truths.

This Emersonian theory provides the unstated philosophical rationale for Thoreau's constant sense of analogies between the natural world and the human perceiver: not just between owls and dark corners of the mind, but between the Concord River and "The current of our reflections" (*Week* 158) or between unmapped continents and unexplored regions of the self (*Walden* 320–21). Wherever he travels, whatever he sees, Thoreau finds that "Our external senses consent with our internal" (*Journals* 6: 353).

So, too, Emerson's doctrine lies behind Frost's continuous visceral sense of correspondences between outer and inner. It is not just leaves that parallel "darker moods"; "A season-ending wind" answers to the "deathward" impulse of the poet's despondency (336); or, in a similar but better-known instance, the "desert places" in a winter landscape are analogous to the poet's own spiritual emptinesses. Not all of the changes of season and weather correspond to such dark moods, of course; natural phenomena provide equally useful correlatives for more positive states, even for love. The same storm wind that frequently images distress still, on other occasions, "seems like the time when, after doubt, / Our love came back amain" (27). In sum, "The weather's alternations, summer and winter," effectively correspond to "love's alternations, joy and grief" (317).[7]

Clearly, one of Frost's favorite metaphors for the correspondence between external and internal circumstances is the similarity between "outer" and "inner weather," the parallelism which he explores in "Tree at My Window." Here the correspondences are so thorough, the man inside the window and the tree outside balanced so symmetrically, that the two realms virtually mirror each other. (That symmetry is reflected in the verse itself, in the almost Augustan balance between lines—"tree, I have seen you taken and tossed," "You have seen me when I was taken and swept"—and chiasmus within lines—"Tree at my window, window tree"—as well as in the *a-b-b-a* rhyme scheme.) The essential kinship between man and tree is underlined not only by their proximity and symmetry, but also by the constant personification of the tree—a "Vague dream-head" with "light tongues"—and by the unusual intimacy of the poem's central trope, the chatty apostrophe to the tree.

The setting of the poem points to Frost's moderate epistemological assumptions: the tree is unmistakably distinct from the poet, seen through a perceptual window, but Frost insists that such a medium is no impermeable barrier between perceiver and perceived:

Tree at my window, window tree,
My sash is lowered when night comes on;
But let there never be curtain drawn
Between you and me.

This companionable object is a "window tree" not only because of its location, but also because of its potential utility: the poet may see something through it. Frost jokes that "Not all your light tongues talking aloud / Could be profound," but the implications of the metaphor itself are serious: to see the tree's leaves as tongues and the sound of their rustling as talking is surely to imply a good deal about the potential intelligibility of the natural world to the human mind.[8] Such intelligibility, in orthodox Emersonian fashion, depends on the essential parallelism between tree and poet:

tree, I have seen you taken and tossed,
And if you have seen me when I slept,
You have seen me when I was taken and swept
And all but lost.

The "if" here is typical of Frost's precision in his claims for the kinship of human and natural: though the poet watches the tree, he is too well versed in country things to yield to the conceit that it watches him with similar concern. But regardless of its solicitude, the tree, "taken and tossed" by the wind, is a precise reflection of the sleeping poet, "taken and swept / And all but lost" in the welter of dream activity.

Of the figurative elements in "Tree at My Window," not the least important is the submerged romantic metaphor that goes back at least as far as Coleridge's "Eolian Harp" (1795): just as the wind moves the tree's leaves, so some kind of mental impulse moves the sleeping poet's mind—the real "dream-head" here—in the nocturnal variety of imagining. If there is any doubt that the poem is about the workings of the imagination, we need only note the introduction in the last stanza of a third force, which is credited with having arranged the symmetry of tree and poet: "Fate" and "her imagination." That fated imagination is both the agency and the ultimate goal of the conspiracy between the natural and the human; imagination sees self and tree as "putting their heads together" and "conspiring" precisely in order to imagine—to make the images that constitute—the world we live in.

2.

This deep-seated sense of correspondences helps to explain why for Frost, as for so many other American nature writers, natural phenomena are almost never purely physical or random; they seem to have been "put there" as signs or messages for the human observer. The "frozen-ground-swell" undermining stones and mortar is taken (by one of the characters in "Mending Wall") to be evidence of "Something" in nature "that doesn't love a wall"; it "makes gaps even two can pass abreast," as if hinting broadly that it favors, not artificial barriers between men, but human fellowship. A single flower, spider, and dead moth are assumed (until the last line of the poem) to have been arranged in a grim tableau by another force, which has "brought" the spider and "steered" the moth to the same flower even in the night— all with the apparent design of teaching the observer about the dark side of nature. A stray Dalmatian who wanders in to the poet's house is taken (tongue in cheek, to be sure) to be a messenger from the dog star, "A symbol," "An intimation" of "A meaning I was supposed to seek" (421). The chirping of a thrush in the woods is "Almost like a call to come in / To the dark and lament" (334).

Again it is Emerson who provides the essential philosophical rationale for such an attitude toward sights and sounds: because they correspond to spiritual truths, such phenomena may serve, in Emerson's most characteristic terms, as symbols or emblems of those truths. As he writes in *Nature,* in the central chapter on "Language," "Nature is the symbol of spirit. . . . Every natural fact is a symbol of some spiritual fact" (*Collected Works* 1: 17,18). It is the poet, of course, who most thoroughly perceives the emblematic meanings of objects and, by using them symbolically, "rides on them as the horses of thought" (*Collected Works* 3: 13). Or, as Thoreau puts it, referring specifically to animals, "They are all beasts of burden, in a sense, made to carry some portion of our thoughts" (*Walden* 225).

In Emerson's theory, natural symbols are often so clear and forceful in their meaning to the human observer that they become at least metaphorically verbal—"a picture-language . . . of beings and duties" (*Collected Works* 4: 66), "a Sanscrit cipher covering the whole religious history of the Universe," "the sublime alphabet" of divine revelation (*Journals* 7: 375; 3: 258), "words of God," "nouns of the intellect, and . . . the grammar of the eternal language" (*Collected Works* 2: 186; *Complete Works* 6: 304).

For Thoreau, such symbols tend to remain only marginally verbal—objects are "runes," "hieroglyphics" (*Week* 251, 159), "unfathomable" "sibylline sentences," "untranslatable aphorisms" (Thoreau, *Journals* 2:392, 1: 380). "The Maker of this earth but patented a leaf," as he suggests characteristically in *Walden* (308); we still need a Champollion to "decipher this hieroglyphic for us, that we may turn over a new leaf at last."[9]

For Frost in our own century natural symbols, not surprisingly, are seldom as forward in conveying their meaning as Emersonian theory might want to make them. Yet they do, on a number of occasions, at least approach the fully human clarity of words. That clarity is suggested in a rudimentary way, for instance, in an unusually Emersonian poem, "Bond and Free," where Frost stresses the earthliness of "Love" (as opposed to the otherworldliness of "Thought"):

On snow and sand and turf, I see
Where Love has left a printed trace
With straining in the world's embrace.

Here Frost seems to be harking back to a displaced version of the (ultimately Augustinian) notion of *vestigia Dei,* the "footprints" or "traces" of God in the created world.[10] The undisplaced metaphor, like correspondences, is a seventeenth-century commonplace; Milton's newly fallen Adam asks, for instance, in something like the archetypal question of the visionary poet: "In yonder nether World where shall I seek / His bright appearances, or footstep trace?" (*PL* 11: 328–29). Frost's version of the idea is distinctly secular but not unassertive: the "printed trace" of Love is readily available in the earth's surface. When he says "printed," Frost is in one sense playing on a familiar translation of *vestigium,* which can be rendered "footprint" as well as "trace." But he is also suggesting another kind of print, of course: the lettering by which Love leaves its message in the natural world.

Exactly the same play on words occurs in a considerably less serious context in "Closed for Good." Tracks in the snow on an abandoned country road become something more than tracks; the road will soon be so deep in snow that even the speaker will "have ceased / To come as a foot printer," leaving it to a mouse or fox to "print there as my proxy." In another similar figure, the poet sees in "A Patch of Old Snow" "a blow-away paper," "speckled with grime as if / Small print overspread it."

A more important instance of this sort of metaphor occurs in "Design," where Frost calls the flower, spider, and moth "Assorted characters of death and blight." "Characters" is doubly metaphorical: it sees these three things not only as living presences, *dramatis personae,* but also as letters in a message that the poet must decipher. Or again, echoing one of Whitman's favorite wordplays, "leaves" in the sense of foliage are also pages in the vegetable text: fossilized remains, which Frost calls "leaves of stone," are "The picture book of the trilobite" (364), an age-old natural encyclopedia.

In itself no one of these instances would be greatly significant, perhaps; but cumulatively, all of these (and other) plays on and metaphors of "print" and "characters" and "leaves" surely project an implicit view of the created world as a kind of text. The trope becomes explicit on two occasions. "My Brother's Keeper," the bookstore owner in *A Masque of Mercy,* insists that, for all the difficulties facing the seer, "there's no lack of light"—

> A light that falls diffused over my shoulder
> And is reflected from the printed page
> And bed of world-flowers . . .

This source of reflected illumination, this "printed page / And bed of world-flowers,"[11] is none other than the secular half of the twin books of revelation upon which Milton and his contemporaries relied. In the words of Sir Thomas Browne, "There are two bookes from whence I collect my Divinity; besides that written one of God, another of his servant Nature, that universall and publik Manuscript, that lies expans'd unto the eyes of all; those that never saw him in the one, have discovered him in the other" (20–21).[12] Francis Quarles, in another typical formulation, likewise argues that the Bible is not the only text of revelation: "Before the knowledge of letters, GOD was knowne by *Hierogliphicks;* And, indeed, what are the Heavens, the Earth, nay every Creature, but *Hierogliphicks* and *Emblemes* of His Glory?" Milton laments his blindness above all because it extinguishes one source of revealed wisdom, "the Book of knowledge fair" constituted by "Nature's works" (*PL* 3: 47–49).

But again, as in the case of correspondences, the crucial metaphor of nature as a text of revelation is transmitted from the seventeenth century to Frost chiefly through Emerson and Thoreau. Emerson, as usual, formulates the idea more systematically: "Nature is language & every new fact that we learn is a new word; but rightly seen, taken all together it is not merely a language but the language put together into a most significant & universal book. I wish to learn the language not that I may know a new set of nouns & verbs but that I may read the great book which is written in that tongue" (*Journals* 4: 95).

The sources of the metaphor are suggested with unusual clarity in the most explicit version of it in Frost's poetry, in that important sonnet "Time Out." The wanderer, as we have seen, pauses and realizes:

> The mountain he was climbing had the slant
> As of a book held up before his eyes
> (And was a text albeit done in plant).
> Dwarf cornel, goldthread, and *Maianthemum,*
> He followingly fingered as he read . . .

Given the fact that this poem was probably written in 1939 (Thompson and Winnick 390n.5), the archaism of the crucial parenthetical line —"(And was a text albeit done in plant)"—amounts almost to a bow to the venerable tradition that descends from the seventeenth century. But the last two quoted lines show clearly how that tradition has been filtered through Frost's nineteenth-century American forebears: both the naturalist's attention to the species of plant involved and the hands-on "fingering" of those plants represent Frost at his most Thoreauvian.

3.

The assumptions which lie behind the metaphor of "Time Out" help to explain one of the defining traits of Frost's poetic activity, the constant effort to "read" the meaning implicit in objects and scenes encountered in the natural world. Brad McLaughlin, the comic hero of "The Star-Splitter," insists that "'The best thing that we're put here for's to see.'" For Frost, as for Emerson, sight is the most important sense because it always, at least potentially, involves reading, and therefore vision.

The effort to "read" natural objects, which, I argue, is central to Frost's nature lyrics, is also dramatized in a number of the narrative poems. The longest and most important section of "West-Running

Brook," for instance, consists of the husband's attempt to read in the brook and its wave a kind of "annunciation" (to use his wife's term) of the life current in the human spirit. The young man and woman in "The Generations of Men" are drawn together by their common efforts to get the meaning, first, of the "old cellar hole" that remains from their ancestral home and then of the "purer oracle" delivered by a nearby brook. The heroine of "Maple" spends most of her life trying to decipher the meaning of her name and of the tree that it stands for; she knows only that her mother wanted her to "'be like a maple tree. / *How* like a maple tree's for us to guess.'"

Despite the profoundly Emersonian presuppositions that motivate these constant efforts to "get the meaning of" hillsides or flowers, brooks or trees, the enterprise is inevitably more problematic, strenuous, and precarious for Frost than for Emerson or Thoreau. Frost dramatizes that fact (among others) in "For Once, Then, Something," one of the best of his allegories about the reading process. Conning one of those sources of water that recur in such allegories (most notably in "Directive"), the poet finds that it is difficult both to perceive any underlying reality in the phenomenal world and to be sure of its meaning if we do catch a glimpse of it.

> *Once,* when trying with chin against a well-curb,
> I discerned, as I thought, beyond the picture,
> Through the picture, a something white, uncertain,
> Something more of the depths—and then I lost it.

Frost's image for his epistemological uncertainty here is remarkably close to a figure that Wordsworth uses in *The Prelude* (4: 256–70) to describe the complications of memory, which at times "cannot part / The shadow from the substance." Frost, however, is not talking about recollection but about perception itself, and his uncertainty involves not only the operations of the mind but external reality. Here the natural world, in fact, actively discourages the poet's efforts to see:

Water came to rebuke the too clear water.
One drop fell from a fern, and lo, a ripple
Shook whatever it was lay there at bottom,
Blurred it, blotted it out.

This source of water is far from oracular; because of its willful refusal to let him see the fundamental whiteness that it covers, Frost can only wonder: "What was that whiteness? / Truth? A pebble of quartz? For once, then, something."

The zeugma of the final line strikes some readers as typical of Frost's own willful refusal to clarify; only a skeptic or worse, presumably, would threaten to equate "truth" with "a pebble of quartz." But the near equation works two ways. Not only does it, at first glance, threaten to trivialize "truth." If we keep in mind the inordinate fondness of American poets for the commonplace, and Emerson's faith that "there is no fact in nature which does not carry the whole sense of nature" (*Collected Works* 3: 10), the equation may also, at second glance, imply the potential transcendental significance of a pebble of quartz: perhaps in that seemingly insignificant whiteness does lie an emblem of truth itself. Thus the overall burden of the poem, like its title, is not wholly skeptical, but problematic.

The sources of such post-Emersonian complications in the reading process are numerous; one of them, in fact, is Frost's very animism. Not surprisingly, the sense that the external world is inhabited by spirit—or spirits—is not always reassuring. As a result, the natural world often has a mysterious, even eerie menace in Frost which is found only rarely in his nineteenth-century predecessors. An urban couple, newly arrived in the country, may view the new moon as a kind of guardian spirit—but may also feel the need to keep an uneasy eye on the woods outside their kitchen window, "'Waiting to steal a step on us whenever / We drop our eyes or turn to other things'" (114). An old man alone in an echoing house may sense—in the demonic equivalent of the symmetry described in "Tree at My Window"—that "All out-of-doors looked darkly in at him" (108). In "Directive" the would-be seer must be prepared to undergo "the serial ordeal" of passing by the work of a glacial giant, "Of being watched from forty cellar holes / As if by eye pairs," and of "the woods' excitement over you." Not only the ocean, in "Once by the Pacific," but the land itself, in "Sand Dunes," may monstrously assault the human; the dunes rise up to try to "bury in solid sand / The men" whom the ocean "could not drown."

This side of Frost's animism certainly adds to the difficulties inherent in the reading process. An even more important complication, however—and a distinctly post-Emersonian one—results from the impact of twentieth-century science; indeed, that impact is more substantial on Frost's work than on that of his more obviously modernist contemporaries—Pound, Eliot, Stevens, Yeats, and even Williams.[13]

As both the poems and the biographical evidence demonstrate, Frost is familiar not only with the general directions taken by contemporary science but also with a remarkable number of specific developments. "A Passing Glimpse," for instance, dramatizes one of the cardinal epistemological notions of modern physics. Trying to fathom the meaning of the natural world, Frost suggests, is like trying to distinguish the species of flower glimpsed from a train speeding by:

> I name all the flowers I am sure they weren't:
> Not fireweed loving where woods have burnt—
>
> Not bluebells gracing a tunnel mouth—
> Not lupine living on sand and drouth.
>
> Was something brushed across my mind
> That no one on earth will ever find?

The intensity of the poet's will to apprehend natural truth is indicated by the Thoreauvian concern with species (even of flowers which the poet is certain he hasn't seen) as well as by the particular varieties listed: like the wished-for vision of natural truth, they all blossom brightly in apparently unpromising ground. But the lesson that Frost draws from this speeding half-sight is genuinely skeptical: "Heaven gives its glimpses only to those / Not in position to look too close." That lesson is an exact application to the realm of reading the vegetable text, or of epistemology generally, of Heisenberg's uncertainty principle from quantum mechanics.

But, for the most part, Frost's view of nature is affected relatively little by physics (or by chemistry). The atomistic, mechanistic, and therefore deadened view of the natural world which the findings of these microsciences might suggest is not Frost's view to any great extent. It is instead the macrosciences—geology, archaeology, and above all astronomy—that consistently fascinate Frost (like Emerson before him) and, by the very breadth of their perspectives, lead him to a distinctly less anthropocentric view of the natural world and its accessibility than he might otherwise have.

For Emerson, characteristically, the discoveries of nineteenth-century geology seldom have a dispiriting effect;[14] for the most part, they expand his perspective on the past in such a way as to confirm his faith in the purposiveness of natural process and the supreme role of human beings in natural history. Geology, he reports enthusiastically, demonstrates the "sublime" fact "that Man who stands in the globe so proud and powerful is no upstart in the creation, but has been prophesied in nature for a thousand thousand ages before he appeared; that from times incalculably remote there has been a progressive preparation for him; an effort, (as physiologists say,) to produce him." When we study geology, like other contemporary sciences, "our views are expanded and our sentiments ennobled" (*Early Lectures* 1: 29, 3: 168–69).

For Frost, by contrast, archaeology and geology, in the course of expanding his view, seldom ennoble his sentiments; instead, by demonstrating the eccentric place of humans in the order of nature, these sciences tend to make time and natural process seem impersonal, indifferent, even chilling. "Our Hold on the Planet," with its conclu-

15

sion that nature is only "a fraction of one percent" more "in favor of man" than opposed to him, is only a marginal exception to the rule; typically, geological time strikes Frost as almost sardonically unconcerned about merely human fates. Methodically rearranging continents, time remains unmoved itself, and the human observer is unlikely to be greatly comforted by its "lack of joy or grief / At such a planetary change of style" (335).

The tone of Frost's quasi-geological poems therefore tends to be that of a grim joke. The poet jokes—defensively, surely—about the insignificance of human life in the face of geological processes like erosion ("In Time of Cloudburst") or mud slides. In "On Taking from the Top to Broaden the Base," the joke is clearly on foolish defiance of natural forces, on a complacently anthropocentric perspective. The poem begins with humans hurling defiance at a mountain which looms over their home, and which they mistakenly judge to be too old to muster another avalanche. But time and the mountain, of course, have the last laugh; "even at the word" of the human taunt, a mud slide comes to bury the people who have so badly underestimated geological forces. It comes, ironically, "in one cold / Unleavened batch"—the kitchen metaphor the final rebuke to the excessively domestic imagination. Having begun by speaking in the voice of the foolish humans, the narrative ends with an inhuman, impersonal, essentially geological perspective—something close to that of the mountain itself: "none was left to prate / Of an old mountain's case." The poem thus enacts just the shift of perspective, from comfortably domestic to vast and impassive, which renders the natural world ominous in so many of Frost's geological poems.

An equivalent shift—spatial rather than temporal—has an equivalent chilling effect in most of the poems involving astronomy. The effects of Frost's lifelong fascination with astronomy, in fact, offer a particularly good illustration of the differences between his imaginative circumstances and Emerson's. Just as pre-Darwinian notions of evolution serve chiefly to reinforce Emerson's ameliorism, so the vast perspective of astronomy largely corroborates his spiritual and moral idealism. Emerson is confident that "the atmosphere was made transparent with this design, to give man, in the heavenly bodies, the perpetual presence of the sublime," "a perpetual admonition of God & superior destiny" (*Collected Works* 1: 8; *Journals* 4: 267).

For Frost, again by contrast, the cosmic perspective serves chiefly to reduce the individual human being to insignificance. "Stars," a very early paradigm of that effect, begins, like "On Taking from the Top to Broaden the Base," with an essentially anthropocentric perspective; it speculates that the countless stars "congregate" above the "tumultuous snow" of earthly life "As if with keenness for our fate." But, within a few short lines, the poem purges that anthropocentric view and recognizes that the stars in truth are clustered "with neither love nor hate." "Marble" both in their lack of feeling and in their lack of "the gift of sight"—two of the definitive human faculties—these stars are a far cry from Emerson's perpetual beacons of the sublime. But such impassivity crops up again and again throughout Frost's astronomical verse. Human experience, with all its ups and downs, strikes no responsive chord in extraterrestrial bodies; we must "look elsewhere than to stars and moon and sun / For the shocks and changes we need to keep us sane" (268).

Eventually, the consequence of expanding his spatial perspective to galactic proportions is not merely to make Frost's sky indifferent. As in the case of the geological poems, impassivity can begin to verge on something more sinister. In "A Loose Mountain," the poet finds astronomical evidence not just for a kind of sullen, unfeeling Prime Mover in the distant reaches of space—"The heartless and enormous Outer Black." He also wonders, with his characteristic brand of dark humor, whether the great "star shower known as Leonid" may not be cosmic punishment aimed at man. Frost is too thoroughly modern to be frightened, like Pascal three centuries earlier, by "le silence éternel de ces espaces infinis"; he insists that "They cannot scare me with their empty spaces / Between stars" (296). But his remarkable familiarity with contemporary astronomy, by making the natural world far less "sublime" and far less involved in human "destiny" than it generally is for Emerson, inevitably lessens the ease with which the natural text may be read.

That final—and crucial—effect comes close to dominating the otherwise hortatory "Take Something Like a Star." For more than half of the poem the speaker protests the abstruseness of this stellar emblem. Though he is willing to allow the star "some obscurity of cloud" because of its great "loftiness," he insists that being "wholly taciturn . . . is not allowed"; he demands a clear lesson from the star.

> Say something to us we can learn
> By heart and when alone repeat.
> Say something! And it says, "I burn."
> But say with what degree of heat.
> Talk Fahrenheit, talk Centigrade.
> Use language we can comprehend.

Again, as in "On Taking from the Top to Broaden the Base," one of the things involved here is a kind of joke about the speaker's excessive anthropomorphism—ironically underlined by the very act of apostrophizing a star. Frost himself, well aware of the profound otherness of celestial bodies, is hardly one to admire the sort of queasy, reductive anthropocentrism that wants a star to "Talk Fahrenheit, talk Centigrade." Yet behind the mockery of such an attitude—which may, after all, be a species of self-mockery—lies a genuine if complicated epistemological nostalgia: natural revelation will not be unimpeded when the human observer and the natural phenomenon are no longer perceived as having a common medium of communication; in our century, it is up to the human observer to translate the star's burning into Fahrenheit or Centigrade.

Knowing a good deal of contemporary science, and recognizing the limitations that it entails for the reading process in his time, Frost nonetheless—in a thoroughly characteristic reaction—accepts and even values those limitations. For one thing, he finds them spiritually appropriate. It is true, as the penultimate stanza of "Sitting by a Bush in Broad Sunlight" tells us, that natural revelation in our time will be un-Mosaic in its reticence. But, with something akin to a seventeenth-century theological perspective, Frost views the distance between human beings and the source of revelation as spiritually and epistemologically functional. "The Infinite's being so wide / Is the reason the Powers provide" natural boundaries, he suggests—one's "hide," one's dwelling, one's nation, all are necessary "defenses" "Between too much and me" (348–49).[15] "My Brother's Keeper" in *A Masque of Mercy* comes close to the conventional theological argument that the source of truth must be "accommodated" to human perception. He suggests, as we have seen, that "there's no lack of light" in the world—but that it must be "diffused" and "reflected from the printed page / And bed of world-flowers so as not to blind me."

> If even the face of man's too bright a light
> To look at long directly (like the sun),
> Then how much more the face of truth must be.
> We were not given eyes or intellect
> For all the light at once the source of light—
> For wisdom that can have no counterwisdom.

The notion of accommodation here, though secular, is stated in terms and images remarkably close to Milton's (*PL* 3: 374–89): light may be available to our eyes only as it is "reflected" from the natural text, but that indirection, designed as it is to spare our limited sight, is a necessary instrument of, rather than a hindrance to, any revelation we may experience.

But Frost, of course, is even more interested in the artistic than in the spiritual uses of perceptual adversity. He describes the modern situation almost melodramatically—"The background in hugeness and confusion shading away from where we stand into black and utter chaos"—in order to make the point: "against the background any small man-made figure of order and concentration. What pleasanter than that this should be so? . . . we like it, we were born to it, born used to it and have practical reasons for wanting it there. To me any little form I assert upon it is velvet" (*Letters* 419; rpt. *Selected Prose* 107).

One of the most important of those practical reasons for relishing modern complication is that it presents opportunities for drama—opportunities which Frost, of course, takes advantage of not only in the narrative poems but in the lyrics. The drama in the nature poems arises in large measure, as we will see, from the fact that, for Frost, the process of reading the natural world regularly involves struggle and uncertainty. Such struggle, and such drama, are particularly clear by contrast with Emerson's poetic practice. Despite his systematic theories of correspondences and of the natural world as a text, Emerson's dominant philosophical idealism generally undermines the dialectics of what we normally call nature poetry. The result has been aptly characterized by Harold Bloom: "The mature Emerson wanted a humanized nature so badly that he made his poems, or the bulk of them anyway, egregious short-cuts to that end" (*Ringers* 222).

For Frost, with his unquestionable "proof of being not unbounded" (331), such shortcuts seldom threaten the lyrics; on the contrary, the drama of imaginative struggle is a constant poetic resource. Frost assumes with Emerson that there are ties, even analogies, between observer and vegetable text. But, because the exact nature and extent of such correspondences are neither constant nor immediately apparent, because Frost cannot conceive of the external world as "only a realized will,—the double of the man" (*Collected Works* 1: 25), the process of deciphering the text is both necessary and functional. It is in that very process, in the drama of its twists and turns, its unforeseen successes and failures, that the modern maker of emblem poems discovers and forges the underlying ties between himself and the natural text.

CHAPTER 2

"Eyes Seeking the Response of Eyes"

"Things must expect to come in front of us
A many times—I don't say just how many—
That varies with the things—before we see them. . . .
Our very life depends on everything's
Recurring till we answer from within." (147)[1]

1.

"The face of truth" is accommodated, and all revelation made possible, not only by the "bed of world-flowers" which indirectly reflects that dazzling light, but also by the remarkable powers of the human eye. That organ alone is capable of "concentrating earth and skies" to human dimensions "So none need be afraid of size." In dramatizing this process in "All Revelation," Frost stresses the active role that the eye and mind must assume. If we are successfully to negotiate the "Cyb'laean avenue" of natural revelation, a human head with its penetrating gaze must assertively "thrust in" to any given natural phenomenon (the sexual metaphor making mind the father of perception, mater-ial nature the mother). The object may turn out not to be "impervious" to understanding; it may responsively "glow" "In answer to the mental thrust." But that active human thrust must initiate the visionary process. It is only human "Eyes seeking the response of eyes"[2] that can "Bring out the stars, bring out the flowers"; only the percipient mind, that is, actively seeking the response of something alive and akin to itself, which can either stir a correspondent reaction in the natural world (like the "glowing" of the geode here) or at least "bring out"—visually pick out or look out for ("exspectare")—stars, flowers, or any other natural object of perception. The repeated verb—"Bring out, bring out"—underlines the creative role of perception. In the context of this poem, at least, "All revelation has been ours" means only secondarily that all revelation has been given us; chiefly it means that all the vision we have has been and must be forged by our own imaginative efforts.

Such an emphasis on imaginative self-reliance obviously adds to the responsibility which the mind must bear for the success or failure of the visionary enterprise. Frost often demonstrates his awareness that contemporary difficulties in understanding nature cannot result solely from the intractability of matter, or from the reluctance of stars to "Talk Fahrenheit, talk Centigrade." The vegetable text itself, presumably, has changed little since the time of Emerson and Thoreau; if its language now seems cryptic, that must be at least partly because the imagination has lost some of its seventeenth- or nineteenth-century literacy. Frost worries about that possibility while trying to "read" a prehistoric artifact in "A Missive Missile." Its message is "So almost clear and yet obscure"; surely some of that obscurity must lie in his own inadequate perception:

How anyone can fail to see
Where perfectly in form and tint
The metaphor, the symbol lies! . . .
Oh, slow uncomprehending me . . .

With his modern stress on the active role which the mind must play in creating nature, and still more in getting any meaning from it, we should not be surprised that Frost devotes a considerable amount of attention to the question of how the human observer can best improve his chances of visionary success. Essentially, Frost suggests, the observer who wants to see more in nature than an inanimate cold world needs to cultivate three interrelated conditions. These preparatory states are scarcely modernist, however; all three are deeply rooted in Thoreau.

The would-be reader of the natural text must first, almost inevitably, isolate himself temporarily from normal contact with other human beings. In most of the best of Frost's lyrics, including those in which revelation is most fully achieved, natural education—even when it involves lessons about social ties—can most profitably be pursued by the individual consciousness isolated against the surrounding landscape. (Here, of course, Frost is following not only Thoreau but the whole predominant tradition of Protestant and romantic writing: all of the English romantics, with the occasional exception of Coleridge, as well as Cooper, Bryant, and Emerson in Frost's native tradition.) Whether it is in poems as early as "My Butterfly" or, to jump forward nearly seventy years, as late as "In Winter in the Woods Alone"; whether the vision achieved is as bright as those in "The Tuft of Flowers" and "The Quest of the Purple-Fringed" or as dark as those in "Design" and "Desert Places," the great majority of Frost's most penetrating insights are won in isolation. (There are, of course, important exceptions to this general tendency. Some important visions are achieved in the presence, and with at least the passive help, of a companion figure, as in "A Boundless Moment" or "Iris by Night," and still others—the most acute case is "Two Look at Two"—in conjunction with the wife figure. But these are comparatively rare instances.)

Frost's worries about the excessively social forces of twentieth-century American life—"We're too unseparate out among each other" (324)—and his recurrent dramatizing of the pursuit of solitude are based on one half of the traditional view of American nature writers. He does not share Cooper's or Bryant's assumption that human society is inherently corrupting; but he does accept the traditional view that it is likely to hamper the imagination's efforts to explore. Separation, on the other hand, is likely to heighten the mind's alertness to natural revelation; the flower nymphs of "In a Vale," for instance, speak to the youth precisely because "they wist, / One so lonely was fain to list." As Thoreau emphasizes, such separateness from other people, and the spiritual alertness that comes with it, prepare the solitary for the discovery of ties that are at least as important as those usually called social. Alone at Walden, Thoreau says, "I experienced sometimes that the most sweet and tender, the most innocent and encouraging society may be found in any natural object" (131). In what is usually called solitude, the individual may rediscover his ties, not only with natural objects, but with the vital source lying behind them. "What do we want most to dwell near to? Not to many men surely, . . . but to the perennial source of our life" (133).

As the process of preparing for visionary experience is acted out again and again in Frost's lyrics, solitude is to be accompanied—and preserved from sterility—by a second state, a kind of imaginative adventurousness. The importance of this condition to Frost's visionary efforts has—not surprisingly, perhaps, in view of the predominant ironist assumptions—been regularly underestimated by his critics.[3] Many readers find a regrettable spiritual reserve, even timidity, in Frost's recurrent pulling back from encounter with the darker profundities of natural experience. A case often cited is the poet's refusal, at "the edge of the woods," to accept the thrush's possible invitation to enter the nocturnal forest:

> I would not come in.
> I meant not even if asked,
> And I hadn't been. (334)

Frost likewise rejects natural "invitations to grief" in "Storm Fear" and "A Leaf-Treader," among others. But the significance of these rejections is two-edged: they reveal not only an obvious reluctance to enter but also (paradoxically) an underlying openness to natural darknesses; only a poet who is at least partly attracted by "invitations" from the threatening side of natural experience has any need of resisting them.

On the other hand, when circumstances are less demonic, Frost is capable of remarkable visionary adventurousness or natural exploration. In fact, as various critics, most notably Richard Poirier (87–111, 135–72), have pointed out, a large number of his poems are built around the pattern of going out from the domestic center into the recesses of the natural world in order to win new insights into the self and its relationships.[4] This pattern is so thoroughly characteristic of Frost, from "Into My Own" through "In Winter in the Woods Alone," that the first line of "The Wood-Pile" is probably as close as any to a paradigm of the opening of a Frost lyric: "Out walking in the frozen swamp one gray day . . ."

Like the pursuit of solitude, Frost's "extravagance" is of course Thoreauvian, rooted in the same impulse that Thoreau feels in his writing as well as in his living: "I fear chiefly lest my expression may not be *extra-vagant* enough, may not wander far enough beyond the narrow limits of my daily experience, so as to be adequate to the truth of which I have been convinced. *Extra vagance!" (Walden* 324).[5] Without that impulse to wander beyond the narrow limits of daily experience and the domestic routine, to encounter new experiences in a realm different from and larger than oneself, home would grow stale and solitude be purposeless if not destructive. In two of his most important poems treating "extra-vagance," Frost stresses that the activity, though designed to fructify the relationship with nature, is uniquely human.

"The Sound of Trees" might almost have been written to explicate a sentence in Emerson's second essay on "Nature": "the trees are imperfect men, and seem to bemoan their imprisonment, rooted in the ground" (*Collected Works* 3: 106). For Frost, too, trees are inferior to human beings because they are incapable of extra-vagance: "They are that that talks of going / But never gets away." Watching them swaying in the wind, the poet—again as in "Tree at My Window"—mirrors the trees in some respects: "My feet tug at the floor / And my head sways to my shoulder." But that fact serves to emphasize the deeper contrast between these trees, with their tameness and fixity, and the poet, who extra-vagantly sides with the clouds (the dream-heads of this poem) in choosing exploration:

> I shall set forth for somewhere,
> I shall make the reckless choice
> Some day when they are in voice
> And tossing so as to scare
> The white clouds over them on.
> I shall have less to say,
> But I shall be gone.

Certainly there is some of Frost's characteristic irony here: the poet, too, "talks of going / But never gets away." But the poem's chief assertion is that something uniquely human—whether poet or the impulse that leads people to prefer "the noise of" trees close to their dwellings—calls us to extra-vagance. Only the imagination (suggested by the submerged Eolian image of the wind blowing through the trees), can convert that "noise" into a meaningful invitation, and thus give the trees "voice"; without imagination, of course, the trees can not even "talk of going."

A similarly Emersonian contrast lies at the center of "Misgiving," where the emblems of natural timidity are leaves. Unlike those in "A Leaf-Treader," with their centrifugal "invitation to grief," these leaves, like Shelleyan impulses which lose their nerve, soon give up their daring flight because of their fear of the unknown:

> All crying, "We will go with you, O Wind!"
> The foliage follow him, leaf and stem;
> But a sleep oppresses them as they go,
> And they end by bidding him stay with them.

These leaves, which "had promised themselves this flight" ever since the spring, now, in the face of flight itself, want only to cling to the domestic "sheltering wall." The almost explicitly Shelleyan "summoning blast" of the wind finally moves them only to "a little reluctant whirl / That drops them no further than where they were." They suffer, in short, a crucial "misgiving"—not only a queasy apprehensiveness about the unknown, but a consequent inability to give themselves up to extra-vagance. Again, by contrast, the poet is determined to make the reckless choice of exploration, regardless of the cost:

> I only hope that when I am free,
> As they are free, to go in quest
> Of the knowledge beyond the bounds of life
> It may not seem better to me to rest.

The wind which Frost welcomes is again the Eolian wind of inspiration; but it may also connote, like Shelley's, death and destruction—as witness the autumnal setting, the "sleep" that "oppresses" the leaves, the "summoning blast," and the thought of "knowledge beyond the bounds of life." Imaginative exploration, as the careers of poets from Shelley through Anne Sexton suggest, potentially involves all of these things; but, at least in this poem, the prospect of physical death is less appalling to Frost than that of the imaginative death that results from excessive clinging to the familiar.

We have not sufficiently appreciated this remarkable side of Frost—an impulse emphasized by the rare rhetorical heightening of phrases like "reckless choice," "summoning blast," and "quest / Of the knowledge beyond the bounds of life." Though the extra-vagant journey remains only prospective in both "The Sound of Trees" and "Misgiving," as it does also in "Into My Own," it is actually made in the recurrent fictions of numerous other lyrics. I cite only a single instance, "An Encounter," which demonstrates the intensity of the impulse to extra-vagance by dramatizing its frustration. When the poet, in his familiar excursion, first becomes entangled in a cedar swamp, he is "sorry I ever left the road I knew," but he soon realizes that in fact he has not left the familiar far enough behind. He encounters, not an untamed natural source of wisdom, but an annoying reminder of "civilized" routine, a telephone pole, even here in the middle of an apparent wilderness. Echoing Thoreau's sardonic view of the telegraph, Frost speaks to this "barkless specter" of a denatured tree: "'You here?' I said. 'Where aren't you nowadays? / And what's the news you carry—if you know?'" The point is double: not only that the "news" transmitted by telephone wires is likely to be trivial ("the Princess Adelaide has the whooping cough"), but that the poet can discover no really fresh insights—no genuine news—until he succeeds in traveling even more extra-vagantly. His final words to the telephone pole almost literally call for such extra-vagance:

"Me? I'm not off for anywhere at all.
Sometimes I wander out of beaten ways
Half looking for the orchid Calypso."

"Calypso" is in fact a rare type of orchid, but it is also, not incidentally, the name of an exotic nymph who keeps voyagers from returning home to "beaten ways."

Like Thoreau, Frost knows that, without constant exploration beyond the road we know, "Our village life would stagnate" (*Walden* 317). He is well acquainted with the most unextra-vagant side of the psyche, the squeamish and fearful kind of attitude toward the wild which he generally takes to be symptomatic of neurosis.[6] This is true of the unhappily married woman in "The Hill Wife" sequence, with her obviously Freudian worries about the "dark pine" outside the couple's bedroom and her fears "in an oft-repeated dream / Of what the tree might do" inside the room (128). It is true in the case of another "prude afraid of nature," the broadly satirized "runaway from nature" in "New Hampshire." Though armed with an ax, he turns and flees from the woods, a partisan of "sheer Matthew Arnoldism" and another victim of "dendrophobia."

> He knew too well for any earthly use
> The line where man leaves off and nature starts,
> And never overstepped it save in dreams.

It is true, finally, of an entire contemporary mentality in "A Brook in the City," where urban builders imprison a stream "Deep in a sewer dungeon" simply because it has shown the fearlessness of that which is natural. The consequences of the city dwellers' own fears are predictable in standard Freudian terms: repression can only lead to a building up of hydraulic pressure, with the consequent poisoning of what was once pure (the once flower-strewn brook now runs "In fetid darkness"). And the townspeople can neither work nor sleep because the unresolved fear which they have repressed is a fear of life itself — "an immortal force."

Against such varieties of fearfulness, squeamishness, excessive fastidiousness, and repression, Frost insists that imaginative health demands the most extra-vagant kind of openness to the nonhuman. "At the same time that we are earnest to explore and learn all things," as Thoreau puts it, "we require that all things be mysterious and unexplorable, that land and sea be infinitely wild, unsurveyed and unfathomed by us because unfathomable" (*Walden* 317–18). If the seeker is to achieve the deepest kind of educational encounter with the natural world, he needs at least on occasion to pursue extra-vagance until he achieves yet a further stage of visionary readiness. Like young Isaac McCaslin in his efforts to see a legendary bear, the explorer needs to relinquish willful control of his progress—however unsettling the prospect may be—and become lost, in order to find himself more truly and more strange. "In our most trivial walks, we are constantly, though unconsciously, steering like pilots by certain well-known beacons and headlands, and if we go beyond our usual course we still carry in our minds the bearing of some neighboring cape; and not till we are completely lost, or turned round,— for a man needs only to be turned round once with his eyes shut in this world to be lost,—do we appreciate the vastness and strangeness of Nature. . . . Not till we are lost, in other words, not till we have lost the world, do we begin to find ourselves, and realize where we are and the infinite extent of our relations" (*Walden* 171).

Frost echoes this idea in "Lost in Heaven." Following the yearning of his "impatient sight," the poet looks up at the stars through a break in the cloud cover. Again the astronomical perspective is disorienting: because he can see few stars, and no identifiable constellations, the poet cannot determine where he is astronomically. But his reaction, far from dismay, is "not ungrateful consternation":

Seeing myself well lost once more, I sighed,
"Where, where in Heaven am I? But don't tell me!
O opening clouds, by opening on me wide.
Let's let my heavenly lostness overwhelm me."

The notion of cooperating with natural forces in order to be "overwhelmed" by and ultimately lost in them, to one's "heavenly" benefit—a notion inspired partly, no doubt, by the New Testament and partly by the very immensity of the American wilderness—is a cardinal one in our whole tradition of nature writing, at least from Cooper to Faulkner and Frost. It lies at the heart of two of Frost's best-known poems, which span almost the entirety of his career. In "Into My Own," the first poem in his first volume, the poet—far from shrinking from the depths of the woods this time—only regrets that those depths are not greater, only wishes that, instead of being "the merest mask of gloom," the old dark trees "stretched away unto the edge of doom." Like Thoreau, Frost wants woods that are "infinitely wild," "mysterious," "unfathomable," precisely so that he can lose himself in them. Had he such "a pitch-dark limitless grove" of trees, as he puts it elsewhere (443),

> I should not be withheld but that some day
> Into their vastness I should steal away,
> Fearless of ever finding open land,
> Or highway where the slow wheel pours the sand.

> I do not see why I should e'er turn back . . .

Frost wants to wander beyond the restraints of domestic society, the measured space of open fields and the measured time associated with well-traveled roads, because he is convinced that by losing himself in the natural vastness he will in a deeper sense find himself. Should his friends, from whom he has almost surreptitiously had to "steal away," dare to follow the poet in their own explorations of the natural depths, "They would not find me changed from him they knew— / Only more sure of all I thought was true." The self is lost or overwhelmed in order to be clarified.

More than thirty years later, in the more allegorical terms and hieratic voice of "Directive," Frost reaffirms the visionary uses of lostness. The poem is Frost's most explicit attempt to describe preparation for vision or revelation as a secular equivalent of traditional religious initiation, but its ideas and language probably owe as much to

Walden as to the New Testament. Drawing on both sources, for instance, it stresses the need for innocence, suggested both by the children's playhouse and by the "broken drinking goblet like the Grail" taken from it. Above all, "Directive" insists that the initiate, if he is to find his destination and his destiny, must first lose himself. The bardic speaker offers himself as an unusual sort of guide for the novice, "a guide . . . / Who only has at heart your getting lost." The goal of the quest here, like the dark woods of "Into My Own," is a realm beyond conventionally measured time and space. The guide is to lead the initiate "Back out of all this now too much for us, / Back in a time made simple by the loss / Of detail." And the physical end of the journey is essentially a nonplace:

> a house that is no more a house
> Upon a farm that is no more a farm
> And in a town that is no more a town. . . .
>   where two village cultures faded
> Into each other. Both of them are lost.
> And if you're lost enough to find yourself
> By now, pull in your ladder road behind you
> And put a sign up CLOSED to all but me.
> Then make yourself at home.

Only after he has thoroughly lost himself by arriving at this nonplace with its nonhouse in a nontime will the spiritual wanderer discover his true home, true self, and true sustenance: "Here are your waters and your watering place. / Drink and be whole again beyond confusion." It seems only appropriate that, after all the earlier emphasis on Thoreauvian isolation, innocence, and lostness as means of finding these "original" waters of vision, the waters themselves should turn out to be Emersonian. Frost's last line distinctly echoes Emerson's "Two Rivers": "So forth and brighter fares my stream,— / Who drink it shall not thirst again" (*Complete Works* 9: 248).[7]

2.

Frost's desire to explore extra-vagantly in nature, and ultimately even to lose himself in it in order to discover himself anew, attests again to his strong sense of the otherness, the substantial external reality, of the creation. In the final analysis, that sense preserves him from the ultimate bane of modern theories of perception, and the greatest possible threat to any theory of natural revelation, the danger of solipsism. Characteristically, however, this is not to say that Frost never worries about or experiences that danger. Any poet who believes that perception depends on the active thrust of the mind, and that all revelation must be substantially the result of our own imaginative efforts, must at least consider the possibility of solipsism. And there are surprising moments in Frost (as I have suggested especially in chapter 6), in which the imagination becomes genuinely Promethean in its domination of natural fact. A lyric like "The Freedom of the Moon"—an almost Stevensian exercise in perspectivism—provides a foretaste of that Promethean mood. The moon, a Coleridgean symbol of the active imagination, illuminates the natural landscape as the poet wills: "I put it shining anywhere I please." As in "All Revelation," the serial verbs stress the imagination's active control, indeed its manipulation, of what it perceives:

> By walking slowly on some evening later
> I've pulled it from a crate of crooked trees,
> And brought it over glossy water, greater,
> And dropped it in, and seen the image wallow,
> The color run, all sorts of wonder follow.

The metaphors in the poem stress the speaker's ownership of imagination and its light: he takes it out of a crate, carries it to a convenient location, and drops it (like a tablet of dye) into the water, just as earlier in the poem he "tries" it in various locations, "As you might try a jewel in your hair." The freedom of the moon is the freedom of the self, owning imagination, to use it in any fashion that satisfies its sense of beauty and order.

If the illuminating mind is thus able, at least occasionally, to shape a "natural" scene so powerfully, a self-conscious poet will inevitably need to be alert to the dangers of subjectivism. It is just those dangers that Frost warns against in several of his most fully developed emblem poems (see chapter 7). One of those typically raises that concern in trying to "read" the markings on a prehistoric artifact:

> The meaning of it is unknown,
> Or else I fear entirely mine,
> All modern, nothing ancient in't,
> Unsatisfying to us each. (328)

Though he often acknowledges the possibility of it, however, Frost never accepts subjectivism as inevitable. In "The Generations of Men," the woman may be doubtful about the source and authority of the "'voices'" that she and her "stranger-cousin" are trying to hear in the brook: "'It's as you throw a picture on a screen: / The meaning of it all is out of you; / The voices give you what you wish to hear.'" But against this prospect, which would preclude any kind of learning from nature, the masculine figure insists that the brook's voices, and their meaning, are wholly autonomous: "'Strangely, it's anything they wish to give.'"

For the poet himself, the truth undoubtedly lies somewhere between these two extremes, one yielding to pure subjectivism, the other denying the imagination any power or freedom. "For Once, Then, Something" raises the possibility that the poet who seeks to read the natural world, and draw sustenance from it, may, like Narcissus, be seeing only the superficial reflection of himself in the phenomenal world:

> Others taunt me with having knelt at well-curbs
> Always wrong to the light, so never seeing
> Deeper down in the well than where the water
> Gives me back in a shining surface picture
> Me myself . . .

33

But the first two words of the poem suggest that the worry is less Frost's than others'—presumably those who are unsympathetic to the whole enterprise of reading the vegetable text. Frost acknowledges the active role which the imagination plays in shaping the reality it perceives: surely there is something attractive in the idea that he sees his reflection "in the summer heaven, godlike, / Looking out of a wreath of fern and cloud puffs"—both exalted and belaureled in his Apollonian creativity. But he also insists that, at least "*Once*," he has succeeded in apprehending a less superficial and subjective reality, "Something more of the depths," "beyond the picture," something (if only a pebble) genuinely other.

The need to avoid the subjectivist extreme is the obvious point of "The Need of Being Versed in Country Things," where human nostalgia for the lost past threatens to misread the phoebes' song as a lament—the imagination almost fails to draw that necessary "line where man leaves off and nature starts." But Frost is also aware that, in seeking to avoid subjectivism, the observer may run the risk of falling into an opposite error which equally impairs his vision—the error of drawing the line so heavily that he fails to see, in the otherness of nature, any kinship or value. That is the overreaction portrayed in "The Most of It."

The protagonist here is not altogether naive. He has learned the lesson of "The Need of Being Versed," and thus refuses to accept a "natural" sound that is in fact strictly human, simply a projection of himself; he is not content with "the mocking echo of his own" voice "From some tree-hidden cliff across the lake."

> Some morning from the boulder-broken beach
> He would cry out on life, that what it wants
> Is not its own love back in copy speech,
> But counter-love, original response.

Surely Frost shares that desire to evoke "counter-love, original response" from the creation. But the melodramatic terms of the description—"He would cry out on life"—like the genesis of the poem,[8] make it clear that Frost's attitude toward this character is largely parodic. The parody is aimed at the character's excessive self-conscious-ness and (despite his intentions) its anthropocentric consequences. Because he hears the echo of his own voice, "He thought he kept the universe alone"—a burden which, whatever others he may bear, never weighs Frost down. This character is like another figure (also satirized) who fears that "No one was looking at his lonely case" in the cosmos, and therefore "hugged himself for all his universe" (396). Similarly wrapped up in himself—ironically, because of the self-consciousness of his very desire to avoid the anthropocentric error of believing that phoebes weep—this protagonist falls into the opposite error, a failure suggested by the poem's original title, "Making the Most of It." Hav-ing called out for an original response, he is too self-conscious to real-ize, and so make the most of, it when it does occur:

> nothing ever came of what he cried
> Unless it was the embodiment that crashed
> In the cliff's talus on the other side,
> And then in the far-distant water splashed,
> But after a time allowed for it to swim,
> Instead of proving human when it neared
> And someone else additional to him,
> As a great buck it powerfully appeared . . .

That is of course a heavily loaded "Unless." Like the boulders that break up the emptiness of the beach earlier in the poem, this "great buck" is a fundamental natural reality, "crashing" his way "power-fully" toward the observer. He certainly represents an "original re-sponse" from the nonhuman, and—especially if we think of the deer in "Two Look at Two"—he is even an "embodiment" of a kind of "counterlove," evidence that earth returns, or at least reflects, man's concern with vitality. But the excessively self-conscious observer on the beach can see him only as a brutal, alien force, who "crumpled" the water, "stumbled through the rocks with horny tread, / And forced the underbrush." It is as if the human, sexually assaulted by

35

the natural, somehow overlooks the significance of the event. Having avoided the pitfall of subjectivism, the character nonetheless fails to make the most of the genuine otherness of the natural world.

As the full drama of his emblem poems demonstrates, Frost's own ultimate goal is to avoid any of these extremes and to achieve a delicate middle ground. Certainly the extremes are a genuine part of Frost's own experience in coming to grips with the external world: at certain moments natural fact threatens to overpower the human spirit (see especially chapter 4), and at certain others the mind threatens to dominate natural fact (see especially chapter 6). But Frost characteristically seeks to strike a balance between such extremes, so that the natural world as imaginatively perceived will be neither a mere echo of the human voice nor a brute fact alien to the mind. The potential for balance—even active cooperation—between natural fact and imagination is suggested by the Eolian metaphor which Frost inherits from Wordsworth and Coleridge and Shelley: the same motion and spirit that rolls through all things may also impel all thinking things, and particularly inspire the mind of the poet. We have seen a submerged form of the metaphor in "Tree at My Window"; it appears explicitly in "To the Thawing Wind." The poet, frozen in imaginative winter and enclosed in the "narrow stall" of potentially solipsistic isolation from nature, invokes the springtime wind to melt that ice and "Turn the poet out of door," where he may creatively, perhaps even extra-vagantly, explore new ground.

A more significant Eolian metaphor is Frost's distinctly modern variation in "The Aim Was Song." The traditional figure of the Eolian harp implies a kind of imaginative passivity; just as the language of "The Most of It" makes the human observer female to the buck, it makes the poet female to the male wind.[9] In this poem, however, Frost "converts" the figure to suggest that natural inspiration and imaginative activity may go hand in hand—may in fact be the same thing. Without active human assistance, nature seems to labor to no point; "Before man came to blow it right / The wind once blew itself untaught," unable to make anything except noise. But man—in a surprising reversal of the traditional pedagogical relationship—can teach nature and make the wind humanly meaningful:

> Man came to tell it what was wrong:
>> It hadn't found the place to blow;
> It blew too hard—the aim was song.
>> And listen—how it ought to go!

> He took a little in his mouth,
>> And held it long enough for north
> To be converted into south,
>> And then by measure blew it forth.

> By measure. It was word and note . . .

The repetition of "by measure," like the "converting" of the wind into something far different from what it first was, suggests a surprisingly Stevensian view of the relationship between imaginative activity and natural fact. We may be reminded of the sea and singer in "The Idea of Order at Key West":

> The song and water were not medleyed sound
> Even if what she sang was what she heard,
> Since what she sang was uttered word by word.

Frost shares with Stevens the insistence that a natural fact or sign "translated" into human music or language is something distinct from nature. But, despite that important similarity, the ultimate implications of "The Aim Was Song" are closer in spirit to Thoreau and the less idealist side of Emerson than to "Order at Key West." Stevens's poem stresses the creative autonomy of the imagination so heavily that it creates a virtual opposition between sea and singer, natural sign and human translator. But Frost's poem, taking a characteristic middle way, views the imagination even at its most active and creative as still a part of a larger reality that also includes the natural. "The aim" of song here is not only man's, but ultimately nature's as well; the song breathed back out by the poet, however distinct from the "untaught" wind, is not antagonistic to it:

> It was word and note,
> The wind the wind had meant to be—
> A little through the lips and throat.
> The aim was song—the wind could see.

The wind has successfully been humanized and, like the poet, can now participate in the definitively human activity of seeing; but the imagination here, as usually in Frost, works less in opposition to nature than in cooperation with it. The active mind does no violence to natural fact in shaping it so that it may be humanly meaningful (and thus pleasing), for such meaning is ultimately the fact's "own"—and its only—meaning: "The wind the wind had meant to be." Frost may not go as far as Thoreau's assertion that "A writer, a man writing, is the scribe of all nature; he is the corn and the grass and the atmosphere writing" (*Journals* 2: 441). But he comes close, at least in this poem, to celebrating with Emerson "the naturalness of knowing" and imagination's role as "nature's finer success in self explication" (*Journals* 7: 507). As Frost puts it in another poem, the chief purpose of Eve's being created is to help shape bird song, to add a human "oversound" to nature's previously meaningless chirping, "Her tone of meaning but without the words" (338). Or, as he puts it in his most pertinent prose statement, speaking of "form and the making of form": "the world . . . not only admits of it, but calls for it. We people are thrust forward out of the suggestions of form in the rolling clouds of nature. In us nature reaches its height in form and through us exceeds itself" (*Letters* 418; rpt. *Selected Prose* 106).

CHAPTER 3

Synecdochism

How anyone can fail to see
Where perfectly in form and tint
The metaphor, the symbol lies!
Why will I not analogize?
(I do too much in some men's eyes.) (327)

1.

If it were simply a metaphor that he uses in trying to make sense of the natural world, the "book of nature" trope would represent an interesting strand of Frost's thought—not only for what it suggests about the ultimate intelligibility of the external world, but also for what it tells us about Frost's roots in a nineteenth-century American version of a seventeenth-century English tradition. But Emerson not only domesticates that metaphorical view of nature; he also insists on "the instant dependence of form upon soul" (*Collected Works* 3: 3)— and, in the combination of those two notions, in effect provides Frost with the basis for a poetics. As this and the four following chapters seek to demonstrate, throughout the nature lyrics, the metaphor of the "vegetable text" helps to shape not only Frost's vision of the relationship with nature, but also the recurrent structures of the poems. The form of the lyrics—the characteristic structure which I have called the emblem poem—depends instantly, in other words, on the soul of the activities which they dramatize—the efforts to read the natural text. The crucial poetic idea that makes possible this "instant dependence of form upon soul," this essential link between structure and vision, is the Emersonian conception of the symbol or emblem—or what Frost more often calls synecdoche.

Especially in the earlier years of his career, Frost occasionally describes himself as a symbolist—and invariably intends the term in an Emersonian sense. In a letter to Louis Untermeyer in 1917, for instance, he objects to the label of "Yankee realist"—in effect, local colorist—which had been applied to him by critics such as Amy Lowell. "I wish for a joke I could do [i.e., describe] myself," he writes, "shifting the trees entirely from the Yankee realist to the Scotch symbolist" (*Letters to Untermeyer* 63; rpt. *Selected Letters* 225). "Scotch symbolist" is meant to suggest the habits of mind which Frost inherited from his mother, particularly his early exposure to Swedenborgian doctrines. As he notes elsewhere, "I was brought up a Swedenborgian. I am not a Swedenborgian now. But there's a good deal of it that's left with me. I am a mystic. I believe in symbols" (Lathem, *Interviews* 49, quoted in Thompson, *The Years of Triumph* 694n.23). That such symbols are to be understood in the Emersonian sense is clear in a late essay, where Frost describes his efforts during half a century to understand Emerson's "Brahma": those efforts, he writes, have made him "a confirmed symbolist" (*Selected Prose* 97).

On one occasion toward the end of his life, Frost is reported by Untermeyer to have disclaimed the symbolist label—no doubt because the word is too likely to be understood in a *symboliste*, rather than Emersonian, sense. Yet even in rejecting the label in its usual twentieth-century sense, Frost implicitly invokes the Emersonian or Thoreauvian brand of symbolism out of which his poetry does rise: "I can't hold with those who think of me as a symbolical poet, especially one who is symbolical prepense. Symbolism is all too likely to clog up and kill a poem—symbolism can be as bad as an embolism. If my poetry has to have a name, I'd prefer to call it Emblemism—it's the visible emblem of things I'm after."[1]

Most characteristically, however, Frost calls himself neither emblemist nor symbolist, but synecdochist. In a letter to Untermeyer written about 1915, he grants: "If I must be classified as a poet, I might be called a Synecdochist, for I prefer the synecdoche in poetry—that figure of speech in which we use a part for the whole" (Untermeyer 180).[2] The same term crops up in several later comments reported by Frost's first biographer,

Elizabeth Shipley Sergeant. In 1931 the poet notes: "I started calling myself a Synecdochist when others called themselves Imagists or Vorticists. Always, always a larger significance. A little thing touches a larger thing." A few years earlier, he reports: "I believe in what the Greeks called synecdoche: the philosophy of the part for the whole; skirting the hem of the goddess. All that an artist needs is samples" (*Robert Frost* 325, "Good Greek" 148).[3] As the very language of these statements suggests, when Frost calls himself a synecdochist, he is referring to a great deal more than simply a preferred variety of figurative speech.

Emerson normally uses the term *symbol* to describe both a poetic and an epistemological theory. Not only is verbal expression symbolic ("Words are signs of natural facts"), but the creation itself is symbolic ("natural facts are symbols of . . . spiritual facts" [*Collected Works* 1: 17]). As Charles Feidelson has noted—and here we touch on an idea central to Frost's thinking about poetry and nature—*symbol* is not the only term which Emerson uses in both a stylistic and an ontological sense. "When he declares that 'there is no fact in nature which does not carry the whole sense of nature' [*Collected Works* 3: 10], that 'the entire system of things gets represented in every particle' [*Collected Works* 2: 57], he is defining synecdoche" (147).[4]

Frost, though always less radical than Emerson in his formulations, likewise uses "symbol" and "synecdoche" in more than a linguistic sense. On the one hand, synecdoche is of course a kind of trope—"that figure of speech in which we use a part for the whole." On the other hand, when Frost describes himself as "a mystic" and a believer in symbols in a Swedenborgian context, he is surely suggesting that things themselves may be seen as symbolic or synecdochic. So with the claim that he believes in "the philosophy"—presumably a carefully chosen word—"of the part for the whole; skirting the hem of the goddess." When we look at the poems themselves, we find that they are shaped by Frost's "synecdochism" at every level, from style to structure to the very manner of perceiving reality which is incorporated in them.

Local rhetorical manifestations frequently involve a kind of sophisticated punning in which a term refers simultaneously to a literal object and to a broader, figurative reality—the sort of thing we have already seen in Frost's use of "character" or "print." A model example occurs in "After Apple-Picking," where "Essence of winter sleep is on the night, / The scent of apples." "Essence," clearly, is not only the literal perfume, "The scent of apples"; for Frost, that scent physically embodies, or synecdochically represents, the essential qualities of winter sleep, of the postharvest state of mind with which the poem is concerned. The same kind of synecdochic pun is central to "Fragmentary Blue." In the first stanza of the poem, "heaven" is used literally, meaning simply "sky": "heaven presents in sheets the solid hue" of blue. But in the second stanza (indeed in the very next line) the word takes on an expanded, figurative meaning as Frost answers the question why men should cherish that particular color: "Since earth is earth, perhaps, not heaven (as yet)." The play on "heaven" in the literal sense and "heaven" in the figurative sense reflects precisely what the poem is about: the relationship between earthly, "fragmentary blue" and the larger realm of spiritual fulfillment which that blue synecdochically emblems. Comparable double meanings occur in the titles of two of Frost's volumes. A "mountain interval" is both a literal "intervale" (a tract of low, open land between mountains) and a momentary pause between imaginative climbings. (In fact, when urged by a well-meaning friend to spell the word "intervale," Frost insisted on "interval" precisely because of "its double meaning.") And "a further range" is not just a more distant group of mountains but also the further range of experience that they image out.[5]

Plays like these on "essence," "heaven," "interval," and "range" are not superficial rhetorical games; they all suggest that the physical part manifests a more than physical whole. Such synecdochism may be most obvious when it shows itself in verbal plays, but it pervades Frost's lyrics even when it does not rise to the surface of the language. The very materials of the poetry—the natural objects, events, and situations, and the way they are managed—are synecdochic.[6] Undoubtedly this is above all what Frost has in mind when he describes himself as a synecdochist: "All that an artist needs is samples"; "Always, always a larger significance. A little thing touches a larger thing." We see the phenomenon clearly in a well-known poem like "Stopping by Woods on a Snowy Evening." The poem, with its familiar lines, has been the object of a remarkable amount of critical interpretation, reader after reader seeking to define the numerous levels of meanings embedded in the poem's apparent simplicity. The poem in its entirety contains no surface difficulties, no obscurities of language or syntax, no esoteric allusions, virtually no figurative language, no "symbolism prepense." Yet every reader senses meaning beyond the obvious and literal—precisely because the very *things* of the poem are synecdochic. Pausing to rest on a dark, cold evening; contemplating a realm which is both beautiful and dark, attractive and eerie; having promises to keep; being in the midst of a journey at the end of which lies sleep— all of these situations and activities are symbolic in the Emersonian sense—synecdochic, to use Frost's preferred term. Every one of them is a concrete, partial embodiment of a whole realm of experience; that is why the poem invites us to read it not only as a simple narrative but also as a meditation on such matters as duty, will, and temptation.

The method of "Stopping by Woods" is typical of a number of Frost's more reticent lyrics, in which the concrete vehicle of the synecdoche is stated, the abstract tenor only hinted at. The technique of "After Apple-Picking" is similar: the poem talks explicitly about a specific harvest, implicitly about aspiration, harvest, and satiety in a much broader sense. Likewise in "Peril of Hope": the written poem is a very spare description of one stage in the budding and blossoming of fruit trees; the poem between the lines, to which the title directs our attention, is about the dangers which may beset fruition in a more general sense.

My chief interest, however, lies neither in the local rhetorical manifestations of Frost's synecdochism nor in the synecdochism of his subject matter, but in the synecdochism of his poetic structures. Frost's well-known dictum on "The Figure a Poem Makes" tells us: "It begins in delight and ends in wisdom. . . . It begins in delight, it inclines to the impulse, it assumes direction with the first line laid down, it runs a course of lucky events, and ends in a clarification of life—not necessarily a great clarification, such as sects and cults are founded on, but in a momentary stay against confusion. It has denouement. It has an outcome that though unforeseen was predestined from the first image of the original mood—and indeed from the very mood" (*Selected Prose* 18). Frost is talking here chiefly about the process of composing, how a poem gets written; but the pronouncement describes equally well the imaginative structure of a typical Frost lyric.

If (to put the matter in seventeenth-century terms) a natural object or scene is a kind of text, then the observer's response to that scene is likely, in the manner of a sermon, to fall into two parts: reading of the text and commentary on its lesson. This epistemological movement may also be stated in rhetorical terms as the movement from description of the natural vehicle to commentary on its implications (the tenor); or, in more specifically Frostian terms, from description of the natural part to commentary on the more than natural whole. Thus, "the figure"—a word that may mean both underlying metaphor or synecdoche and underlying structure—which "a poem makes" begins in the "delight" of observing a particular object or scene or action; it ends in the "wisdom" of grasping the larger human insight of which the observed phenomenon is the partial embodiment. It "assumes direction from the first line laid down" because the observed vehicle of any natural synecdoche inherently hints at the general tenor; that is why its "outcome," the lesson read in the natural emblem, "though unforeseen was predestined from the first image." And because the observed fact with which the poem begins reflects in miniature "the whole sense of nature," as Emerson puts it, the unfolding of the larger significance of that fact will almost inevitably offer a "clarification," a "denouement," a "momentary stay against confusion." (This fact in turn helps to explain why many of Frost's lyrics close, as many of Emerson's do also, epigrammatically or aphoristically. As Frost adds, just after the passage cited above: the poem "finds its own name as it goes and discovers the best waiting for it in some final phrase at once wise and sad.")

In short, the Emersonian conception of symbolism—what Frost prefers to call emblemism or synecdochism—provides both an episte- mological rationale for the process of reading the "text albeit done in plant" and a formal means of dramatizing that process. The structures of most of Frost's nature lyrics are related in one way or another to the fundamental synecdochic design of what I call the emblem poem: they begin with the observation of a specific natural fact or emblem and lead through one process or another to a recognition of the larger imaginative reality implicit in it. The two underlying parts of such an em- blem poem, description and commentary, or vehicle and tenor, reflect what Emerson calls the "natural fact" and its corresponding "spiritual fact." The movement from one to the other not only reflects but, in many cases, acts out the process of "reading" the natural emblem.

Throughout his nature lyrics, Frost explores an enormous number of variations on this basic structural outline. The natural phenomenon or vehicle in which the poem originates may be generalized, habitual, or typi- cal (as in "Nothing Gold Can Stay"); or it may be a specific, particular- ized object or scene or event, as in "Design." The movement from natu- ral text to its lesson may be direct, as it is in both of these poems; may follow a more circuitous process of meditation, as the poet explicitly speculates on the meaning, for instance, of "Birches"; or, while the poem's fiction again acts out the movement "from sight to insight" (as Frost puts it elsewhere),[7] may involve, not an internal meditation on the natural emblem, but a direct discovery or revelation of its meaning, as for instance in "The Tuft of Flowers." Whatever the variations—and they are of considerable interest in themselves—the basic synecdochic structure remains a formal constant in most of Frost's nature lyrics.

2.

Emerson provides Frost with the basic epistemological and linguistic ra- tionale for writing emblem poems but not with many practical models. Ultimately because of his philosophical idealism, Emerson in his own po- ems tends to use natural objects more nearly allegorically than emblem-

atically; indeed, I find in all his poems only three which might meaning-
fully be called emblem poems: "The Humble-Bee," "The Rhodora," and
"The Titmouse." (Significantly, two of these three poems find echoes in
Frost's own verse—"The Rhodora" in "A Young Birch," "The Titmouse" in "Dust of Snow" and numerous other winter lyrics.)

A more useful structural model for Frost is Bryant. With his substantial number of genuine emblem poems—"The Yellow Violet,"
"The Rivulet," "March," "To a Waterfowl," "Sonnet—October,"
"To the Fringed Gentian," and "Hymn to the North Star," to name
only a few of the clearest cases—Bryant, despite the considerable differences in many of their philosophical attitudes, helps to shape a remarkable number of Frost's lyrics.

Yet, as Frost himself is aware, the specific images and sensuous
textures of his emblem poems (as of many of his ideas about how best
to prepare for natural revelation) more frequently echo Thoreau than
either Emerson or Bryant. (Frost writes of *Walden* that it "surpasses
everything we have had in America," and acknowledges that parts of
it "must have had a good deal to do with the making of me" [*Selected
Letters* 278, 182].) The reasons for this influence are not only tem-
peramental but structural: again and again in *Walden*, as in Thoreau's
other writings, we encounter prose versions of Frost's preferred synecdochic structure—what might be called "emblem passages," in which
Thoreau observes seemingly trivial objects or events, ponders their significance, and draws anything but trivial lessons from them. This is true,
for instance, in the opening chapter of *Walden*, in Thoreau's springtime
description of a striped snake which is able to survive for some time
submerged beneath the water of a pond—"perhaps because he had
not yet fairly come out of the torpid state. It appeared to me that for
a like reason men remain in their present low and primitive condition;
but if they should feel the influence of the spring of springs arousing
them, they would of necessity rise to a higher and more ethereal life"
(41). This is not the most predictable lesson which might be drawn
from a snake under water. Still more importantly, in the last and greatest emblem passage in *Walden*, Thoreau chooses what would seem to

be a particularly unpromising emblem: "a strong and beautiful bug which came out of the dry leaf of an old table of apple-tree wood, which had stood in a farmer's kitchen for sixty years." Considering that emblem with his naturalist's concern for details—the dating of the egg deposit by counting annual rings in the wood, the possible causes of the egg's hatching after many years—Thoreau concludes triumphantly by reading in that homely event what is for him the paramount lesson of human experience: "faith in a resurrection and immortality" of the human soul (333).

As surely as Emerson's theories of symbolism, such passages in *Walden* lie behind a poem like "Nothing Gold Can Stay," which might well serve as the structural prototype of Frost's nature lyrics:

> Nature's first green is gold,
> Her hardest hue to hold.
> Her early leaf's a flower;
> But only so an hour.
> Then leaf subsides to leaf.
> So Eden sank to grief,
> So dawn goes down to day.
> Nothing gold can stay.

The basic structure here, though extraordinarily compressed,[8] is typically synecdochic. In the first five lines Frost describes the concrete vehicle: the delicate, yellow, flowerlike beginning of a bud, followed by its "subsiding" from that brilliant, unlimited potential to the comparative green dullness, and the inevitable limitations, of the actual leaf. These lines begin the poem with some of the "delight" which comes from a Thoreauvian familiarity with the minutiae of natural process; but—were we dealing with anyone except an American nature writer—they would scarcely prepare us for the next line. Suddenly, in a startling expansion from physical part to more than physical whole—the synecdochic analogy made explicit in the "So"—Frost moves from a detail of vegetable growth to the history of human failure and suffering. We need to remind ourselves how remarkable it is to see so slight a vehicle expanded into such a weighty tenor. And yet such an expansion is, as we have just seen, not without precedent in American nature writing: Thoreau provides a clear structural and epistemological model when he reads, in the story of the "beautiful bug" in the apple-wood table, proof of the immortality of the soul. And Emerson, in a statement that serves very well to gloss "Nothing Gold Can Stay," speaks of "the catholic character which makes every leaf an exponent of the world" (*Collected Works* 1:125). In short, the seemingly incongruous terms of Frost's analogy have their own kind of logic; the trope reflects Frost's characteristic way of perceiving reality, an angle of vision which is rooted in a tradition of American nature writing.

The seventh line of the poem avoids anticlimax for two reasons: because it adroitly contracts the scope of the analogy from cosmogony back to the realm of Thoreauvian natural fact (a fact which, like that in the first five lines, is also implicitly synecdochic); and because the implied idea is surprising. Here, as in "Spring Pools" and "The Oven Bird," Frost suggests an almost Blakean view of natural process or experience: that it traces an essentially and consistently downward curve from its beginning. Finally, in the closing line, Frost recapitulates his postlapsarian point: "Nothing gold can stay." Again, as he does with "heaven" in "Fragmentary Blue," Frost has used a key word synecdochically. In the first line, "gold" signifies chiefly a color; by the last line, it connotes not merely yellowness but wealth or perfection in numerous senses.

The expansive potential of a poem like "Nothing Gold Can Stay"— of the synecdochic method itself—helps to explain why Frost, unlike many of his modern contemporaries, is essentially content to write a large number of short lyrics, rather than aspire to the great long poem of which *Paterson* is an exemplum. One might hypothesize a priori that Frost's production of numerous short poems suggests an atomistic view of reality. But Frost does not, in fact, accept such a view; even as brief a lyric as "Nothing Gold Can Stay" projects a fairly comprehensive vision of experience. It is rather his synecdochic view of reality, and his synecdochic structural tendencies, which make Frost attempt to capture part of an overarching truth in each of a large series of short poems. If, as Emerson assures us, "Every moment instructs, and every object: for wisdom is infused into every form" (*Collected Works* 3:113–14), then even the most "trivial" natural phenomenon, properly perceived, can serve as the springboard for a significant poem. On at least one occasion, in fact, Emerson comes close to advancing an explicit rationale for the poetic practice of relying on synecdochic miniatures as a valid means of expressing larger truths: always, he says, "does the World reproduce itself in miniature in every event that transpires, so that all the laws of nature may be read in the smallest fact. So that the truth speaker may dismiss all solicitude as to the proportion & congruency of the aggregate of his thoughts, so long as he is a faithful reporter of particular impressions" (*Journals* 7: 302–3; cf. *Collected Works* 2: 201).

3.

In the four following chapters, I examine in some detail the structure and vision of several dozen of Frost's nature lyrics, all of them variations of the emblem poem epitomized by "Nothing Gold Can Stay." I have divided these nature lyrics into four groups according to certain structural tendencies involving the particularity with which they describe the natural emblem and the means by which they move from that description to a reading of the emblem's significance. Specifically:

I. "Nothing Gold Can Stay" is a good example of a number of poems which might be labeled "fablelike" emblem poems. This type of poem begins by describing a generalized, typical, or habitual phenomenon in nature and, without acting out a process of discovery, directly expands the synecdoche to conclude with the stated or implied significance to be found in the natural fact. I discuss these poems in the following chapter.

II. "Design" is a representative member of a class of poems, discussed in chapter 5, which might be called "prototypical" emblem poems. This sort of poem is similar in its movement to the fable-like poems: that is, it moves without any intermediate process of exploration or discovery from the observed natural emblem or vehicle to a reading of its significance or tenor. The prototypical emblem poem, however, differs from the fable-like poem in that it originates in the description of a specific, particularized object or scene or event.

III. Poems like "Birches" I have labeled meditative emblem poems and discussed in chapter 6. A poem of this sort differs from fablelike and prototypical emblem poems in that it acts out the process of learning the significance of the natural emblem with which it originates. In the fictions of these meditative poems, the process of comprehending the lesson occurs explicitly in the poet's contemplation; the lesson is learned mediately, through the poet's speculation inspired by the natural sign.

IV. Finally, needing a serviceable term, I have called works like "The Tuft of Flowers" and "The Thatch" "heuristic" emblem poems (from the Greek *heuriskein,* "to discover"). This type of poem begins with a specific sight or sound or incident; like a meditative emblem poem, it acts out the process of discovering the significance of the natural emblem or synecdoche; but it differs from the meditative poems in that such significance is not arrived at through an explicit process of speculation by the human observer, but, in terms of the poem's fiction, is discovered directly in or, in some cases, seems to be revealed directly by, the natural emblem itself.

Clearly, any critic who proposes such a set of categories and labels needs to apply them with a good deal of tact, lest the critical machinery bend and stretch the poems to fit preconceived criteria. All such categories need to be taken with several grains of salt; they are as much practical conveniences (they enable the critic to group poems together and thus discuss a large number of poems in manageable fashion) as substantive realities. Obviously other critics might devise other, equally useful, structural categories for the same poems. These categories, moreover, are by no means wholly discrete. As will become clear, the criteria which I propose simply establish a kind of spectrum on which the poems may be located. Some poems fit the criteria neatly, while others are borderline cases, and might be put in either of two of my proposed groupings. The chart opposite lists specific emblem poems grouped according to the criteria enumerated above.

FROST'S EMBLEM POEMS: A STRUCTURAL GROUPING

FABLELIKE POEMS

"Acceptance"
"The Armful"
"Beech"
"Desert Places"
"In Hardwood Groves"
"In Winter in the Woods Alone"
"Lodged"
"The Middleness of the Road"
"One Step Backward Taken"
"Our Hold on the Planet"
"Nothing Gold Can Stay"
"November"
"Sitting by a Bush in
  Broad Sunlight"
"Spring Pools"
"The Strong Are Saying
  Nothing"

PROTOTYPICAL POEMS

"Bereft"
"The Cocoon"
"Design"
"Hyla Brook"
"A Loose Mountain"
"Moon Compasses"
"Mowing"
"On a Bird Singing in Its Sleep"
"Once by the Pacific"
"The Onset"
"Our Singing Strength"
"The Oven Bird"
"Pod of the Milkweed"
"Something for Hope"
"Unharvested"
"A Winter Eden"
"A Young Birch"

MEDITATIVE POEMS

"Birches"
"Bond and Free"
"A Boundless Moment"
"The Census-Taker"
"On a Tree Fallen Across the
  Road"
"On the Heart's Beginning
  to Cloud the Mind"
"Sand Dunes"
"A Soldier"
"There Are Roughly Zones"
"To a Moth Seen in Winter"
"West-Running Brook"
"Wild Grapes"

HEURISTIC POEMS

"Afterflakes"
"A Considerable Speck"
"Dust of Snow"
"Iris by Night"
"I Will Sing You One-o"
"Looking for a Sunset Bird
  in Winter"
"A Missive Missile"
"My Butterfly"
"The Need of Being Versed in
  Country Things"
"The Quest of the Purple-Fringed"
"Take Something Like a Star"
"The Thatch"
"The Tuft of Flowers"
"Two Look at Two"
"An Unstamped Letter in Our
  Rural Letter Box"
"The Wood-Pile"

I have ventured into the sticky area of structural categories in hopes of accomplishing several things in the next four chapters: studying in some detail the numerous variations of structure which Frost works on the basic synecdochic pattern exemplified by "Nothing Gold Can Stay"; demonstrating the relationship between these various patterns, particularly certain more complicated forms, and the process of reading natural emblems; considering the question of processiveness in the structure and movement of Frost's lyrics; and, not least importantly, suggesting that the myriad structural variations tend—not without exceptions—to be consistently and understandably linked to the stages of an overall imaginative struggle which they represent, the varying degrees and kinds of success in the poet's effort to make "all revelation" his. To oversimplify, these four structural groupings correspond for the most part to four stages in a great imaginative struggle in the nature lyrics: the wintry moment of those poems treated in chapter 4, in which the imagination threatens to be overwhelmed by a massive and alien natural world, and finds itself with no effective resources with which to manage that world; the expanded perspective of the poems treated in chapter 5, which begin to see natural process as more favorable to human beings and the commonplace as worthy of deep appreciation; the Promethean stirring of the imagination in a number of poems (chapter 6) in which mind rises up, casts off, and momentarily dominates natural fact; and the final reconciliation of the imagination and its objects in chapter 7. I have attempted, in other words, to give some meaning in terms of practical criticism to Emerson's insistence on "the instant dependence of form upon soul," to suggest how the structure and movement of Frost's nature lyrics are linked to their soul or vision.

CHAPTER 4

"Too Absent-Spirited to Count"

In winter in the woods alone
Against the trees I go. (470)

1.

In Frost, there is a stage of the imagination's life in which the natural world seems huge, overwhelming, and mindless in the worst sense— not only unsympathetic to all human endeavor, but incapable of registering human concerns. Worse yet, the imagination itself in this stage seems enervated or dispirited, scarcely capable of responding to, much less transforming, the unpromising circumstances in which it finds itself. Some of these poems (e.g., "Desert Places" or "In Winter in the Woods Alone") use winter as a trope to dramatize this stage of imaginative torpor, just as Stevens does in poems like "The Dwarf" and "No Possum, No Sop, No Taters." But, surprisingly enough—in a twist characteristic of Frost's relationship to many conventions—the seasonal cycle in these poems is manifested at least as much in spring as in winter. (Conversely, some of Frost's brighter visions of imaginative assertiveness or of the relationship with the external world are dramatized in winter poems, as I have suggested in chapters 6 and 7.)

Structurally, the poems which I want to consider in this chapter share two characteristics. They describe the natural emblem (the vehicle of the synecdoche) in little detail: the emblem, in other words, is generalized, typical, or habitual—though the degree to which this is true certainly varies, from the very generalized phenomena of "In Hardwood Groves" or "Nothing Gold Can Stay" to the more nearly particularized emblems of "The Strong Are Saying Nothing" or "Acceptance." Secondly, all of these poems are nonprocessive; in terms of their fictions, they move immediately from natural emblem to natural lesson, without dramatizing the discovery of that lesson.

In both of these respects, such poems might well be called fablelike. Frost's few true fables ("Haec Fabula Docet," "A Drumlin Woodchuck," "The Bear"), as well as his poems which are closer to true fables than to emblem poems (works like "The White-Tailed Hornet," "Departmental," "Waspish," "Two Leading Lights," "The Egg and the Machine"), strike me as almost uniformly among his least engaging. One reason for their lack of power may be precisely their generalized description of blind man, woodchuck, bear, ant, or wasp—though the description of the white-tailed hornet is less generic. (It is also true, however, that generalized description is no hindrance to the real power of occasional poems, like "Nothing Gold Can Stay," as we've seen, or "Sand Dunes," as we will see in chapter 6.)

What debilitates Frost's true fables more than their generalized descriptions, I think, is that they are manufactured to illustrate a preconceived point (all too often political). In Frost's emblem poems, however—and this is an essential characteristic of what he calls emblemism or synecdochism—the natural emblem has a life of its own. Unlike a true fable, an emblem poem always begins, or gives the impression of beginning, not with a moral to point, but with a natural object or scene or event to observe and record. The fabulist views the natural world essentially as allegory, while the emblemist or synecdochist sees it as sacrament in Thoreau's sense.[1] Frost himself may best have summarized this essential quality of all of his emblem poems, even those which are closest to fable, as opposed to the essential nature of genuine fable. Speaking of yet another label applied by some of his early critics, he writes: "A realist I may be if by that they mean one who before all else wants the story to sound as if it were told the way it is because it happened that way. Of course the story must release an idea, but that is a matter of touch and emphasis, the almost incredible freedom of the soul enslaved to the hard facts of experience. I hate the story that takes its rise idea-end foremost, as it were in a formula" (*Letters* 179).

2.

In terms of Frost's paradoxical prescription, the vision of the fablelike emblem poems focuses much less on the almost incredible freedom of the soul than on its enslavement to the hard facts of experience. For the most part, nature in these poems, whether manifested in nightfall, the coming of winter, or even the potentially Eolian wind, is indifferent if not hostile to human concerns. Though only two of these poems even approach Frost's astronomical or geological perspective ("Desert Places" and "Our Hold on the Planet," respectively), nature here is still close to the massive, powerful, unmalleable force that dominates those astronomical and geological lyrics.

There is almost surely a link between the dark vision of nature in these poems and their structural tendencies. Generalized description itself may have something to do with the apparent massiveness of nature here. When nature is seen in the aggregate, it may well lack some of the attractiveness and accessibility which it gains in a closer view, with more detailed description; it is in those particular details, in the actual texture of the natural world, that the American nature writer is most likely to find something approachable and "friendly." Moreover, the generalized description in these poems may itself result from the fact that most of the natural phenomena being described are either typical (as in "November" or "Spring Pools") or clearly habitual (as in "Desert Places"). Many of them, particularly those involved with the seasonal cycle, suggest natural process; and, in the imaginative mood represented by these poems, natural process (like human process, for that matter) tends to seem machinelike, unalterable, and hence alien.[2]

In several respects "Lodged" is as basic an emblem poem as one could imagine. Though it does not deal with natural process, it is typical of those fablelike poems which see nature as massive and inimical to individual concerns. It melodramatically personifies the wind and rain as malevolent conspirators that "push" and "pelt" and "smite" the object of the poet's concern, a bed of flowers. These, thoroughly vanquished by the storm (they "actually knelt"), can at most barely survive the onslaught and lie "lodged—though not dead." For Frost, with all his figures of home, the irony of that participle is substantial: the flowers are "lodged" only in the sense of being violently embedded in the mud—quite the opposite of being domiciled or received as guests. The tenor of the poem's synecdoche is minimal: the final line, in minimalist language, simply tells us that the defeated and battered flowers are a fitting synecdoche for the poet's own buffeted condition: "I know how the flowers felt."

Logically—or ironically—enough, it is precisely at the low point in the relationship with nature represented by these fablelike poems that Frost raises the issue of faith in the operations of the natural world most explicitly—or, at least in two poems, in the most orthodox terms. Not surprisingly, such poems achieve at best a precarious kind of faith. "Sitting by a Bush in Broad Sunlight," attempting to read the significance of a ray of sunlight on the poet's hand, offers a distinctly post-Mosaic view of revelation, natural or otherwise. Biologically, it reasons, "All creatures still warmly suspire" from "that one intake of fire" when sunlight first somehow spawned life in the earth's primal broth. So, by analogy, though God "spoke to people by name" on only a single occasion (that of the burning bush), the effect of that original revelation still "persists as our faith." For a synecdochist, at least, theology recapitulates phylogeny. Still, the emphasis in this poem is on the recalcitrance of natural revelation, on "how final a hush" "descended of old on the bush" after the original burning revelation.

Likewise "In Hardwood Groves," despite its almost explicitly Christian hints about the way in which death may lead to further life, emphasizes the suffering and difficulty involved in that process. Here Frost sees the leaf-fall as part of a larger cycle, so that we witness each autumn "The same leaves over and over again!" But this cyclical view of leaf life does not stress the promise of rebirth, despite language reminiscent of the Apostles' Creed:

Before the leaves can mount again
To fill the trees with another shade,
They must go down past things coming up.
They must go down into the dark decayed.

They *must* be pierced by flowers and put
Beneath the feet of dancing flowers.

The references to "being pierced," to "going down into the dark decayed" before being able to "mount again," surely have Christological as well as dendrological implications. But, for all of those hints of rebirth in some larger sense, the poem emphasizes, not the glory of renewal and "things coming up," but the necessity of suffering before such rebirth. Not only is there something demonic about those next year's flowers, "dancing" on the graves of this year's leaves; but the tone of the last two lines—"However it is in some other world / I know that this is the way in ours"—is essentially that of resignation, only a muted version of the conclusion of "In Time of Cloudburst." There, too, cyclicality suggests, not so much renewal, as "endless . . . repetition," which is all too likely to make one "tired and morose / And resentful of man's condition" (286).

It tells us something about the darkness of the vision of the fablelike poems that it is not only autumn poems, like "November" and "In Hardwood Groves," or winter poems, like "Desert Places," in which the natural world seems to threaten human hopes. In this group of poems, even those which deal with the conventionally brighter side of the seasonal cycle, with the return of spring, offer a sobering view of experience. While "In Hardwood Groves," an autumn poem, offers at least the hope of a balance of natural powers, three spring poems, far from fulfilling that hope, effectively dash it.

"The Strong Are Saying Nothing," a synecdochic account of spring farming, offers an all but explicitly agnostic view of final matters. The description of the natural emblem here is both more extensive (fourteen of sixteen lines) and more nearly specific than that in most of the fablelike group. But it insinuates some fairly bleak notes: in the hoe's indifference to the survival of individual plants; in the isolation of the farmers doing the planting (their "lots" are "far apart"); in the figure of one farmer "stumbling after a halting cart" on his "harrowed" plot of land; in the possibility that the early plum blossoms may not come to fruition. Even the wind, which "goes from farm to farm" and might inspirit and unite the farmers and help to pollinate the blossoming plants, fails in its constructive missions: it "carries no cry of what is hoped to be." In its closing two lines, the poem explicitly deduces the meaning of this scene: on the basis of this picture of life, in what would conventionally be its most promising state, the poet can only stress the uncertainty of what lies beyond life: "There may be little or much beyond the grave, / But the strong are saying nothing until they see."

Recurrently in these fablelike poems, in fact, the potentiality of spring seems to be a burden rather than a blessing. "The Strong Are Saying Nothing" worries that the potential may not be realized; "Nothing Gold Can Stay," as we have seen, suggests that even if the potential is realized, actuality will be a diminishment or impoverishment rather than fulfillment; hence spring, like fall in more predictable poems, is associated with the Fall. Even more emphatically in "Spring Pools," the springtime potential seems to be as much destructive as creative. The pools are described in the opening stanza, in an image reminiscent of certain charged moments in Wordsworth, as earthly (and synecdochic) reminders of more than earthly perfection: "though in forests," they "still reflect / The total sky almost without defect." (The chiasmus of the poem's next-to-last line—"These flowery waters and these watery flowers"—also suggests the possibility that natural elements might reflect each other harmoniously.) But these prelapsarian tokens, ironically, are involved in another kind of vernal Fall. The pools "Will like the flowers beside them soon be gone"; the perfect symmetry and stasis pictured in the opening lines will inevitably be broken by the unremitting seasonal cycle. Though the pools will go to give life to the trees, Frost sees that transformation as loss rather than gain, and the new leaves that the water will nourish as "dark foliage" which will "darken nature." The second half of the poem generalizes the scene only implicitly, by calling on the trees to "think twice" before they drink up the spring pools. But this of course is a futile hope—a sentimental wish, the wish of one not sufficiently versed in country things. That fact is especially clear in view of the emphasis in this poem, again, on the mindless or instinctual quality of natural process, which never thinks once, let alone twice. The inexorability of such process is reemphasized by the poem's final line, which notes that the spring pools themselves have been created only at the expense of the "snow that melted only yesterday." Thus it suggests that life inevitably and universally necessitates death—and so, ironically, the spring poem tends toward an even darker view of the same process which is at the center of the autumn poem, "In Hardwood Groves"[3]—and, implicitly, toward a more ironic view of the vast "waste" lamented in "November."

In fact, in these fablelike poems, the most optimistic view of nature may, ironically, lie in the minimalist assertion of "Our Hold on the Planet," another poem (like "Lodged") about rain. This poem grants that, as all of the other fablelike poems remind us, "There is much in nature against us." But it concludes that "nature altogether since time began"—natural fact clearly taking on a kind of massiveness—"must be a little more in favor of man" than opposed to him— "Say a fraction of one percent at the very least." This faith, if it can be called that, seems to be that of the statistician or the actuary—a far cry from what we might expect of a descendant of Thoreau.

3.

As even the minimal synecdoche of "Lodged" suggests ("I know how the flowers felt"), the perception of natural hostility inevitably tells us

less about the natural world than it does about the perceiving imagination. The fundamental problem in these poems, clearly, must result
less from the condition of the natural world than from some insufficiency in the imagination or spirit. The real problem in "Lodged" is
not what the wind and rain do to the flowers but what other forces—
emotional, psychological, or spiritual—do to the poet.

The extent of the human malaise in the fablelike poems begins to
become clear in a remarkably effective little autumn poem called "November." (The number of coming-of-autumn poems in Frost's canon
must be second only to that in Dickinson; but his tend to be dominated not so much by regret or nostalgia for the golden summer as by
a dark fear of what lies ahead.) Again, as in "Lodged," the objects of
concern are battered: the leaves "Get beaten down and pasted / In
one wild day of rain. / We heard 'Tis over' roaring." But the synecdoche here soon expands remarkably, in the manner of "Nothing
Gold Can Stay." In this single day, with its "year of leaves" simply
"wasted," Frost sees an emblem of much vaster sorts of waste. The
mind may "make a boast of storing, / Of saving and of keeping" that
which it treasures, through love or memory or art;[4] but the boast is an
empty one in this poem, made

>   only by ignoring
> The waste of moments sleeping,
> The waste of pleasure weeping,
> By denying and ignoring
> The waste of nations warring.

In view of the fact that "November" was first published in 1938, it is
perhaps not surprising that Frost should see a synecdochic parallel between autumnal loss and "The waste of nations warring." (And in fact
"Our Hold on the Planet," published two years later, insists that nature "Includ[es] human nature, in peace and war.") But Frost expands
that sense of waste even more vehemently to include both grief and

sleep; he sees natural process, political process, emotional process—half of every element of human experience, apparently—as sheer waste; any repetitive or cyclical process, whether natural or emotional or political, involves loss and destruction as surely as it involves springtime or peace or joy or waking. Thus the surprising power of this little poem derives from very characteristic Frostian sources: the enormous expansion from unextraordinary synecdochic vehicle (rain-beaten autumn leaves) to remarkably broad tenor—devastation in a very broad sense; and the haunting rhymes and rhythms of these fifteen short lines. Only two lines here use masculine rhyme, so that the extra unaccented syllable at the end of the other thirteen lines breaks the potentially sing-song rhythm of iambic trimeter; while one of the rhymes recurs three times (keeping, sleeping, weeping) and one recurs, exactly or approximately, in eight of the poem's fifteen lines: glory, migratory, story, roaring, storing, ignoring, ignoring, warring. With such repeated rhymes, the poem imitates the cyclicality which is its subject.

"November" suggests clearly that the underlying darkness or enervation or "waste" in the fablelike poems is internal; outer weather, as always, is an index to inner. No poem makes that point more memorably, perhaps, than "Desert Places."[5] The familiar scene—the poet out wandering as winter and night come on—is described in the melodramatic tone which recurs in the fablelike poems and some of their near cousins (see chapter 5): "Snow falling and night falling fast, oh, fast." The first three stanzas record what appears to be the total winter emptiness promised in "November"; the snow rises in the woods and, like sand dunes, threatens to eradicate activity and particularity; the ground is "almost covered smooth in snow, / But a few weeds and stubble showing last." As in "Sand Dunes," the fundamental threat of the natural assault is to mental activity, as the third stanza makes clear. There the poet foresees a greater desolation, including his own imaginative paralysis, before winter is over: "A blanker whiteness of benighted snow / With no expression, nothing to express."

But for Frost, as "Sand Dunes" makes explicit (see chapter 6), natural assault cannot annihilate imaginative activity if the mind and will resist; the ultimate threat here must be internal ("nearer home"), a failure of the spirit itself. That of course is exactly the danger in these three stanzas; the poet reacts to the threat of the snow not with flight or struggle but with a kind of exhausted indifference; he is "too absent-spirited to count"—either to enumerate the disappearance of particulars around him or to matter.

> They cannot scare me with their empty spaces
> Between stars—on stars where no human race is.
> I have it in me so much nearer home
> To scare myself with my own desert places.

The use of correspondences here is double. In the first three stanzas, Frost uses them in a traditional Emersonian fashion, to suggest that the natural world's desert places are emblematic of his own emptinesses, his own "absent-spiritedness." In the last stanza, in the defiant "They cannot scare me," Frost uses correspondences in a post-Emersonian fashion to make the ultimate claim for the depth of his own imaginative tenebrae—namely, that nature, even when viewed astronomically in the next to last couplet, provides no desert places dark or empty enough to image out those of the spirit. "Absent-spiritedness," in fact, is the ultimate theme of the fablelike poems—just as the triumph of "mind" or "heart" or "spirit" is the central focus of the Promethean poems discussed in chapter 6.

If, in the grip of such absent-spiritedness, the strong are saying nothing, what might the imaginatively strong do? How might they cope with such unpromising circumstances? Even in this darkest, coldest, or lowest stage of the imaginative struggle, there are momentary yearnings for escape or reconciliation—but they are doomed to be frustrated. The natural emblem in "The Middleness of the Road," for instance, seems to offer both sorts of satisfaction. The emblem, a rural road, "at the top of the rise / Seems to come to an end / And take off into the skies," the "universal blue" of which seems to offer the promise of perfect exaltation or "absolute flight." Conversely, "at the distant bend" the road "seems to go into a wood, / The place of standing still," the "local green" of which is an emblem of "absolute . . . rest." Thus the road seems to offer a choice of satisfactions—either the sort of extra-vagance and freedom which the mind feels in the Promethean poems or the sort of rest, of true home, of being genuinely "lodged," which the mind achieves in the heuristic poems. But the central point of the poem, made clear in the synecdochic expansion of the second half, is that "the absolute flight and rest" for which "Fancy" may yearn are both unavailable to the human. The natural world may seem to offer rest in the green of the woods or perfect freedom in the blue of the sky, but the wayfaring human mind can attain neither certainty; it is condemned to middling alternatives that "Are limited" to human ways and "deal" only "with near and far"—relative, not absolute, dimensions. (In more triumphant moods, of course, Frost relishes just such limitation; here the tone is one of disappointment.)

Or again, in "Beech," the possibility of asserting human forms in the face of natural fact—probably the activity which most characteristically delights Frost in other moods—seems less heroic than precarious. The poem begins by describing the corner marker of a property line, but even in locating that marker it manages to suggest the deflection of imaginative yearning by natural fact: "Where my imaginary line / Bends square in woods." The last four lines describing the emblem begin, implicitly, the synecdochic expansion of the significance of the property line, which seems to define—and limit—not only physical ownership but the self as well:

One tree, by being deeply wounded,
Has been impressed as Witness Tree
And made commit to memory
My proof of being not unbounded.

The poem thus recognizes both the separateness of the individual (reminiscent of the isolation of the farmers in "The Strong Are Saying Nothing") and the cost of that separateness: the beech, a kind of natural alter ego, has been doubly "impressed"—both notched and dragooned—and "deeply wounded" in order to express the boundary line of property and selfhood (two kinds of limitation which are also seen as analogous in "Triple Bronze" and "A Drumlin Woodchuck"). The explicit expansion of the synecdoche in the closing lines moves from the ethical plane to the epistemological and ontological. As a plot of property, or as one's selfhood, must be asserted against the indefinite other,

> Thus truth's established and borne out,
> Though circumstanced with dark and doubt—
> Though by a world of doubt surrounded.

There is certainly a positive side to this poem; property, selfhood, truth, each, as Frost would say, is a "small man-made figure of order and concentration" asserted against the "background in hugeness and confusion shading away from where we stand into black and utter chaos." Yet there is something very somber in these lines, too: surrounded by that "world of doubt," the "deeply wounded" beech testifies both to the separateness of the individual and to the precariousness, the madeness—the "middleness"—of truth itself.

And "Beech," like "The Middleness of the Road," represents one of the more heartening impulses in the fablelike poem. Thus "circumstanced"—with "dark and doubt" "standing around" it—the imagination tends for the most part to be simply daunted—"repressed and moody with the weather," as Frost puts it elsewhere (240). When faced with the coming of night (like the coming of autumn) in these poems, the imagination may resort simply to a kind of resignation, which is ironically called "acceptance" in the poem of that name.

In each of the two movements in "Acceptance" from description of natural emblem to implied assessment of its meaning—the more general movement of the first five lines and the more specific reenactment of the last nine—the poem's irony derives from the contrast between excessive human concern in the descriptive portions and natural impassivity in the implicit commentary—a contrast, of course, that also interests Frost in "The Need of Being Versed in Country Things" and "Loneliness" from "The Hill Wife" sequence. The opening description of the sunset, though highly generalized, has a peculiar kind of vividness, again notably melodramatic: "the spent sun," as if defeated by powers of darkness, helplessly "throws up its rays on cloud / And goes down burning," like a battered ship, "into the gulf below." Against this melodramatic description of the sunset Frost juxtaposes the reaction of the natural world—an instinctive impassivity and "acceptance":

> No voice in nature is heard to cry aloud
> At what has happened. Birds, at least, must know
> It is the change to darkness in the sky.

Again in the second movement, the description is heavily charged with concern, chiefly in the personification of a lone bird—"some waif"— almost caught far from its nest when the sun sets. But again that concern is undercut by the reaction of the natural world—ironically expressed in the highly anthropomorphic "thoughts" of that bird:

> "Safe!
> Now let the night be dark for all of me.
> Let the night be too dark for me to see
> Into the future. Let what will be, be."

If the poem is in fact affirming an "acceptance" of natural process and apparent loss, the affirmation is even more muted than that in "Sitting by a Bush in Broad Sunlight" or "Our Hold on the Planet." The bird's "thoughts" represent a kind of acceptance which is both fatalistic and willfully ignorant—the acceptance, in other words, of natural

65

instinct, not of thought at all in any human sense. A bird cannot "think" once any more than trees can "think twice"; to genuine human thought or feeling—"the heart of man"—it is inevitably "treason" "To go with the drift of things" "And bow and accept the end / Of a love or a season" (30) or, by parallel, a day. Moreover, as Reuben Brower reminds us, "The last two lines [of 'Acceptance'] were printed in *West Running Brook* under the heading *Fiat Nox,* as an epigraph to a group of poems that included beside this sonnet 'Once by the Pacific,' 'Bereft,' . . . and 'Acquainted with the Night'" (101)—heavy irony even by Frost's standards.

Again, a link between structure and vision suggests itself. The fablelike emblem poems almost unanimously begin, as we have seen, with unpromising or threatening natural circumstances. The very fact of their nonprocessiveness—the fact that the poem's movement is directly from natural emblem to lesson, with no room allowed for extended meditation on or exploration of the problem—comes close to prohibiting a triumphant imaginative response to those circumstances.[6]

But "acceptance" or resignation, though suggested by the tone of many of these fablelike poems, is not a response that Frost is much given to living with, even in the dark moods of these poems. His most characteristic response to the "doubt and dark" surrounding him in the fablelike poems is suggested by a very late winter lyric, "In Winter in the Woods Alone." In the imaginative mood or stage which these fablelike lyrics represent, no part of the seasonal cycle fulfills the mind's yearnings. Spring is predominantly a moment on the verge of collapse into a withered kind of actuality; summer, with its conventional fruition, seems not to exist at all; autumn and the coming of winter are seen (more expectedly) as threats to life itself. Thus it is appropriate that a winter lyric should come close to summarizing the almost embattled vision of the imaginative situation which dominates this group of poems. There is no melodrama in this poem's view of natural fact; after cutting down a maple, the poet returns home at sunset: "I link a line of shadowy tracks / Across the tinted snow." That chain of footprints surely suggests an underlying bond between woodsman and woods, and the synecdochic expansion of the last lines makes the idea explicit:

> I see for Nature no defeat
> In one tree's overthrow
> Or for myself in my retreat
> For yet another blow.

Unlike the "sheer Matthew Arnoldist" of "New Hampshire," the protagonist of this poem does not draw the line between human and natural so deeply that he quails at the sight of arboreal blood and runs for shelter.

Yet for all that moderation, this remains a poem about the opposition between human effort and natural fact. The ax-bearer, a far cry from Isaac McCaslin relinquished of gun, watch, and compass, "goes against" the trees, "overthrows" and "lays [one] low," and looks forward to another day and "yet another blow." His situation, once again, is essentially one of cold isolation: "In winter in the woods alone," finally "retreating" into himself and cutting short his Thoreauvian extra-vagance. But these are the kinds of circumstances in which the imagination typically finds itself in this group of poems. Recurrently for Frost, when the imagination is operating in something like a fable-making fashion, spiritual adventurousness such as we will see in chapter 6 and fruitful involvement with the natural such as we will see in chapter 7 seem to be beyond its reach. In the wintry stage of the imaginative struggle which these poems reflect, the spirit can only withdraw to its own fundamental center, husbanding its resources for a warmer day.

CHAPTER 5

"What to Make of a Diminished Thing"

Well, something for a snowstorm to have shown
The country's singing strength thus brought together,
That though repressed and moody with the weather
Was nonetheless there ready to be freed
And sing the wild flowers up from root and seed. (240)

1.

Of the four groups into which I have divided Frost's nature lyrics, the prototypical emblem poems are among the most numerous; many of them are among Frost's most representative and best-known poems. A prototypical emblem poem differs from a fablelike poem in one essential: it originates in the observation or description of a particularized object, scene, or event, rather than a generalized or habitual phenomenon. Obviously the distinction between "generalized" and "specific" is relative, not absolute. Some of the more nearly specific descriptions in the poems discussed at the end of the previous chapter—"The Strong Are Saying Nothing," for instance, or "Acceptance"—lie on the borderline of the distinction, as do certain lyrics—"Once by the Pacific" or "A Winter Eden"—which I call prototypical emblem poems. But, on balance, the latter poems, as a group, deal with noticeably less generalized emblems than the fablelike poems as a group. Chiefly because they seem to grow out of more specific situations, the prototypical poems have more of the narrative impact of modern fiction than the comparatively statuary impact of fable. In reading these poems, we seldom if ever have the sense that we are witnessing the allegorical illustration of a preconceived moral—as we might have in reading "Our Hold on the Planet," say. Rather, these poems create the effect of reporting par-

68

ticular, actual scenes or events, and of deriving their final insights, whether stated or implied, from the details of the original incidents.

"Prototypical" suggests itself as a name for these emblem poems for two reasons. First, because the natural sign described in such a poem is more particularized than that in a fablelike poem, it is more thoroughly characteristic of Frost's practice; it evinces Frost's instinctive interest, like so many other American nature writers, in the particularities, the individuality, of a tree or a flower or a scene. Secondly, this kind of poem (like the fablelike) represents, in terms of structure and organization, the simplest and most basic model of an emblem poem: it describes a natural phenomenon in greater or lesser detail, and then directly articulates the lesson or significance implied by that emblem. In this respect it is unlike a meditative or heuristic emblem poem, each of which is processive. The simple bipartite structure of a prototypical emblem poem involves no *movement,* whether contemplative or apocalyptic, from natural emblem to lesson; it simply, statically, juxtaposes the two. The meditative and heuristic emblem poems might be viewed as building on or complicating this "prototypical" structure by adding process—by acting out the movement—between description of the emblem and realization of its meaning.

The prototypical emblem poems give the impression of being simple, basic, or preliminary models for the processive groups in two other ways. First, the quality of the drama in these poems is different from, and probably less striking than, that in the meditative or heuristic emblem poems. The greater particularity of the natural emblems in the present group of poems tends to make them more striking, on the whole, than the fablelike poems; but both of these sets of poems rely on the drama of recognition, when the poet perceives what a natural object signifies, rather than the drama of struggle to uncover that meaning. The kind of imaginative effort or conflict which is central to both meditative and heuristic emblem poems is by definition excluded from a nonprocessive emblem poem. The "prototypical" form may begin with a similar observation and may even conclude with a similar insight, but the drama of the struggle to get from the beginning to the end has essentially been omitted, or has taken place outside the confines of the poem proper.

Secondly, perhaps more surprisingly, when we study these proto-typical emblem poems in detail, we find that their vision of experience is for the most part less heartening, less assertive, less unified than that of the processive emblem poems examined in the next two chapters. Unless this phenomenon is a remarkable coincidence, the very lack of processiveness in the prototypical emblem poems must have some-thing to do with their more limited vision—as I have tried to suggest in some detail at the end of this chapter.

On the other hand, it would surely be an exaggeration to imply that the brighter side of Frost's vision is achieved *only* in processive em-blem poems. As I suggest elsewhere in this chapter, there are some prototypical emblem poems—"Hyla Brook" is a clear case—that are far removed from the fablelike vision of distance or opposition be-tween the human and the natural. The fact that such poems—a few, at least—are nonprocessive may suggest that the very idea of "imagi-native struggle" is not always applicable. If a poem like "Hyla Brook" can read a profoundly affirmative natural lesson without any process of struggle, it may attest to Frost's sense—at least on some occasions—of the ready availability, even the ease, of a kind of natural revelation. Such a poem may be nonprocessive, may lack movement and struggle, not because such struggle is impossible, but because it is unnecessary.

2.

Given my assumption that structure and vision are linked in all the emblem poems, and given the structural similarities between the first two groups of poems, it is not surprising that some of the prototypi-cal emblem poems share the fablelike vision of antagonism between spirit and natural forces. Indeed, two of these poems describe two of the more massive instances of natural assault in Frost's canon. In no other poem, perhaps, does his astronomical perspective lead to a grim-mer view of natural hostility than in "A Loose Mountain," subtitled "Telescopic." The phenomenon which the poem begins by observing is an annual meteor shower, "the star shower known as Leonid."

Frost's first, tentative translation of the meaning of that phenomenon sounds only partly serious, an almost jokingly literal commentary on man's Promethean accomplishments; the meteor shower has been "No doubt directed at our heads as rebels / In having taken artificial light / Against the ancient sovereignty of night." But the almost Miltonic tone of that last line hints at an underlying seriousness; and the second half of the poem reads a genuinely chilling astronomical lesson. The annual meteor shower results when the earth's orbit intersects the orbit of a comet and grains of dust, detached from the comet's tail probably many years earlier, enter the earth's atmosphere. Though such a "star shower" is harmless in itself, Frost says, it "constitutes a hint" about the damage which might be inflicted if the actual comet—the "loose mountain" of the poem's title—were to strike the earth:

> it constitutes a hint
> That the loose mountain lately seen to glint
> In sunlight near us in momentous swing
> Is something in a Balearic[1] sling
> The heartless and enormous Outer Black
> Is still withholding in the Zodiac
> But from irresolution in his back
> About when best to have us in our orbit,
> So we won't simply take it and absorb it.

The last line suggests again, in deadpan language and not without a characteristic touch of admiration, that the cause of such potential destruction is cosmic offense at the Prometheanism of human science—the power of mind itself, which might metaphorically "absorb" a lesson or insight and thus physically enable earth to absorb the impact of the comet. But the poem's stress is less on the power of science than on the astronomical punishment which it may call down on humans; and, in that emphasis, the interstellar forces of the physical universe take on a genuinely monstrous shape—that "heartless and enormous Outer Black" bent on annihilating the human race with the mountainous comet in "his" galactic sling, and only toying with the earth until its position makes his task foolproof.

Of course, this is not Frost's best-known personification of vast natural forces as a monster threatening to assault the human; that occurs in "Once by the Pacific." The ocean and clouds there are not only monstrous; like the "Outer Black," they are malevolent. The waves, pacific in name only, "thought of doing something to the shore / That water never did to land before"; the ultimate darkness that they threaten is an age of "dark intent," inspired by nonhuman "rage." Against this backdrop of huge malevolence, the almost cozy domestic tone of "God's last *Put out the Light*" rings with grim irony—an irony redoubled by the submerged and inverted allusion to the original "Fiat lux." (The same inverted allusion occurs, of course, in the title of the section of *West-Running Brook* in which the poem was first collected: *Fiat Nox.*) Whether or not we accept the details of Norman Holland's psychoanalytic reading of "Once by the Pacific" (Holland speculates that the poem may be a reaction to various fears aroused when a child sees his parents in the sexual act [16–23]), we can surely agree that it must represent a kind of projection of the poet's psychological fears onto the natural world (32). But that fact does not make the ocean in the poem any less threatening, or lessen the importance of the natural world in the economy of Frost's imagination.

Projection or not, it is not surprising that a poet should feel menaced by a comet or the ocean; these represent nature at its most massive, and might well be expected to instill a sense of human fragility. But, in the best known of the dark prototypical poems, Frost confronts nature on a much more local scale—indeed, the poem hinges on the diminutiveness of the natural emblem—and still reads in it one of his most chilling lessons. "Design" is a crucial, and multiply ironic, enactment of and commentary on the whole Emersonian outlook which lies behind Frost's method of making nature lyrics. It continually invokes, and yet simultaneously questions, the entire American literary tradition which authorizes the process of emblem reading. For a basic understanding of the poem one still cannot do better than to read Randall Jarrell's account (88–91); I want merely to add a few remarks about the sonnet as an emblem poem.

Structurally, "Design" is as clear a model of the American emblem poem as we could ask for, its movement "from sight to insight" reflected in the conventional division of the sonnet into octave and sestet and underlined by the typographical separation of the two parts. The encounter with the natural emblem in the octave is essentially Thoreauvian: the poet, evidently, is out wandering alone in nature, and the time is early morning. Many of Frost's darkest insights into the natural order occur at the emblematic moment when night descends; but the impact of the macabre scene in "Design" is made more acute by the bright expectations of what Thoreau calls "the most memorable season of the day, . . . the awakening hour" (*Walden* 89), when the poet encounters these "Assorted characters of death and blight / Mixed ready to begin the morning right." The natural "characters" represent a startling apparent violation of natural order: a wildflower which would normally be blue, a spider which would likely be dark, and a moth which might be almost any color[2] are all the same color—and, with Melvillian irony, that color is the white of purity or innocence. As Jarrell notes, much of the descriptive detail in these lines is intended to heighten the grim contrast between the potential innocence—from the "dimpled" spider to the "dead wings carried like a paper kite"—and the actual horror of the scene.[3]

Such inverted innocence, in such a small, even delicate scene, serves only to render the message that Frost reads in this tableau all the more dismaying: the evident "design of darkness to appall." Even that brief formulation is steeped in irony. As "The Onset" suggests (see below), shaped whiteness—the whiteness of design—may ordinarily be heartening to Frost; it is the indefinite and formless whiteness of snow (as in "Desert Places"), of Melvillian chaos, which usually dismays. Here, however, the shaped whiteness of a small emblem turns out to be not the whiteness of normal design, but of "design of darkness"; its effect is to "appall" the observer, to make him turn pale or white with dread of such dark whiteness.

Were "Design" to end with its thirteenth line, it would be a powerful and ironic but relatively straightforward emblem poem. The final verse, however, threatens to call all in doubt—not just the evident lesson of natural darkness, but the entire epistemological basis of reading the book of

73

nature. That line—"If design govern in a thing so small"—questions the result and method of the rest of the poem, and the presuppositions of emblem reading, in the way Frost regularly questions his inherited assumptions. Neither in the context of this poem nor in the context of Frost's whole canon, however, does the last line deny the omnipresence of design.

This sonnet might almost have been written as a characteristic reaction by Frost to what he would consider the excesses of Emersonian optimism, as for instance this serene assertion: "I am not impressed by solitary marks of designing wisdom; I am thrilled with delight by the choral harmony of the whole. Design! It is all design. It is all beauty" (*Early Lectures* 1: 49).[4] Frost is too Thoreauvian in his familiarity with natural fact, including its dismaying side, to accept so sweeping a concept of design. In the poem's first thirteen lines, he simply extends the logic of the traditional argument from design; as Jarrell puts it, "If a watch, then a watch-maker; if a diabolical machine, then a diabolical mechanic" (89).[5] But the last line—"If design govern in a thing so small"—seems to threaten to undermine not just the previous lines of this sonnet, but Frost's entire "synecdochist" poetics—as well as a long and central tradition of American nature writing. Frost invokes just that tradition in the eleventh and twelfth lines of "Design": "What brought the kindred spider to that height, / Then steered the white moth thither in the night?" The question echoes both Emerson in "The Rhodora" ("The self-same Power that brought me there brought you") and, behind that line, Bryant in "To a Waterfowl" ("He who, from zone to zone, / Guides through the boundless sky thy certain flight . . . , / Will lead my steps aright"). Frost's couplet, in other words, simultaneously rings in and questions the nineteenth-century American poetic tradition of providential design.

The original version of the last line, reported by Thompson (*The Early Years* 582), reads: "Design, design! Do I use the word aright?" That question still lingers in the "If" of the revised final line. If we look at the poem as a whole, clearly design of some sort *does* "govern in a thing so small"—in the masterfully crafted sonnet itself, in its description in the octave which both heightens and ironizes the drama, in its sestet which simultaneously invokes and questions the tradition of the argument from design. The real question which the last line raises is whose design this is—whether that of God or nature or "darkness," on the one hand, or that of the observer, on the other. As William James puts it in *Pragmatism:* "the abstract word 'design' is a blank cartridge. It carries no consequences, does no execution. *What* design, and *what* designer? are the only serious questions" (quoted in Abel 66–67). The implication for Frost, I think, is that the "design of darkness" or of nature or of God *is* the design made by the perceiver, by the poet. Only the human eye can make or find any design in the natural world. Though the narrator's role in the drama is intentionally and ironically minimized, it remains crucial in the two opening words of the poem: "I found" (or in the "curious eye" "Saw" of the draft version). Like all revelation, all design "has been ours."[6]

As the revised version of the last line of "Design" suggests, for a temperament as willful and feisty as Frost's, the occasional sense of the potential hostility and violence of the physical world, such as we see in "A Loose Mountain," "Once by the Pacific," and the first thirteen lines of "Design," is ultimately less appalling than the threat of emptiness or indifference. That fact is made clear not only in the fablelike poem "Desert Places," but also in two prototypical poems from the *Fiat Nox* section of *West-Running Brook*. "Bereft" is a minor coming-of-autumn poem, melodramatic both in its tone and in its lesson—an uncharacteristic sense of having been abandoned, "Word I was in the house alone," "Word I was in my life alone." A more interesting poem, "A Winter Eden," describes winter as a state of emptiness and devitalization—the external equivalent of the state which "Desert Places" sees as both external and internal. The tone of "A Winter Eden," far from the melodramatic whispering of "Bereft," is appropriately dry and deeply ironic. The poem is set in an ironic winter "garden" (in fact "an alder swamp") in which the rabbits ironically "come out to sun and romp." This "garden"

> lifts existence on a plane of snow
> One level higher than the earth below,
> One level nearer heaven overhead,

only in an ironic, literal, reductive sense: it physically elevates "a gaunt . . . beast," paradoxically "luxuriating" in this barren paradise, high enough to "hold his highest feast / On some wild apple-tree's young tender bark." This "highest feast" is of course a mark of the animal's desperation—and may, by girdling the young apple tree, destroy it. Like the lone beast, the "loveless birds," having been ironically elevated to a stage of necessity where "all pairing ends," attempt to sustain themselves on buds, again feeding on the future life of the trees. This irony-filled winter Eden is, in sum, "As near a paradise as it can be / And not melt snow or start a dormant tree"—as nearly Edenic as it can be, that is to say, and still be virtually lifeless. Here there is no need for a divine order to "Put out the light"; the woodpecker's "double knock" signals 2 P.M. and the end of the day. Even the closing couplet, which sees in this winter barrenness an implicit synecdoche for all of life, cannot resist stating the idea with heavy irony, particularly in its final word: "An hour of winter day might seem too short / To make it worth life's while to wake and sport." Such a poem is not far removed from the "absent-spiritedness" of the fablelike group.

3.

It is an interesting fact, however, that, beyond the five lyrics which I have just discussed, the rest of Frost's prototypical emblem poems, with very few exceptions, deal with natural reality in such a way as to find it neither appalling nor empty. When we contrast the vision of the rest of these poems with the antagonism between mind and nature which dominates the fablelike poems, it is impossible not to conclude that the substantial difference in their visions is significantly related to the difference in their descriptive approaches. When natural reality is perceived in the generalized or habitual emblems of the fablelike class—e.g., in "November"—it tends to seem alien and intractable. Perceived in local manifestations and specific details, however, natural fact can be, if not transformed—that operation occurs only in the processive poems of the two remaining groups—at least studied attentively, "followingly fingered," known, to some extent understood. Like so many other American poets (not just those who write of nature), like so many American writers of fiction, like so many American painters, Frost seems to find a sort of reassurance in the very touch of individual grains of experience, in what Richard Wilbur calls "true textures, . . . true / Integuments" ("Objects"). It is those particularities which lift the perceiving mind and nurture "the almost incredible freedom of the soul enslaved to the hard facts of experience."

This is certainly not to say that there are no exceptions, even important exceptions, to the general tendency. Some generalized phenomena reassure (as in "I Will Sing You One-O"); some particularized emblems dismay (as "Design" amply demonstrates). The description of "The Oven Bird" is no less specific and detailed than that of "Hyla Brook"— indeed the two emblems are remarkably similar in many respects; yet the desiccated reality which both synecdochically represent strikes the poet as basically regrettable in one poem, eminently acceptable in the other.

As we have seen, the most extraordinary part of Frost's myth of the seasons is his sometimes negative view of spring. In many poems spring has for him the traditional implications of renewal; yet in several—"Peril of Hope" as well as "Nothing Gold Can Stay" and "Spring Pools"—spring is associated with fall in the religious sense, the moment of realization or incorporation when the golden potential of life lapses into withered actuality. "The Oven Bird" extends that view by seeing summer, not as the full fruition of vernal promise, but as the ultimate running down of potentiality into actuality. The devitalized reality which characterizes winter in "A Winter Eden" here characterizes the opposite season; for the warbler to be "a mid-summer and a mid-wood bird" is to be firmly locked in the rundown stasis of fallen existence, where "the highway dust is over all." The full foliage of summer is not a triumph of vitality but, as in "Spring Pools," a dark reality; "leaves are old" and flowers only one-tenth as plentiful as they were in spring. Thinking of flowers in particular, Frost locates this midsummer day at an equal distance from the poignant fall of spring and the more obvious, final fall of autumn:

He says the early petal-fall is past,
When pear and cherry bloom went down in showers
On sunny days a moment overcast;
And comes that other fall we name the fall.

It is this nostalgia for "the early petal-fall" (described in the poem's most powerful lyric passage), this implied sense of springtime beginnings as the peak of the annual cycle, which makes midsummer seem a time, not of fulfillment, but of impoverishment, appropriately expressed in the booming, unmelodic call of the oven bird: "The question that he frames in all but words / Is what to make of a diminished thing."

That question is essentially answered in "Hyla Brook," one of Frost's greatest lyrics and the poem immediately preceding "The Oven Bird" in *Mountain Interval*. (Frost is characteristically too circuitous to have reversed the order and made the relationship obvious.) Beginning with a similar midsummer emblem—really a more unpromising emblem than the oven bird's call—and using in part the same imaginative strategy, Frost makes something altogether different of diminished summer reality. Much of the first half of the poem describes the midsummer brook, like the oven bird, in terms of contrast with its past, especially its springtime past: it has now lost the "song and speed" of previous months; now that it has disappeared, so has the music of the peepers, "the Hyla breed / That shouted in the mist a month ago." But the effect of memory here is exactly the opposite of that in "The Oven Bird." There recollected spring serves only to increase the poignancy of the present sense of loss; here recollected spring helps to redeem the present diminished reality: because it was once a beautiful and vital stream, this "brook"—now, in fact, nothing but a "bed . . . / Of dead leaves stuck together by the heat"—is still worthy of being cherished; it is still "A brook to" those—if only those—"who remember long."

Memory in "Hyla Brook" is redemptive partly because it is more inclusive than in "The Oven Bird." There it reaches back only to spring; by contrast, midsummer is diminishment. Here it encompasses winter, too: the croaking frogs in the mists of May were "Like ghost[s] of sleigh bells in a ghost of snow." Implicitly the poet is thinking of the brook in terms of the whole annual cycle, and in those terms the present moment of desiccation is justified. That wholeness of perspective also enables him to imagine the brook as a vital reality beyond its literal end in time; the "present" brook described in the first twelve lines is entirely imagined: "Sought for much after" its physical drying up, it is "found" either invisible "underground" or visible only figuratively, "flourishing" in the jewelweed which it has gone (like the spring pools of that poem) to water. When in the final line Frost is able to assert that "We love the things we love for what they are," his imaginative accomplishment is doubly or triply understated. In fact, the brook is dried up and gone, yet the poet loves it because, in what he imagines it to be now, he sees explicitly what it was and implicitly what it will again become in the following winter and spring.

"Hyla Brook" is especially important as an answer to "The Oven Bird" if we consider the basic emblems of the two poems: if the modern singer wants to know "what to make of a diminished thing," the answer lies in an examination of that dried-up reality which, if he can see it not only in its present form (or nonform) but in its past and future forms, too, he may succeed in finding a genuine brook, a true source of imaginative vitality. And of course it is true that we love the things—and the people—we love in just this way—because we give them a breadth of vision which enables them to exist not just in their present selves, but in their past selves (child, young woman, youthful friend) and in their future selves as well. The poem offers some central insights into both imagination and love—the workings of both and the central relationship (for Frost) between them.

Nearly forty years after "Hyla Brook" and "The Oven Bird," Frost returns to the question of midsummer loss, and deals with it in broadly similar terms, in "Pod of the Milkweed." Even in the opening lines of the detailed description—of a scene of countless "butterflies of every race" flocking almost manically to the milkweed blossom—the meaning of the emblem begins to seep in: precisely as in "November," "The theme of wanton waste in peace and war." Just as the oven bird attracts the poet's attention because its song is uniquely unmusical, so the milkweed of all summer flowers catches his eye by its colorlessness: "drab it is its fondest must admit." In both cases, of course, the dullness of the natural emblem is appropriate to the drained vitality which Frost senses in these midsummer moments. Again, such drabness begins to take on intimations of a fallen world; the milkweed, Frost notes, is scarcely the flower of the promised land;

> although it is a flower that flows
> With milk and honey, it is bitter milk,
> As anyone who ever broke its stem
> And dared to taste the wound a little knows.

The other assorted characters of this drama are the numerous butterflies, suggestively personified as "intemperate," assaulting the milkweed blossom "With thirst on hunger to the point of lust." More precisely, the butterflies remind the poet of men at war;[7] they make a "tumult" over the flower and raise an almost epic "cloud / Of mingled butterfly and flower dust / That hangs perceptibly above the scene." "Many shall come away . . . struggle-worn / And spent and dusted off of their regalia."

In this poem midsummer involves a more paradoxical variety of loss than the simple desiccation of "The Oven Bird" and "Hyla Brook"—that of excess and waste. For all the drabness of the milkweed blossom and the bitterness of its milk, it is paradoxically *too* bountiful, on this one midsummer's day, for the good of the ravenous butterflies.

> In being sweet to these ephemerals
> The sober weed has managed to contrive
> In our three hundred days and sixty-five
> One day too sweet for beings to survive.

Again, as so often in his emblem poems, Frost's language applies equally well to vehicle or to tenor of the synecdoche—to butterflies or to other beings, other ephemerals.

The poem's second stanza describes the aftermath of the butterflies' day of frenzy:

all the good they did for man or god
To all those flowers they passionately trod
Was leave as their posterity one pod
With an inheritance of restless dream.

This pod, which resembles both a "Guatemalan parakeet" and a meta-morphosed butterfly, "hangs on upside down with talon feet / In an in-quisitive position"; "Something eludes him. Is it food to eat? / Or some dim secret of the good of waste?" The personified questioner here is his own answer. The only "posterity" of the profligate butterflies is this pod, but that, as the title might suggest, is the point of the poem: the "dim secret of the good of waste" is precisely that, with the help of the butter-flies' pollination, the milkweed flower has yielded fruit—the seedpod. The poem ends, like "The Oven Bird," with what appears to be a question about fallen reality: "He seems to say the reason why so much / Should come to nothing must be fairly faced." But the milkweed pod, by its very existence, answers that question. As originally published, the poem car-ried a footnote to the last line: "And shall be in due course." In due course, the pod will burst and sow other milkweed plants; "so much" lepidopterous activity will not in fact "come to nothing."

Beyond its obvious similarities to "The Oven Bird," then, espe-cially in its long, hard look at the problem of apparent waste, "Pod of the Milkweed" adopts the basic imaginative attitudes and strategies of "Hyla Brook"—or of traditional theodicy. It succeeds in coming to grips with apparent summer waste and loss—even, in the ultimate im-plication, that of war—by expanding its perspective to encompass the whole annual cycle. The first stanza, rather like "The Oven Bird," looks only at the midsummer moment of "lust" and destruction and "waste." But the point of view of the second stanza has subtly altered to focus on a time after the butterflies' midsummer madness and to examine not the milkweed flower but its fruit, the pod. And the foot-note, with its reference to "due course," implicitly looks ahead to the following spring. Thus the midsummer moment, however profligate and even destructive in itself, may be seen to be worthwhile in the context of the natural cycle: "waste was of the essence of the scheme." In the human analogy, Frost implies, even the waste of war is somehow essential to some larger (unspecified) "scheme."

"Pod of the Milkweed" presents an instructive contrast to another poem about natural waste and war, the fablelike "November." There, seeing the autumnal moment of leaf-fall in isolation, Frost can read only the lesson that waste appears to be an inevitable and lamentable part of all experience—not just of the seasonal cycle and war, but of human life and emotion as well. When, however, as in "Pod of the Milkweed" or "Hyla Brook," the moment of waste or loss is seen in the total context of natural process, it becomes an acceptable stage of the recurrent cycle. That same outlook informs several other prototypical emblem poems, and suggests another general characteristic of this second group of lyrics: the natural world seems less alien in them not only because it is perceived in terms of particularized emblems, but also because those detailed emblems are understood or "read" in terms of a larger natural context. (There are two distinct axes involved here: the greater specificity of observation pertains to the emblem itself; the expanded perspective pertains to the poet's understanding of the emblem, the natural lesson.)

"Unharvested," "The Onset," "Something for Hope," and "On a Bird Singing in Its Sleep" all repeat the basic imaginative strategy of "Hyla Brook" or "Pod of the Milkweed": beginning with a phenomenon which would suggest excess, waste, or loss in itself, each redeems that phenomenon by placing it in the larger context of natural process (the very villain of so many of the fablelike poems). In the end-of-summer poem, "Unharvested," the poet is drawn "to leave the routine road" by the odor of ripe apples, but discovers that the entire production of an apple tree lies unpicked on the ground—a scene which, more obviously than the oven bird's call or the frenzy of butterflies, might be taken as an emblem of waste. In this poem, however, Frost's faith in the overall beneficence of natural cycles—suggested by the orderly "circle of solid red" in which he perceives the apples—is complete. Knowing that there will be other summers and other harvests, he can view the "waste" as freedom from utility: the tree has "eased itself of its summer load" and is now "of all but its trivial foliage free." Like Thoreau—"I love to see that Nature is so rife with life that myriads can be afforded to be sacrificed" (*Walden* 318)—Frost not only accepts but relishes the fact that some things remain beyond human control:

> May something go always unharvested!
> May much stay out of our stated plan,
> Apples or something forgotten and left,
> So smelling their sweetness would be no theft.

Thus, in the confidence of some plan larger and wiser than our own, Frost sees in the fallen apples evidence not of waste but of nature's profligate bounty.

Again in "The Onset," expanded perspective enables Frost to accept the loss and overcome the fear which are so often associated with the coming of night and winter. The particular onset of winter here is seen, as in many of the fablelike poems, as typical or habitual—"Always the same." The tone of the description of that onset is, as in other such moments of natural threat, melodramatic: the night is "fated," the woods are "dark," the snow is "gathered" in a kind of conspiracy, and falls with a demonic "hissing." (And of course an "onset" is not just a beginning but a kind of assault.) Synecdochic expansion seeps into the description of the arrival of winter, which soon becomes emblematic not only of death but of a failure of moral will (always a deep fear in Frost), and so a waste of life itself:

> I almost stumble looking up and round,
> As one who overtaken by the end
> Gives up his errand, and lets death descend
> Upon him where he is, with nothing done
> To evil, no important triumph won,
> More than if life had never been begun.

In the second section of the poem, however, the explicit translation of the emblem's full meaning, Frost expands his perspective to see the coming of winter in the larger context of the seasonal cycle of death and renewal: "all the precedent is on my side: / I know that winter death has never tried / The earth but it has failed." If the echoes of legal language ("tried," especially "precedent") suggest a kind of abstract faith in the ultimate triumph of spring over winter, rather like the statistician's faith in "Our Hold on the Planet," the poem's final assertion has the power of specific descriptive detail, returning to the landscape in its imagined springtime state:

> I shall see the snow all go downhill
> In water of a slender April rill
> That flashes tail through last year's withered brake
> And dead weeds, like a disappearing snake.
> Nothing will be left white but here a birch,
> And there a clump of houses with a church.

The details, and the tone, of this closing description are a far cry from those of the first five lines. The only white left in the vernal landscape will be not the formless white of the snowstorm but the heartening shaped white of a birch tree (always associated with aspiration in Frost), a church, and "a clump of houses"—the human domestic center as natural a part of the scene as a clump of trees. And though the metaphorical snake that flashes its tail through the dead vegetation inevitably recalls both the "hissing" of the fifth line and the serpent of Genesis, it is surely a transformed serpent—both "disappearing" and doing so in the form of a springtime rill, a quintessential Frostian source of life.

The almost theodicial use of expanded perspective in these prototypical poems can be applied not only to the annual cycle but to larger (and potentially more daunting) periods as well. In "Something for Hope," that perspective—what Frost calls "foresight"—assures the poet of the ultimate beneficence even in "A cycle . . . of a hundred years" of vegetable growth in a field. First wildflowers, beautiful but "not good to eat," crowd out the useful "edible grass"; then, over a period of many years, trees come to crowd out the wildflowers; and finally the farmer may harvest the trees' timber, leaving the field for grass once more—and the cycle will begin all over. Obviously the farmer who harvests the timber at the end of the hundred-year cycle will not be the same one who watches "the meadowsweet / And steeple bush" crowd out the grass at the beginning of the cycle. There is a certain irony lying beneath the poet's advice to the farmer here, similar in its subject to the irony of "In Time of Cloudburst." But the tone of that poem is "tired and morose / And resentful," because Frost sees the broad expanse of time from the perspective of the individual farmer. In "Something for Hope," by contrast, by viewing the hundred-year cycle from a perspective broader than that of any individual—the perspective of "foresight" (formerly called Providence)—he is able to perceive the value of each stage in the cycle; even the "wasteful weed" brings "lovely blooming," and as part of the total cycle turns out not to be wasteful after all. Thus again, as in "Unharvested," Frost is content to rely on natural process beyond any human control—on a kind of natural "laissez-faire": "Patience and looking away ahead, / And leaving some things to take their course."

This kind of faith in natural process can even, on rare occasions, extend to the scope of eons, as it does in Frost's poem "On a Bird Singing in Its Sleep." Avian instinct strikes the poet as inhuman, almost unnerving, in "Acceptance," but here his view is positive—even though the immediate manifestation of such instinct (a bird singing "halfway through its little inborn tune" in the middle of the night) might at first seem unusually discordant. But the same instinct which leads the bird to sing out of season also gives it "the inspiration to desist." Whatever its momentary slip-ups (as in "The White-Tailed Hornet"), Frost is confident in this poem that animal instinct, as an important part of "the long" evolutionary "bead chain of repeated birth," can safely be relied on; his perspective, almost geological in its vastness, for once does not appall, but (as in "Our Hold on the Planet") justifies the present moment and its aberration. Nor is instinct entirely inhuman in this poem; the same evolutionary forces which have worked over eons to enable this bird "To be a bird" have also worked to enable us to be "men on earth," with our own songs. Frost almost seems to be echoing, in a characteristically muted fashion, the providential tradition of "To a Waterfowl" and "The Rhodora," to be suggesting that the same power, if only biological, that brought us here brought this bird. In a sense, then, "On a Bird Singing in Its Sleep" responds to "Design," the poem immediately preceding it in *A Further Range*.

4.

In the fablelike poems, and in some of the prototypical emblem poems, no season of the year is free of peril: spring represents a lapse from potential vitality, summer a further diminishment and waste, autumn a threat of destruction, and winter an appalling emptiness. But the imagination, adopting a broader perspective and invoking the whole seasonal cycle, can redeem the apparent waste of both midsummer (in "Hyla Brook" and "Pod of the Milkweed") and late summer or early autumn (in "Unharvested"). Two important prototypical emblem poems, using that implied broader view, find even in late autumn a promise of renewal to come and in spring a triumph of vitality over deathliness.

"The Cocoon" is a remarkable little poem in which Frost once again turns to a seemingly bleak natural emblem. As in many of his darkest lyrics, the time of year is autumn, with winter clearly approaching; the time of day is twilight. In this most ominous moment of the natural and imaginative cycle, the poet beholds a lonely and barren dwelling, "one poor house alone, / With but one chimney it can call its own." To complete the bleakness of the scene, the dwelling is seen as a retreat into isolation for its inhabitants (precisely as characters are isolated in fablelike poems such as "The Strong Are Saying Nothing" and "Beech"); the house is

> So close it will not light an early light,
> Keeping its life so close and out of sight
> No one for hours has set a foot outdoors
> So much as to take care of evening chores.

The imagined inhabitants of this barren house live in apparently hermitlike secrecy and withdrawal from human commerce. The poet speculates that "The inmates"—a word that inevitably suggests imprisonment as well as residence[8]—are "lonely womenfolk."

Were the natural and human scene here composed solely of these sterile details, the lesson to be learned from it would almost inevitably be the disheartening autumnal kind which Frost learns in "November" or "Bereft." The central fact of the scene here, however, is a connecting and transforming presence, an "autumn haze / That spreading in the evening air both ways / . . . pours the elm-tree meadow full of blue." Not only does the "haze"—actually the smoke from the house—infuse the otherwise barren meadow with heavenly blue; it also links the otherwise lonely cabin with the surrounding countryside. As an unmistakable sign of human activity, it is the positive equivalent of the nonsmoke which issues from the wood-pile in the poem of that name, also a sign of human activity and creativity which "warm[s] the frozen swamp . . . / With the slow smokeless burning of decay." (The smoke or haze here has additional implications as well; see the discussion of "On the Heart's Beginning to Cloud the Mind" in the following chapter.) As a result of the smoke, this central living presence in the landscape, the lesson which Frost reads from the scene is not at all the bleak, atomistic lesson that we might otherwise expect. The lesson is not read explicitly, but implied in the vehicle of the poem's central metaphor, the cocoon to which the poet compares the massing smoke:

> I want to tell them that with all this smoke
> They prudently are spinning their cocoon
> And anchoring it to an earth and moon
> From which no winter gale can hope to blow it—
> Spinning their own cocoon did they but know it.

The implications of this "cocoon" figure (reflected in the poem's own spinning of a single sentence over the first ten lines) are largely Thoreauvian. It suggests not only protection of the house and its inhabitants during the coming winter, but also metamorphosis and rebirth: after the wintry pupal stage, the women's lives will emerge full-blown and beautiful in the spring. The details of the figure also suggest that in their wintertime cocoon the women will be warmed by a vision which connects "earth and moon," natural fact and Coleridgean imagination. Finally, the metamorphosis of the women will implicitly involve reunion with a human community, a breaking out of their present isolation; that is why the poet "want[s] to tell" the women of their unconscious spinning.

The value of the "cocoon" metaphor, clearly, is that, like the pod of the milkweed, it directs our attention forward to a future stage in the seasonal cycle: the women are spinning their cocoon "prudently," a word etymologically related to "providently"; they are foreseeing. As in "Something for Hope," "foresight" or providence makes the apparent sterility of the present moment an acceptable part of the larger whole. In "Our Singing Strength," something like foresight in-heres in the very landscape; even in the midst of a snowstorm Frost rediscovers the springtime resilience of nature and man. The martial language of the opening description makes it clear that, as in "The Onset" and other poems, the snowfall is a threatening presence, though it comes at the beginning of spring rather than of winter. The "Hordes" of snowflakes assaulting the warm earth at first "could find no landing place to form," and "failed of any lasting hold." After sunset, how-ever—always the moment of greatest peril in the winter poems—the snow renews its attack, and "Next day the scene was piled and puffed and dead. / The grass lay flattened under one great tread." (Later in the poem, the birds tire of trying to alight on the snow-covered tree limbs "And setting off their heavy powder load.") Even in this first descriptive passage, however, the landscape shows at least the possi-bility of resisting the snowy assault. Before sunset, the snowflakes "made no white impression on the black. / They disappeared as if earth sent them back." Even on the following morning, though all else is smothered in snow, the road holds out against the onslaught.

In the second descriptive stanza, the poem's focus narrows from the general landscape to the plight of the birds caught unawares by the unseasonable snowstorm. This scene may seem at first glance to be purely bleak, an ornithological drama of excess, confusion, and imprisonment; unable to land in the trees, the myriad birds are trapped in the still unfrozen road, and "there they let their lives be narrowed in / By thousands the bad weather made akin." The chaotic scene even suggests a sort of antagonism between the birds and the solitary human observer, "me, the Drover," who passes along the road forcing the trapped birds to fly ahead of him endlessly, subjecting them to "the same driven nightmare over."

Yet these descriptive passages, examined more closely, reveal hints of the positive lesson which the poet will draw from the scene. Not only does the earth itself resist the snow's assault in the first stanza; but the birds' retreat before the poet in the second stanza, though panicked and disorganized, is seen in terms not of frozen death but of a life-giving brook: "The road became a channel running flocks / Of glossy birds like ripples over rocks." This image of spring vitality in the midst of winter cold recalls an earlier image of the snow-laden trees: "The rangey bough anticipated fruit / With snowballs cupped in every opening bud." This is not, in short, simply a scene of winter; it is an image of spring life within winter (and, as such, akin to the opening scene in "Birches"). The birds, for all their "apathy of wing," do in their very scurrying teach the poet something about the indestructibility of life:

> Well, something for a snowstorm to have shown
> The country's singing strength thus brought together,
> That though repressed and moody with the weather
> Was nonetheless there ready to be freed
> And sing the wild flowers up from root and seed.

Again Frost's language (like the title of the poem) has double reference: both to the vehicle of the scene, the resilience of the birds, and to the unstated tenor, the indomitability of the imagination. That lesson too has been hinted at in the very description of the scene; the one part of it which has successfully resisted the snow's assault is the one distinctly human element, the road.

> The road alone maintained itself in mud,
> Whatever its secret was of greater heat
> From inward fires or brush of passing feet.

The poem, in sum, is a winter landscape that celebrates the human spirit's power to "maintain itself in mud" even amid that snowy setting—whatever its secret may be "of greater heat / From inward fires" or human contact. Frost's is essentially the same lesson which Emerson learns from a single bird in one of his few genuine emblem poems, "The Titmouse": that a "fire burns in that little chest" which enables an animated creature to resist the assault of external cold and death—or, in human terms, that "'well the soul, if stout within, / Can arm impregnably the skin'" (*Complete Works* 9: 23).[9] We will see that same power asserted more frequently and aggressively in the Promethean poems of the following chapter.

5.

One of the defining impulses of American nature poetry, at least as far back as Bryant's "The Yellow Violet" (probably written in 1814), has been to accept and value the commonplace, that which might appear to an uncaring eye to be a diminished thing. That is also one of the important efforts of these prototypical emblem poems, as we have seen in their affection for a dried-up brook, for steeplebush, or for fallen apples. Moving beyond a vision of natural hostility or emptiness, Frost in a number of these poems rediscovers "the almost incredible freedom of the soul enslaved to the hard facts of experience"—an enslavement that is the perfect freedom of "Love," which "has earth to which she clings" (120).

That willing bondage sometimes takes the apparently hardheaded, matter-of-fact form which we see, for instance, in "Mowing." Just as he explicitly casts aside traditional poetic views of brooks in "Hyla Brook," so in "Mowing" Frost rejects any transcendent perception of fact, any conventional "dream" of "idle hours, / Or easy gold at the hand of fay or elf." He refuses, either as mower or as poet, to be chiefly concerned with the obviously attractive—"Pale orchises" or "a bright green snake." His scythe will whisper to the ground only about matters of fact—"the heat of the sun," "perhaps, . . . the lack of sound"—and the poet will make a poem based ostensibly on nothing "more than the truth." The "dream" he seeks is "The fact"; he leaves the hay to make—not just to become hay, but to make, in its own unadorned reality, his poem.

If that matter-of-fact, utilitarian side is the best-known side of Frost's affection for the commonplace, however, it is certainly not the only one. "A Young Birch," for example, celebrates a delicate kind of natural beauty far removed from the unadorned matter-of-factness of grass or hay. We have seen how, in "Pod of the Milkweed" or "Something for Hope," what might in isolation appear to be waste can be shown to be fruitful in a larger context. In "A Young Birch" (as in "Unharvested"), what might otherwise be considered waste is turned into a positive virtue, a freedom from the narrow, materialistic demands of utility. Here the businesslike attitude of the speaker of "Mowing" is brought up short and made almost deferential by the sheer grace and beauty of a young tree: "The most efficient help you ever hired / Would know that it was there to be admired." The opening description of the growing birch stresses not only its beauty but its delicacy and its "trust":

The only native tree that dares to lean,
Relying on its beauty, to the air.
(Less brave perhaps than trusting are the fair.)

But at least in this poem that trust—in the natural order including human beings—is not misplaced. Like another mower in "The Tuft of Flowers," any worker will inevitably be moved to spare such natural beauty, recognizing that the young birch is "a thing of beauty and was sent"—it has not grown here by accident—"To live its life out as an ornament." Such natural beauty has a higher use than matter-of-fact might recognize; as Emerson puts it in "The Rhodora," a partial source for this poem: "Beauty is its own excuse for being" (*Complete Works* 9: 38). This birch purposefully grows "entirely white / To double day and cut in half the dark"—a far cry from the white of "Design."

Frost's impulse to treasure the fact and to celebrate natural beauty can even lead him to write a remarkable little poem like "Moon Compasses," the first half of which describes an elemental, rather Wordsworthian scene:

> I stole forth dimly in the dripping pause
> Between two downpours to see what there was.
> And a masked moon had spread down compass rays
> To a cone mountain in the midnight haze . . .

The visionary situation might seem unpromising: solitude, midnight, and a momentary "dripping pause" between hard showers. But the scene is completed by the divergent rays of moonlight (like a nondemonic version of Blake's "Ancient of Days") and by a haze that recalls that of "The Cocoon." Now, echoing Donne's most famous conceit, Frost compares those rays to the legs of a compass; the moon has "spread down" its "compass rays" to embrace the mountain

> As if the final estimate were hers;
> And as it measured in her calipers,
> The mountain stood exalted in its place.

That last masterful line implies a wealth of acceptance of earthly reality. The moonlight which encompasses and esteems the mountain, of course, is not only a literal light; it is also the moonlight of Wordsworth and Coleridge, the imagination which illuminates and beautifies the mountain of natural reality. Nor is the echo of Donne's conceit gratuitous, as the final elliptical line of the poem, expanding the synecdochic meaning one step further, makes clear: "So love will take between the hands a face. . . ." The same impulse which leads the mind to illuminate and esteem the natural landscape also lies behind the love of one person for another.[10]

"Moon Compasses" is an instructive member of the prototypical group. Like "A Young Birch" or "Mowing," it shows the capacity of a nonprocessive emblem poem not merely for accepting but for celebrating commonplace natural reality. Even within the confines of a short, nonprocessive poem, Frost can read a powerfully sustaining lesson from a simple scene. Yet the emblems in which these three poems originate are not, of course, foreboding manifestations of the natural order.

When the imagination is faced with more ominous natural signs, it is sometimes reduced in these poems to merely reporting, and perhaps questioning, that fact—as in "Design" or "The Oven Bird." The structural limitations of a nonprocessive poem are almost inevitably associated with certain visionary limitations: faced with an emblem which threatens natural hostility or emptiness, the imagination, by definition, cannot act out the altering or transforming of that emblem in a nonprocessive poem. It is true that several of the most powerful prototypical emblem poems involve something close to transformation of an unpromising emblem: of a dried-up brook, of a solitary cabin, of the warlike frenzy of an army of butterflies. And indeed in such poems imaginative activity is clearly implied, and its effects clearly shown; but the unfolding of the poem itself cannot act out that activity—it occurs only in the pores and interstices of the poem. The placing of the dried-up brook in the context of recollected past and imagined present must be, like Hyla Brook itself, subterranean; it simply seeps into the descriptive portion of the lyric (lines 1–11). Likewise, the imaginative perception of the lonely cabin effectively creeps into the first four lines of "The Cocoon," the description of the "autumn haze" (though the cabin itself is not mentioned until the fifth line). The butterflies' "waste" is unobtrusively placed in the larger context of the annual cycle during the lapse of time which occurs between the two stanzas of "Pod of the Milkweed" and in the footnote to that poem. These poems can hint at imaginative transformation, and they certainly show its effects—but they cannot act it out. For such transformation to be dramatized by the verse itself, a processive structure is necessary—a structure which allows, not merely description of the emblem followed immediately by translation of its meaning, but further thought about, or further exploration of, the emblem *between* that starting point and that terminus. The next two chapters of this study are concerned with two classes of poems that allow just such movement, exploration, and (in many cases) transformation. The meditative poems allow the poet to speculate at some length about the meaning of the emblem before him; the heuristic emblem poems allow him further exploration of the natural text itself.

Those two groups of emblem poems also suggest a second advantage inherent in processive structures. There is certainly drama in some of the prototypical emblem poems, or even in a fablelike poem like "Nothing Gold Can Stay"; but such drama is in a measure circumscribed. The essential component of drama is *agon,* conflict. It is possible for nonprocessive poems to register conflict—for example, the conflict between natural forces and mind in "Design," or between apparent natural emptiness and imaginative coloring of such "emptiness" in "Hyla Brook." But a nonprocessive poem, by definition, cannot pursue the conflict through various twistings and turnings to a final resolution. Only a processive structure allows a poem (to return to Frost's remarks on "The Figure a Poem Makes") to "run a course of lucky events" before it "ends with a clarification of life." This fuller kind of imaginative drama is at least potentially powerful in two respects. First, struggle, reversal, and denouement may simply be more gripping for the poem's audience; that is its theatrical value. Beyond that, the profoundest triumphs of the imagination, or of the mind's faith in the natural order, are likely to be those which are hard-won, which come only after denial, conflict, and reversal. That is the spiritual value of visionary drama.

CHAPTER 6

The Promethean Frost

"It is this backward motion toward the source,
Against the stream, that most we see ourselves in,
The tribute of the current to the source.
It is from this in nature we are from.
It is most us." (260)

1.

After the imaginative struggles of the fablelike and prototypical emblem poems, with their occasional defeats and limited victories, the radical assertiveness of the Promethean poems may come almost as a shock. Indeed, the familiar critical view of Frost might lead us to believe that he is anything but Promethean. For this familiar Frost, as one critic puts it, "guarded epiphanies are more than enough"; the familiar Frost practices "resignation to the gravitational pull of a given reality which confines our will" (Bradford 277). While such phrases might adequately characterize the Frost of the fablelike poems, or even of some of the prototypical emblem poems, they scarcely begin to describe the side of Frost which I want to examine in this chapter. This Frost feels a clear and sometimes irresistible Promethean impulse—an impulse to assert the power of the imagination in the face of, and the superiority of the imagination to, natural fact. But surely it is not so surprising to discover a Promethean side of Frost if we think of the central role of the same impulse in poets like Yeats and Stevens.

The relationship of poetic structure to the Promethean impulse in Frost is a bit complicated. For the most part, Frost's Promethean poems overlap with the structural class which I have labeled meditative emblem poems; but, in this case, I hesitate to claim a strict one-to-one equivalence between structure (meditative poems) and vision (Promethean poems). I classify all but one of the meditative emblem poems—all except "On the Heart's Beginning to Cloud the Mind"—as Promethean, but hesitate to insist that all of the Promethean poems are meditative. Unlike fablelike or prototypical emblem poems, the clearly meditative poems—"To a Moth Seen in Winter," "West-Running Brook," "Wild Grapes," and "Birches" are good examples—do not simply, statically juxtapose tenor and vehicle of the synecdoche, emblem and lesson. They are processive: for the first time, the poem itself now acts out the process of natural education, the visionary dynamic of progressing from object or scene to meaning. (Two clear examples: The simple descriptive portion of "Birches" may consist only of its first three lines. That preliminary description of bent trees is followed by speculation about how they got that way—whether from ice storms [lines 5–20] or from a boy's swinging [lines 23–40]—and by a final meditation on the significance of swinging birches. Or, in "Wild Grapes," the speaker tells the story of a traumatic childhood event in the poem's first three sections [lines 1–91] and then—some years later—draws the moral of that experience in the final section [lines 92–103]). The meditative poems are differentiated from the heuristic emblem poems by the fact that in them the movement from emblem to significance is discursive. In terms of the poem's fictions, the natural lesson is not announced directly by the natural messenger, but is arrived at mediately through the poet-observer's contemplation inspired by that messenger or emblem. Here, in short, the natural emblem is not so much a word to be read as a sign to be pondered, a hieroglyph to be deciphered.

Like Wordsworth, Frost explicitly appreciates the potential value of the contemplative means of arriving at the natural lesson, the very indirection of meditative vision. Wordsworth's explicit theory of composition reflects his tacit theory of imaginative perception: natural experience may inspire "powerful feelings," but only in the meditative pause—only when such "emotion" is "recollected in tranquillity" and "contemplated" by the imagination (*Literary Criticism* 27)—can the seer grasp the full meaning of such experience and feelings. This meditative process is acted out in many of Wordsworth's most powerful visionary moments, from "Tintern Abbey" to the climactic Simplon Pass episode in the sixth book of *The Prelude* (itself a remarkably Promethean episode). Natural phenomena are always most meaningful for Wordsworth when they are contemplated in memory, when they "flash upon that inward eye / Which is the bliss of solitude." Frost suggests a similar theory of vision in "Time Out." The Thoreauvian explorer may realize that a mountain is in fact a text albeit done in plant; but "It took that pause to make him" do so. Reading the text seems virtually synonymous with contemplation of it: the "slope" of the seer's "head," the angle of his vision, is "The same for reading as it was for thought." Under all but the most exceptional of circumstances, the perceiving mind "will have its moment to reflect"—to ponder and thus, in one of Frost's favorite puns, in some sense to mirror, the natural scene.

Again in "Carpe Diem," Frost dissents from the traditional suggestion that life should "seize the present." The mind, he insists in Wordsworthian fashion, can come to grips with the meaning of experience only by distancing itself a bit, chiefly through memory and meditation.

> The present
> Is too much for the senses,
> Too crowding, too confusing—
> Too present to imagine.[1]

Virtually all of the dozen Promethean poems which I want to consider in this chapter are clearly meditative. Despite other differences among them—their dates of composition span most of Frost's productive years, from about 1900 to about 1953; their poetic forms represent a good cross section of Frost's whole corpus; their natural emblems vary from habitual to particular, from objects to scenes to incidents; the details of their structure vary widely—all of these poems are characterized by greater or lesser meditative pauses before the speaker reads the lesson implicit in the emblem. Here again it seems clear that there is a link between structure and vision: the introduction of process in the structures of these poems, particularly the discursive movement in which the mind takes up the natural emblem to contemplate it and forge a meaning from it, offer a rich opportunity for the imagination to assert itself, for the mind not only to contemplate but to dominate the natural text.

But not all of these Promethean poems are as unmistakably meditative or contemplative as "West-Running Brook" or "Birches." In three of them—"Sand Dunes," "On a Tree Fallen Across the Road," and "A Soldier"—the meditative process is telescoped into the narrow span of only fourteen or sixteen lines, so that the poem's processiveness is considerably muted.[2] In any event, whether the meditative pause in these poems is greater or lesser, it clearly *tends* to accompany the remarkably Promethean uprising which they celebrate.

2.

"Kitty Hawk," though not an emblem poem—not, in fact, a nature poem at all in any conventional sense—sheds a great deal of light on the essential vision of the meditative emblem poems. It is a remarkable if not startling poem to have been written by the eighty-year-old Frost: one of his longest poems; one of the dozen or so most important pieces from the last two volumes; surprisingly innovative metrically, working within the tight limitations of the short lines and repeated rhymes of its "three-beat phrases"; and, most remarkably, a radical assertion of the power of mind.

In its fiction, "Kitty Hawk" recounts past and present visits by the poet to the Outer Banks of North Carolina. Part One recalls his first visit to the Kitty Hawk area, in November 1894, when Elinor White had cast the young poet into despair by refusing (temporarily, of course) to marry him. Part Two is set nearly sixty years later, when the speaker returns to Kitty Hawk in 1953 on the fiftieth anniversary of the Wright brothers' flight.[3] Part Two, pondering the historical associations of Kitty Hawk, is an extended, often surprising celebration of western technological thought and achievement—a celebration which, if unexpected in the middle of the twentieth century, nonetheless echoes Emerson's approval of scientific conquest at several points in the 1836 *Nature* and elsewhere.[4] Frost goes so far as to suggest that the Wright brothers' pioneering flight is a synecdoche for the entire history of civilization (lines 258–95), and concludes the poem with a thanksgiving to the "God of the machine, / Peregrine machine." Rewriting Genesis, Frost suggests that God must not altogether condemn the Fall —"Our instinctive venture / Into . . . / The material"[5]—since it only parallels, in human terms, the Incarnation:

> God's own descent
> Into flesh was meant
> As a demonstration
> That the supreme merit
> Lay in risking spirit
> In substantiation.

Here again Frost's stance follows Emerson, who notes in *Nature* that "There seems to be a necessity in spirit to manifest itself in material forms" (*Collected Works* 1: 22). Such an argument, which might at first glance seem materialistic, in fact stands simplistic materialism on its head; the celebration of "substantiation" is, on the contrary, a radical assertion of the preeminence of mind or spirit. It assumes, in Blakean or Stevensian fashion, that material nature is barren unless redeemed by human possession: only mind, acting "Like a kitchen spoon / Of a size Titanic," can "keep all things stirred" and thus vital. The homey tropes which Frost uses here, reminiscent of Edward Taylor, underline the domestication of nature by man; but "Titanic" is surely meant to remind us of Prometheus. Without such mental stirring, nature is stagnant and moribund: "Matter mustn't curd, / Separate and settle. / Action is the word." Only mind, here seen primarily in its scientific aspect, can transform the "waste" of infinite space into a human habitation. Through aviation

> We have made a pass
> At the infinite,
> Made it, as it were,
> Rationally ours,
> To the most remote
> Swirl of neon-lit
> Particle afloat.
> Ours was to reclaim
> What had long been faced
> As a fact of waste
> And was waste in name.

To "conquer" nature is not to defeat but to fulfill it. As for Blake and Milton, man is intended to be the ruler over creation; it is his proper task to name the natural world and to order it with mind—"to master Nature / By some nomenclature." Because nature is barren and meaningless in itself, it waits for human intellectual control to transform and fulfill it. Echoing "The Aim Was Song," Frost suggests that technological control clarifies natural purpose and meaning. "Nature's never quite / Sure she hasn't erred / In her vague design" until human beings, by controlling and domesticating space as aviation does, "Undertake to tell her / What in being stellar / She's supposed to mean." The play on "supposed" makes a Blakean or Stevensian point: nature can be expected to mean only what we assume her to mean.

Thus Frost suggests in "Kitty Hawk" that the constant outreach and grasp of the intellect are properly Promethean, and that they both vitalize and fulfill the created world. We ought to fear not a "fall" into contact with the material, but only a sagging into intellectual stagnation, which would also be nature's loss. The most appropriate or (punningly) "becoming fear"

Is lest habit-ridden
In the kitchen midden
Of our dump of earning
And our dump of learning
We come nowhere near
Getting thought expressed.

The importance of getting thought expressed suggests the underlying link between the philosophical assumptions of Part Two and the personal reminiscences of Part One of "Kitty Hawk." The two sections and their widely separated times are held together, not chiefly by the shared location of Kitty Hawk, but by the metaphor of flight: the aeronautical type of the Wright brothers in Part Two, and the aborted poetical flight of the fledgling poet of 1894 ("a young Alastor") in Part One. The poem's subtitle—"A skylark . . . in three-beat phrases"—underlines the Shelleyan implications of the flight metaphor. Nor is the metaphor an adventitious link; it is meant to suggest that what is true of technology is also true of poetry. The same claims which Frost is overtly making for science he is implicitly making for art; both represent the triumph of mind or imagination over nature. Physically, he grants, earth can do no more than passively reflect the rays of sun and moon; intellectually, we make our own light.

All we do's reflect
From our rocks, and yes,
From our brains no less.
And the better part
Is the ray we dart
From this head and heart,
The *mens animi.*

Thus Frost gives his familiar play on "reflecting" a Promethean twist in this poem. Elsewhere, the mind often reflects in the sense of mirroring the natural. Here, while earth's rocks reflect (the sun) in that usual sense, the brain reflects—i.e., meditates—independently and creatively; that intellectual "ray we dart" from our minds, both in science and in poetry, is the central light which orders the universe and gives it meaning.

3.

Before turning to a number of meditative emblem poems which are obviously illuminated by "Kitty Hawk" and its Prometheanism, I want to consider two which seem at first glance to have little to do with the domination of material nature by the mind. One of these is the earliest written of the meditative poems, "To a Moth Seen in Winter," which was composed "Circa 1900" but not published for forty years. The moth, a "Bright-black-eyed silvery creature, brushed with brown," is described only in the first four lines of the poem; in the remaining twenty lines, the poet meditates on the appearance of such a creature in wintertime.

This natural emblem, almost as clearly as the white flower, spider, and moth of "Design," seems a violation of the natural order; yet, despite that fact, there are promising hints of imaginative intimacy between poet and moth. The speaker not only apostrophizes the natural messenger; he reaches out to extend "a gloveless hand warm from my pocket" to touch the moth and provide it "A perch and resting place"; he endows the moth with the implicit ability to respond to his thoughts ("But go. You are right."). Like Thoreau, the poet observes the markings of the moth in some detail; but the first suggestion of imaginative defeat appears in the poem's lone parenthesis: "(Who would you be, I wonder, by those marks / If I had moths to friend as I have flowers?)" This is not incidental information; this insufficiency of Thoreauvian familiarity with moths already suggests a potential barrier between human observer and natural messenger.

In the middle portion of the poem the portrait of the moth becomes increasingly anthropomorphic, and the inescapable lesson which it teaches begins to infiltrate the narrative. The moth is seeking "love of kind," but in doing so it is "lured . . . with false hope"; the poet foresees its inevitable fate: "Nor will you find love either, nor love you." Finally the poem's meditation makes the lesson explicit. The moth is a natural exemplum of something essentially tragic in the yearnings of the heart—those yearnings which are the central subject of the Promethean poems as a group: "what I pity in you is something human, / The old incurable untimeliness, / Only begetter of all ills that are." The poet learns from the moth, "more simply wise than I," the inescapable destruction which that "incurable untimeliness" will bring. Every creature, whether human being or moth, is irrevocably locked in the prison of his own yearnings, and none can reach out to touch any other with life-giving warmth. The barrier between poet and moth—and implicitly between man and man—which was first hinted at only parenthetically is now acknowledged openly:

> the hand I stretch impulsively
> Across the gulf of well-nigh everything
> May reach to you, but cannot touch your fate.
> I cannot touch your life, much less can save,
> Who am tasked to save my own a little while.

The peculiar tone of the last line, simultaneously melodramatic, self-pitying, and hard-headed, is characteristic of Frost's winter moods long after 1900. The line functions to apply the lesson learned from the moth to the poet's own situation: human yearning, too, is fatally flawed; human beings, too, are trapped in isolation.

An even more powerful sense of isolation, and a more direct suggestion that human enterprise is vulnerable to defeat by external forces, shape "The Census-Taker," an unusual poem which combines the qualities of a lyric with those of Frost's dramatic narratives. The natural object of meditation in this poem, like the moth seen in winter, is an archetypal memento mori in Frost's world: a deserted house. It is set in the midst of an almost lunar barrenness and described in extraordinarily spare language. The census-taker comes one windy autumn evening

> To a slab-built, black-paper-covered house
> Of one room and one window and one door,
> The only dwelling in a waste cut over
> A hundred square miles round it in the mountains . . .
> An emptiness flayed to the very stone.

The trees around this rudimentary house are either cut down or rotting and leafless; inside the cabin, too, all is disuse and decay: "No lamp was lit. Nothing was on the table. / The stove was cold . . ." Everything in the scene, in short, is bare, dislocated, or nonexistent. Despite the noise made by the door blowing on its hinges, there are not even any ghosts or skeletons in this parodic house: "I saw no men there and no bones of men there." The emptiness and lifelessness of all he sees (and doesn't see) are underlined by the irony of the errand on which the speaker has come to this "dwelling": "I came as census-taker to the waste / To count the people in it and found none, / None in the hundred miles, none in the house . . ."

Clearly Frost relishes describing such a barren scene—partly for the virtuosity of describing something that mostly isn't there, but partly also because the situation ultimately offers him a chance to refuse to accept such nothingness.[6] (In both respects this poem is similar to "Hyla Brook.") The obvious lesson which such a scene might teach is the preliminary object of the poem's closing meditation, apparently a simple lesson of sorrow at the defeat of all human enterprise and vitality:

> I thought what to do that could be done—
> About the house—about the people not there.
> This house in one year fallen to decay
> Filled me with . . . sorrow . . .

Again, as in "To a Moth Seen in Winter," there appears to be no effective action which the speaker can take to alter or mitigate this forbidding emptiness. All that he can do, in a setting in which, significantly, his voice cannot even raise an echo, is simply to state the fact of lifelessness, to "declare to the cliffs too far for echo, / 'The place is desert. . . .'"

4.

"To a Moth Seen in Winter" and "The Census-Taker" both describe chiefly the wintry state of the imagination's life, with its sense of isolation and of the fragility, even futility, of human desire and effort in the face of external forces. The latter sense, especially, would seem to be diametrically opposed to the Promethean assertions of imaginative dominance in "Kitty Hawk." I want to return to both of these poems shortly to suggest that this opposition is only apparent—that, even in the wintriest moments of the imaginative stage represented by the meditative emblem poems, the imagination is beginning to stir and to rouse itself from what Blake calls "single vision and Newtons sleep" (693).

The potential for that stirring, awakening, and resistance to massive natural fact is perhaps most famously summarized in the central passage of "West-Running Brook," an unusual emblem poem framed in Frost's narrative-dialogue form. Nature as seen here is chiefly mindless flux or entropy; it threatens not only to isolate human beings ("'It flows between us / To separate us for a panic moment'") and to overwhelm them ("'it flows over us'"), but also to undo itself: "'even substance lapsing unsubstantial; / The universal cataract of death / That spends to nothingness.'" Poised against the general tendency of natural fact "'To fill the abyss's void with emptiness'" is the natural emblem—a perversely westward-flowing brook and, within it, an equally perverse wave with a contrary eastward impulse. The husband reads the emblem in his long meditation; he insists that even in the great deathward flux of natural fact, this wave hints at, is emblematic of, the counter force of human spirit and will.

> "see how the brook
> In that white wave runs counter to itself.
> It is from that in water we were from
> Long, long before we were from any creature. . . .
> It is this backward motion toward the source,
> Against the stream, that most we see ourselves in,
> The tribute of the current to the source.
> It is from this in nature we are from.
> It is most us."

A number of critics have shown this "'backward motion toward the source'" to be associated with Bergson's *élan vital*,[7] but whether we call it that or mind, spirit, imagination, or will, that "counter" force opposes the entire stream of natural flux, "'The stream of everything that runs away'"; and even nature itself shows that this "'throwing back'" is somehow "'sacred.'" Two of the lines quoted above closely echo each other—"'It is from that in water we were from'" and "'It is from this in nature we are from'"; both seem virtually solecistic in their unnecessarily repeated *from*s. But the near solecisms make a point: we are not *from* nature, but *from from something in nature* (or water); we are far removed from nature, even unnatural.

That unnatural human impulse to resist nature is not only asserted but acted out in a masterful little poem, "Sand Dunes," in which the human is again far removed from water. Like "To a Moth Seen in Winter," "The Census-Taker," and many other of these Promethean pieces, "Sand Dunes" is set at a moment when natural fact threatens to become not just massive but oppressive, even murderous. Here the ocean waves which threaten the land in "Once by the Pacific" are demonically resurrected as dunes: "up from where" the waves "die /

Rise others vaster yet, / And those are brown and dry"—clearly associated with death. These demonic waves are determined to assault "the
fisher town / And bury in solid sand / The men" whom the ocean
"could not drown."

But here, against yet another primal assault of natural fact—seen as
more threatening, certainly, than either winter or the depopulation of a
mountainous area of New England—Frost asserts a primal faith in the
persistence of mind. Speaking still of the sea whose spirit lurks in these
dunes, Frost insists with a wonderfully telling verb that "She may know
cove and cape, / But she does not know mankind"—after all, only mankind
can *know* anything in a more than physical sense—"If by any change of
shape / She hopes to cut off mind." Mind is even more Protean than sea:

> Men left her a ship to sink:
> They can leave her a hut as well;
> And be but more free to think
> For the one more cast-off shell.

In this poem, the assault of natural fact clearly does not oppress the human mind or spirit, but strikes a Promethean spark of self-assertiveness
from it. This self-assertion is based on a Thoreauvian freedom which derives from the mind's capacity for constant renewal—for repeatedly leaving former shapes (ship or hut) behind in order to save and renew itself.
Moreover, that freedom and power, as "Kitty Hawk" would predict, help
to transform the natural world at least a bit. Despite the massive threat of
sea and dunes, nature recovers a touch of its Thoreauvian friendliness in
that last quatrain: it is the hermit crab, like the beautiful bug hatched after
sixty years in the applewood tree (*Walden* 333), which serves as model
for the mind of how to survive by leaving the past behind, abandoning an
outgrown shell and outdoing the sea itself in "changes of shape."

The opposition between man and earth is at least equally stark in
a less distinguished poem, "A Soldier," published in the same section

of *West-Running Brook*. (The power of this sonnet is vitiated, to my reading, by an overly insistent tone in the final three lines—a tone which I suspect arises from the personal association of this poem with Edward Thomas, who had died a decade before it was first published.) In "A Soldier," natural obstruction appears to be insurmountable, and spirit, at first glance, thoroughly defeated. The soldier—for Frost, as for Stevens at moments, a figure of capable imagination—is a "fallen lance that lies as hurled, / That lies unlifted now, come dew, come rust." The twice-repeated "lies" suggests the finality of the soldier's death; the repeated verb of "come dew, come rust" suggests by contrast that only the natural cycle, corrosive of human effort, goes on. From the apparent futility of the soldier's death the poem's meditation appears to reason outward to the inevitable defeat of all projections of the spirit:

> Our missiles always make too short an arc.
> They fall, they rip the grass, they intersect
> The curve of earth, and striking, break their own;
> They make us cringe for metal-point on stone.

The trajectory of natural process, "The curve of earth," is not only not the same as our "own," the "arc" of human desiring; that natural trajectory is greater than, and destined to defeat, that "too short" arc of our aims. The spirit's desire, if not pointless, is predestined to come up short against natural fact, to be shattered on what Emerson calls "this cropping-out in our planted gardens of the core of the world" (*Complete Works* 6: 19).

But even in these first eleven lines the poem has proleptically rejected its own preliminary reading of the soldier's death: "If we" judge it to have been pointless, "It is because like men we look too near." In a larger and more Promethean context we would be able to see the indestructibility of spirit; after all, the fallen lance which is the soldier "still lies pointed as it plowed the dust"—"pointed" with human purpose, having "plowed" the dust in an effort to make it fruitful. The harvest of that sacrifice is the burden of the poem's final straining lines:

> this we know, the obstacle that checked
> And tripped the body, shot the spirit on
> Further than target ever showed or shone.

In some sense not readily apparent to us, the defeat of human effort is not final; as in "Sand Dunes," natural obstruction serves ultimately to strike a spark from the spirit, to "shoot the spirit on" toward some supernatural "target," even as the soldier's body was shot in a different sense. Thus the arc of the soldier's intention turns out not to have been "too short" after all—it was aimed at some invisible and immeasurable goal. And the poem's last word, "shone," recalls the assertion of "Kitty Hawk" that the real sun of our world is not a natural ball of gases but the irrepressible reflection of "The *mens animi*." When Frost says that "we know" all of this, he is not only distinguishing human beings from the sea, which "does not know mankind," but also suggesting that "to know" is, at least in the Promethean poems, chiefly a matter of assertion rather than of passive intellectual acceptance. In these poems, we "know" as much through the imagination or through sheer desire as through intellect.

The ultimate desire, as "A Soldier" intimates, is to live and not die, and that fundamental life wish is central to the Promethean poems. We see it in its purest form, perhaps, in "There Are Roughly Zones." The situation described in the opening lines of that poem— night and winter—is a familiar Frost scene: as in "Storm Fear" or "An Old Man's Winter Night," the domestic center is dramatically opposed to threatening external forces: "We sit indoors and talk of the cold outside"; the winter wind "Is a threat to the house. But the house has long been tried." The struggle between human desires and natural forces here involves a hostage, a peach tree which has been planted "very far north" and may not survive the cold, windy night. In pondering the meaning of the peach tree's plight, the poet asks a pair of questions:

> What comes over a man, is it soul or mind—
> That to no limits and bounds he can stay confined?
> You would say his ambition was to extend the reach
> Clear to the Arctic of every living kind.
> Why is his nature forever so hard to teach
> That though there is no fixed line between wrong and right,
> There are roughly zones whose laws must be obeyed?

Though the peach tree, if it is destroyed, "can blame this limitless trait in the hearts of men," the poem, clearly, is not inclined to do so. It will blame, rather, a kind of natural betrayal: "we can't help feeling more than a little betrayed / That the northwest wind should rise to such a height / Just when the cold went down so many below." Like all of the Promethean poems, this one in fact celebrates the obstinacy of "soul or mind" which refuses to accept the rough zones of natural law, celebrates man's yearnings, "That to no limits and bounds he can stay confined." The positive, Promethean implications of that line are clarified by a parallel passage from "Kitty Hawk," where, using the same antithetical rhyme of "mind" with "confined," Frost notes how surprising it is that humans, of all creatures, can fly:

> That's because though mere
> Lilliputians we're
> What Catullus called
> Somewhat (*aliquid*).
> Mind you, we are mind.
> We are not the kind
> To stay too confined.

Thus the most important lesson of "There Are Roughly Zones" is, paradoxically, the value of refusing to learn the obvious natural lesson of caution. Frost relishes the fact that man's "nature," unlike any other part of nature, is "forever so hard to teach" about natural restrictions, because he is confident that "this limitless trait" is no mere anarchic stubbornness; it is an assertion of life: "You would say his ambition was to extend the reach / Clear to the Arctic of every living kind." The imagination, in true Blakean fashion, wants to transform even the waste of the Arctic into a vital garden; that is the ultimate reason why it struggles against dead nature.

Now, if we look back at the two lyrics with which we began our consideration of meditative emblem poems—two apparently unredeemed visions of autumnal and winter bleakness—we can see the same "limitless trait" lying beneath the somber surface even in those poems. "To a Moth Seen in Winter," though chiefly an account of isolation and destruction, is not without an implicit assertion of the will to life. The moth itself is almost an exemplum of yearning, its "wings not folded in repose, but spread" for flight even in the face of winter cold. When the poet foresees that the moth must "Go till you wet your pinions and are quenched," the latter participle may mean either "extinguished" or "slaked," but whether the moth's yearning is thus implicitly fire or thirst, it is essentially Promethean. And the "old incurable untimeliness" which the poet sees and regrets in the moth might, in other moods, be far from regrettable: as both "Reluctance" and "I Could Give All to Time" make clear, time is one of the great imprisonments of the spirit. That "untimeliness" is in fact an analogue of "this limitless trait in the hearts of men."

Again, looking back at "The Census-Taker," we find beneath the surface of lifelessness and human defeat an unextinguished spark of yearning for life, in the speaker himself. The life-giving force of imagination is not absent even from this barren scene, its presence suggested by the Eolian wind on this "cloud-blowing evening," which "swung a door / Forever off the latch, as if rude men / Passed in . . ." With the help of such Eolian activity, "I counted nine I had no right to count / (But this was dreamy unofficial counting)." Though the census-taker "found no people that dared show themselves, / None not in hiding from the outward eye," the inward eye of imagination insists on making its "dreamy unofficial count" of human presences. Its motive, again: "It must be I want life to go on living."

It is accurate to say, in short, that the imagination and its yearning for life and freedom at least partially inform all of these meditative emblem poems. The processive structure of such lyrics reflects the stirring of the imagination, and its Orc-like rebellion (to borrow Blake's terms) against the tyranny of natural "fact."

5.

"There Are Roughly Zones" hints at a surprisingly Promethean use of natural fact which is typical of the poems I am considering: it may educate not only by analogy but also by opposition. One of the poems which most strikingly acts out that process is "On a Tree Fallen Across the Road." This poem, even within the limits of the sonnet, comes close to dramatizing the imagination's struggle with, and the peripeteia in which it overcomes, natural fact. Many of the poems which I am considering hint at a two-part movement. "A Soldier," for instance, embodies a kind of double vision: the narrow vision of the soldier as simply defeated in the first eleven lines, counterpoised by the "knowledge" of the last three lines. "On a Tree Fallen Across the Road" acts out this double vision in its very structure and movement: natural fact poses a crucial question in the first five lines, and the imagination emphatically answers it in the last nine.

The opening lines personify natural facts in order to suggest their purposiveness: "the tempest with a crash of wood / Throws down" the tree "in front of us"; or, as the poem's subtitle suggests, the tree has fallen "To hear us talk." The fallen tree is seen, not wholly as an accident, but as a kind of natural challenge: "not to bar / Our passage to our journey's end for good, / But just to ask us who we think we are / Insisting always on our own way so." Thus storm and tree deliberately raise the central question of self-consciousness: "who we think we are."

In the poem's second movement, in lines 6–14, Frost again attributes purpose to the storm: "She likes to halt us in our runner tracks, / And make us get down in a foot of snow / Debating what to do without an ax." The human traveler, as so often in critical moments of American nature writing,[8] is brought up short and forced to deal directly and nakedly with the natural. Out of this direct confrontation, in the second, larger reading of the event's meaning, in the sestet, comes an answer to the crucial question raised earlier. The storm may throw a tree down in front of us;

> And yet she knows obstruction is in vain:
> We will not be put off the final goal
> We have it hidden in us to attain,
> Not though we have to seize earth by the pole
> And, tired of aimless circling in one place,
> Steer straight off after something into space.

This is a remarkably Promethean moment—asserted, as in every one of these poems, virtually without any heightening of Frost's usual conversational language, without rising above that "everyday level of diction that even Wordsworth kept above" (*Letters* 83–84).[9] The answer to "who we think we are" has already been implied in the next line of the question: "Insisting always on our own way so." Here that answer is underlined. Human beings are defined by the unbounded yearning of mind, spirit, or imagination—again "this limitless trait in the hearts of men"—which, when it begins to feel its true strength, will not be denied by restrictive natural fact, even if it must titanically "seize earth by the pole" and, like Shelley's skylark or like the Wright brothers, leave earth in its flight, "Steer straight off after something into space." Yet, for all its Prometheanism, this poem suggests that natural opposition to human yearning is only apparent, and that a kind of cooperation underlies the apparent assault of physical forces. The storm here, unlike the sea in "Sand Dunes," finally "knows" something—namely, the intensity of human desire and determination. Natural obstruction "is in vain" only in the immediate sense that it cannot stop the active imagination. In a deeper sense it is not futile: natural barriers can serve, paradoxically, to help make the imagination more aware of its own powers. In a sense, the fallen tree does "bar / Our passage to our journey's end for good"—not permanently, but for our benefit. Obstruction may be instruction, may clarify and intensify the spirit and will. As Emerson puts it: "limitation . . . is the meter of the growing man. We stand against Fate, as children stand up against the wall in their father's house and notch their height from year to year" (*Complete Works* 6: 30).

Frost tells a more extended story of spiritual growth by opposition to nature in another remarkable poem, "Wild Grapes." In many details of plot—too many, one may suspect, for coincidence—"Wild Grapes" is reminiscent of Wordsworth's fragment called "Nutting," but the poem's lesson is almost the opposite of Wordsworth's.

While "Nutting" begins its recollection with a sense of blessedness, harking back to "One of those heavenly days that cannot die," the remembrance in "Wild Grapes" seems to inspire at first a sense of fear and trauma. The five-year-old heroine of the poem had begun as an active and fearless child, like Wordsworth's young nut-gatherer extra-vagant in nature: "a little boyish girl / My brother could not always leave at home." But her fearless childhood was apparently brought to an end by an infernal event: "that beginning was wiped out in fear / The day I swung suspended with the grapes, / And was come after like Eurydice."

In the description of that apparently traumatic event, the natural setting is strikingly similar to that of "Nutting." Wordsworth's young nut-gatherer must "force" his way through "tangled thickets" to "A virgin scene!"—"to one dear nook, / Unvisited, where not a broken bough / Drooped with its withered leaves, ungracious sign / Of devastation," but the untouched hazel trees are "with tempting clusters hung." So in Frost's poem the scene is characterized by isolation, peacefulness, and feminine attractiveness: the narrator's brother leads her to "a glade" in which a white birch stands "alone, / Wearing a thin headdress of pointed leaves, / And heavy on her heavy hair behind, / Against her neck, an ornament of grapes."

Soon, however, just as in "Nutting," the tranquility of the virgin scene is disrupted by the human harvester. The girl's brother bends the birch down to the ground to enable her to pluck the wild grapes; but suddenly the appropriation of nature by human is dramatically reversed.

> I said I had the tree. It wasn't true.
> The opposite was true. The tree had me.
> The minute it was left with me alone,
> It caught me up as if I were the fish
> And it the fishpole. . . .

Suddenly the birch snaps back upright, and the terrified little girl finds herself high off the ground, hanging on for dear life. In a preliminary reaction much like the speaker's in "Nutting," this ravishment of human by tree is implicitly seen—at the time—as punishment for violation of the natural order. The brother half-jokingly shouts to the dangling girl not to be afraid of the grapes—"'they won't pick you if you don't them.'" He also tells her that now she knows "'how it feels . . . / To be a bunch of fox grapes, . . . / That when it thinks it has escaped the fox . . . / Just then come you and I to gather it.'" Implicitly, the tree has turned the tables on the human interloper to reprove her assault on the grapes.

If the young Wordsworth's ravishment of nature is a chastening experience, how much more chastening ought this drama to prove— to have been "'run off with by birch trees into space,'" transported like Eurydice to fearful regions of experience. The triumph of "Wild Grapes" is that the experience is finally not chastening at all. In "Nutting," the human assault does not have to be actively reproved: "The

115

silent trees" and "intruding sky" are sufficient to teach the young speaker a lesson in imaginative humility, in restraint of exuberant possessiveness, in "gentleness of heart." In Frost's poem, however, the imagination is in a more Promethean mood. Though the natural emblem would seem clearly to suggest a lesson in humility—though the girl's assault on the grapes has been patently rebuked—the mature woman's meditation on the experience refuses to deduce any such lesson.

In fact, though the plot of "Wild Grapes" is remarkably close to that of "Nutting," both the lesson and the structure of this poem are reminiscent of the climactic Simplon Pass episode of the sixth book of *The Prelude.* There, during the Alpine crossing itself in 1790, Wordsworth is baffled by the natural event, which seems to frustrate his expectations: "I was lost; / Halted without an effort to break through." It is only in retrospect, in a passage added fourteen years after the event, that the poet is able to realize: "But to my conscious soul I now can say— / 'I recognize thy glory'" (lines 596–99). So, in "Wild Grapes," an unusual lapse of time between the natural event, which befalls the five-year-old girl, and the final reading of its significance, retrospectively by the now-grown woman, yields a particularly assertive realization.

Even as early as the opening question of the poem, in the first six lines, it has been suggested that surprising harvests can be found if one knows where to look for them—and the final harvest here is the adult's lesson of the power of desire and imagination. The wild grapes grow high in birches, which always in Frost suggest aspiration, "Mostly as much beyond my lifted hands . . . / As the moon used to seem when I was younger." The "lifted hands" of desire, reaching for the moon which is both an extraterrestrial goal and (for Wordsworth as for Coleridge) a sign of imagination, stretch beyond natural limits and in doing so discover, at least retrospectively, the spirit's true strength. This is what the final meditative section of "Wild Grapes" concludes. The immediate lesson of her childhood experience, the mature woman

suggests, is that she was ignorant: "It wasn't my not weighing anything / So much as my not knowing anything." Again, as so often in
these Promethean poems, knowing and not knowing are crucial issues. But the girl's ignorance is an imaginatively healthy kind of innocence, an ignorance of natural limitation: "I had not taken the first
step in knowledge; / I had not learned to let go with the hands." In
mature reflection, such ignorance or innocence is seen to be a valu-
able trait of the spirit; the lesson which this woman finally draws is the
opposite of that in "Nutting":

> I had not learned to let go with the hands,
> As still I have not learned to with the heart,
> And have no wish to with the heart—nor need,
> That I can see. The mind—is not the heart.
> I may yet live, as I know others live,
> To wish in vain to let go with the mind—
> Of cares, at night, to sleep; but nothing tells me
> That I need learn to let go with the heart.

Here again the ultimate lesson, paradoxically, is the importance of *not*
learning the obvious natural lesson—of discovering, beyond it, the
spirit's own lesson, the power of "this limitless trait in the hearts of
men" and girls and women. The little girl's fearful experience may
have "wiped out" her intrepid youthful "beginning," but the death of
that earlier self was the birth of a second and more triumphant self,
"And the life I live now's an extra life." The girl-woman has been
"translated" (line 45) to a higher realm of experience, "the upper regions" ruled by the heart's desires.

The final lines of "Wild Grapes" oppose "mind," here the instrument of prudential wisdom, to "heart," here the Promethean force
which casts off merely prudential "cares" and limits: it is precisely in
"not knowing anything" in the prudential sense about the conventionally accepted limits of desire, in being ignorant in the worldly

sense, that the girl discovers the power of the heart and its desires. But such an opposition is atypical of the Promethean poems. Taken as a group, these poems celebrate a rich, powerful, and many-sided force, which Frost variously calls "mind," "heart," "soul," and "spirit," and which clearly includes both imagination and sheer desire as well. Indeed, Frost likes Catullus's phrase *mens animi* because it suggests both heart and intellect—"the thoughts of the heart," in Frost's own rendering (Thompson and Winnick 238). The census-taker's intent is not to add up bodies but "to count souls." Frost asks of the force which "comes over a man" and makes him plant peach trees beyond their natural range, "Is it soul or mind?"

This power which informs the Promethean poems, whether we call it the *mens animi* or the *élan vital* or "this limitless trait in the hearts of men," involves above all the primal desire of the self—not letting go with the heart—and a radical kind of self-assertion—"Insisting always on our own way so." But, as in Emerson, in these poems the self is ultimately not selfish. One of its most insistent desires is for freedom, movement, and newness, signified not only by the flight metaphors of "Kitty Hawk" or the determination to "Steer straight off after something into space," but also by the molting metaphor of "Sand Dunes" (we can cast off our shells and "be but more free to think"). "Mind you, we are mind. / We are not the kind / To stay too confined"; the human being is by definition that creature who "can stay confined" "to no limits and bounds."

But the radical freedom from any kind of fixity or limits which these poems celebrate is not an end in itself. It is a means, among other things, to dominate and conquer external nature, which is defined, like the sea, as incapable of "knowing" anything, especially mankind, and, like "the Outer Black," as being "heartless" (361). Through mind, both scientific and poetic, and through heart or desire, the Promethean Frost wants to "seize earth by the pole," to make "the infinite" "Rationally ours." The images of illumination in these poems—of "the ray we dart / From this head and heart," of the "artificial light" which we have "taken" "Against the ancient sovereignty of night" (361)—are images of actively seeking out the unknown, probing into it (as in "All Revelation"), knowing it, naming it ("to master Nature / By some nomenclature"), domesticating it, humanizing it. But for Frost, as for Emerson, to conquer nature in this imaginative assault is not to do it ultimate violence, but to give it meaning and so complete it: "Ours was to reclaim" the "waste" of air and space; we appropriately "Undertake to tell" nature what "She's supposed to mean."

The ultimate goals of the imaginative uprisings in these poems, then, are truly Promethean: to humanize nature and, finally, to assert our deepest wish, that life should prove more powerful than death. "A Soldier" asserts almost baldly that war and earth can "check and trip the body," but cannot impede the flight of "the spirit"; the planter risks the peach tree's life, ironically, because "his ambition" is "to extend the reach / Clear to the Arctic of every living kind." For the author of these poems as for the census-taker, "It must be I want life to go on living."

6.

We have for so long thought of Frost as a poet of the "diminished thing" and the "momentary stay against confusion," as an ironist, as a conservative both temperamentally and poetically, as a poet who "almost always . . . chooses to counterbalance" "transcendent impulses" (Wyatt 89–91), that it is little short of startling to realize how thoroughly Promethean he can be in certain moods—but then, the Romantic predecessor whom he most often echoes verbally is not Wordsworth or Keats but Shelley, a formidably Promethean writer himself. In poems like "There Are Roughly Zones," "On a Tree Fallen Across the Road," and "Wild Grapes," the imagination rises up "To bathe in the Waters of Life; to wash off the Not Human," as Blake puts it (141). Yet it remains true, of course, that these poems represent an extreme stage in Frost's visionary effort. With such poems we reach the limits, remarkable as they are, of Frost's Prometheanism.

In the final analysis that Prometheanism is less Blakean—central, continuous, and polemical—than Wordsworthian. Like Wordsworth's moments of imaginative self-assertion in the Simplon Pass episode, in his description of "spots of time" (*Prelude* 12: 208–23), and in the closing lines of *The Prelude* (14: 448–54), Frost's Promethean moments are peninsular, outgrowths of a larger body of verse which is more moderate in its claims for the power of imagination vis-à-vis natural fact. We need to recognize more clearly than we have the genuinely Promethean or (in Emerson's sense) Orphic side of Frost's poetry. But that side is, on the whole, outweighed by a more characteristic sense of kinship with the created world.[10] That sense is best dramatized, perhaps, in "Birches," which recognizes a Promethean kind of imaginative yearning but ultimately forgoes it in favor of an earthward return to and acceptance of natural reality.

The first twenty lines of "Birches" clearly hint at Promethean tendencies. The poem is set at that time of the natural year which most suggests imaginative stirrings: the springtime moment in the imagination's life when it begins to rouse itself from winter lethargy. Though immobilized by their wintry covering of ice, as the Eolian "breeze rises" the birches move "and turn many-colored / As the stir cracks and crazes their enamel." "Soon," warmed by the sun, they "shed crystal shells," like the human beings of "Sand Dunes" casting off dead external coverings to take on new shapes and new vitality. The evidences of that spiritual molting, as many have noted, echo the Promethean outreach of *Adonais:* "Such heaps of broken glass to sweep away / You'd think the inner dome of heaven had fallen." [11] And, though the birches are permanently "bowed" by the ice storm, they remain suggestive of aspiration: "You may see their trunks arching in the woods / Years afterwards," still straining toward that inner dome of heaven.

In the poem's central fiction, Frost adroitly converts the birches from emblems of Promethean aspiration to emblems of natural fact conquered by that aspiration. Rather than an ice storm, the poet "should prefer to have some boy bend" the birches; this fictive explanation represents more clearly the central presence of *human* activity, and human domination of the natural ("One by one he subdued his father's trees"). The comparison used to describe the care which the boy takes in climbing to the very "top branches" of the birches—"climbing carefully / With the same pains you use to fill a cup / Up to the brim, and even above the brim"—reminds us that this is not only a poem about trees but a celebration of spiritual thirst.

But, in the last third of the poem, where he explicitly reads in the act of swinging birches a lesson for the governance of one's imaginative life, Frost draws back from the Prometheanism implied earlier in the poem: "I'd like to get away from earth awhile / And then come back to it and begin over." As that latter line suggests, the visionary assertion of "Birches" is ultimately less extreme than that of "Wild Grapes." As Richard Wilbur notes, the echoes of Shelley in this poem are ultimately used to argue against Shelley's Prometheanism: "'Birches,' taken as a whole, is in fact an answer to Shelley's kind of boundless neo-Platonic aspiration" (113). The famous closing lines of the poem clearly move toward a reconciliation of human aspiration and earthly reality. The poet hopes that "no fate" will "willfully misunderstand" him "And half grant what I wish and snatch me away / Not to return. Earth's the right place for love."

> I'd like to go by climbing a birch tree,
> And climb black branches up a snow-white trunk
> *Toward* heaven, till the tree could bear no more,
> But dipped its top and set me down again.
> That would be good both going and coming back.

The proper role of the mind or spirit is seen here, not as a conquest of the natural, not as a transcending of earth or a "steering straight off after something into space," but as an integral part of a larger process of give and take, "launching out" and return. The young girl in "Wild Grapes," because of her "not knowing anything" about "letting go," about accommodating natural fact, is carried off by the birch in that poem like a fish caught by a fish pole. The mature speaker of "Birches," on the other hand, knows how to use natural fact to reach its uppermost limits, to climb "*Toward* heaven, till the tree could bear no more," but then to accept the end of the trip and be returned by the tree in a kind of cooperative effort. The imagination here again asserts its freedom and autonomy by dominating natural fact; but then, refreshed by that flexing of imaginative muscle, it "comes back" to natural fact to "begin over," now willing to accept the different but also "almost incredible freedom," as Frost puts it elsewhere, of being "enslaved to the hard facts of experience" (*Letters* 179).[12]

Such a return or reconciliation would, for Blake or Shelley, amount to surrender. But Frost, like most other American nature writers, does not posit Blake's or Shelley's kind of inevitable struggle to the death between imaginative perception and natural fact. Like Thoreau (with certain exceptions), like Emerson in his more restrained moods, Frost believes that, in the final analysis, the two forces are capable of cooperating to achieve meaning. Even apparent natural obstruction of human desire, as in "A Soldier" or "On a Tree Fallen Across the Road," or apparent natural reproof of human overreaching, as in "Wild Grapes," is part of a larger design: nature impedes the mind in order to clarify and intensify its awareness of its own creative powers. In other words, for Frost, as for Wordsworth,[13] even when the mind learns essentially transcendent lessons about its own strength, those lessons are taught, at least indirectly, by nature.

Frost's final assessment of the balance between imaginative outreach and the return to earthly reality is well summarized in "Bond and Free," the poem immediately preceding "Birches" in *Mountain Interval.* "Thought," with its exploratory flight on "dauntless wings" into the farthest reaches of "the interstellar gloom," is not seen here as unambiguously admirable in the manner of the Wright brothers; it is more nearly an Icarus-like overreacher, returning reluctantly to natural fact "With smell of burning on every plume." "Love," on the other hand, "has earth to which she clings / With hills and circling arms about." Though bound to the natural reality of "snow and sand and turf," however, Love is neither dispirited nor deprived of all revelation:

> some say Love by being thrall
> And simply staying possesses all
> In several beauty that Thought fares far
> To find fused in another star.

In his most characteristic moods, Frost ultimately distrusts that momentary impulse of thought or mind or heart to "steer straight off after something into space"—chiefly, I think, because of the dangers of some kind of solipsism in such flight. Love, in this poem as in the famous line from "Birches" or in "The Silken Tent," ties the spirit to earth and natural fact.

The return to natural fact is ultimately characteristic of Frost— but it *is* a return, and is satisfying to poet and reader alike only because it follows the Promethean flight on "dauntless wings." Poirier is essentially right in speaking of "Frost's congenital distrust of the freedom he liked to extol, his ultimate distrust of an imagination set free as it is in Stevens" (79). But that distrust of unfettered imagination would be neither poetically interesting nor spiritually necessary if Frost did not feel, at least from "Reluctance" to "Kitty Hawk," the attraction of Promethean possibilities.

7.

I want finally to look at an unusual meditative emblem poem, "On the Heart's Beginning to Cloud the Mind." While several of the Promethean poems (like "Sand Dunes") represent only borderline instances of processiveness, this poem is, conversely, the only clearly meditative poem which is not Promethean. It is still, however, an instructive example of what can be accomplished within the processive structure of the meditative and heuristic emblem poems. Its processiveness is unusually clear because it is built, more obviously than any other meditative poem, on a dual movement from synecdochic vehicle to tenor: a preliminary, deathly reading of the natural emblem, followed by an imaginative reversal and triumph.

The poem is set in the diurnal equivalent of midwinter, the season of so many of these meditative poems: the poet looks out of his railroad car "In the desert at midnight." The emblem which he sees involves a contrast between the apparent community of other worlds and the apparent isolation of earthly life: "The sky had here and there a star; / The earth had a single light afar." From this suggestive contrast the poet leaps, in the first movement, to a chilling lesson reminiscent of that in "To a Moth Seen in Winter"; that single, distant earthly light he interprets as

> A flickering, human pathetic light,
> That was maintained against the night,
> It seemed to me, by the people there,
> With a Godforsaken brute despair.
> It would flutter and fall in half an hour
> Like the last petal off a flower.

The apparently human light in this nocturnal landscape is not seen as truly human; it is kept with a "brute" lack of hope and will soon "flutter and fall" like a "petal off a [dying] flower." It seems, in short, to belong to the order of nature—those unthinking, mechanistic cycles which so dismay Frost in the fablelike and in some of the prototypical emblem poems. Like the visibilia in "To a Moth Seen in Winter" and "The Census-Taker," it suggests the inevitable defeat of human effort and inspires only pity.

Significantly, however, this poem is less than a third of the way through its imaginative workings. The poet immediately rejects his preliminary reading of the scene; "my heart," he sees retrospectively, "was beginning to cloud my mind." Here "heart" and "mind" would seem to be used in a sense almost the opposite of that in the closing section of "Wild Grapes." There, "heart" suggests human will and aspiration, "mind" the prudential intelligence; here "heart" suggests the sentimental, weak side of the imagination, which has momentarily obscured the potentially powerful light of the visionary side. But now, in the peripeteia of the last two-thirds of the poem, Frost goes on to a second translation of the same scene, "a tale of a better kind," a more triumphant reading. By imagining that the single light which he can see "flickers because of trees" which he cannot see, and particularly that there may have been other earthly lights which were extinguished earlier in the night, "So lost on me in my surface flight," the poet expands his imaginative perspective in a fashion which we saw foreshadowed in the last chapter. By doing so he is able to envision a healthy social order, rather than the isolation of "To a Moth," "The Census-Taker," and the first reading here. This community is represented not only by the unseen presence of lights from other human dwellings—"They know where another light has been, / And more than one, to theirs akin"—but also by the imagined couple whose light the poet does see. "He is husband, she is wife," Frost speculates in a curiously sing-song passage; "She fears not him, they fear not life." As a result of the community which the lone light paradoxically represents in this new reading, the light itself is transformed. No longer is it the quavering, "pathetic" light for which the poet first mistook it, about to "flutter and fall"; now it is a steady glow of human effort lighting the desert midnight as the wood-pile heats the frozen swamp in that poem:

> The people can burn it as long as they please;
> And when their interests in it end,
> They can leave it to someone else to tend.
> Come back that way a summer hence,
> I should find it no more no less intense.

"On the Heart's Beginning to Cloud the Mind," with its insistent couplets and recurrent tendency to aphorism, is not one of Frost's greatest poetic achievements; but it clearly demonstrates the advantages of a processive structure. Had it been a prototypical emblem poem, it would by definition have been limited to the somber, "pathetic" translation of the first twelve lines. Only the processive nature of the poem makes possible the self-admonition of the thirteenth line; only the meditative "time out" enables the poet's imagination to struggle against, and overcome, its earlier, weaker reading of the lone desert light, and so move to the second, brighter reading.

With that triumphant movement in mind, it is possible to see retrospectively that the descriptive portion of the poem contains hints of the powerful lurking presence of the imagination. In the fourth line, for instance, the poet looks "At moonlit sky and moonlit earth"—the moonlight, again, signalling the presence of the Coleridgean imagination which not only illuminates but also connects sky and earth. The epilogue to the poem suggests more obliquely the same lurking power:

This I saw when waking late,
Going by at a railroad rate,
Looking through wreaths of engine smoke
Far into the lives of other folk.

"Waking" is a deliberately active adjective, chosen in preference to the more usual but static "awake"; it suggests especially a dawning awareness of human community—shared, as the last line suggests, not only by the imagined inhabitants of the imagined house, but also by the poet.[14] Most importantly, those seemingly workaday "wreaths of engine smoke"—the medium through which the scene of human persistence and community is perceived—are in fact visionary cousins of Wordsworth's trope for the imagination as "an unfathered vapour that enwraps, / At once, some lonely traveller" (*Prelude* 6: 595–96).[15]

Unlike Wordsworth's, Frost's imaginative vapors are never unfathered; but they recur in several poems—always as adjuncts to the Coleridgean moonlight—to fill and transform otherwise barren scenes. I noted in the last chapter the "autumn haze" which is the most important physical presence in "The Cocoon"; looking at it in greater detail, we can see how effectively it images the visionary power of the mind:

> this autumn haze
> That spreading in the evening air both ways
> Makes the new moon look anything but new
> And pours the elm-tree meadow full of blue . . .

The haze both connects details of the landscape and transforms them. It mingles with the moonlight, not (as it might seem at first glance) to age and yellow it, but to spread its transforming light. Physically, the haze "makes the new moon look anything but new" by diffusing the light to make the moon seem full instead of crescent; imaginatively, it likewise expands the moon's influence, spreading the new light of vision. Moreover, the haze infuses the earthly meadow with the blue of "heaven," as "Fragmentary Blue" puts it. Again in the triumphant vision of "Moon Compasses," though the images are not so carefully detailed, the moon spreads down its measuring and embracing rays "To a cone mountain in the midnight haze."

In all three poems the moonlight illuminates and beautifies, while the vapor fills and transforms, an otherwise bleak landscape into a vision of community (in several senses), of renewal, of acceptance. A kind of human community—of husband and wife in "West-Running Brook," of brother and sister in "Wild Grapes," or of people generally in "On a Tree Fallen Across the Road"—may be implied in many of the Promethean poems; certainly their assertive vision obviates the isolation which dominates "failed" Promethean poems like "To a Moth Seen in Winter" and "The Census-Taker." But, of all the clearly meditative emblem poems, only "On the Heart's Beginning to Cloud the Mind," with its two-part movement and clear triumph of the imagination, foreshadows the central focus of the heuristic emblem poems: not the domination of natural fact by mind or spirit, but the "fellowship" between human beings and, as background for that, between the human and the natural.

To return to the terms used in "Bond and Free," "Thought," or the imagination in its Promethean moods, may seek to assert its power by breaking free from all earthly ties; but Frost instinctively fears the kind of solipsism to which such flight might ultimately lead. As the heuristic emblem poems demonstrate, "Love," or the imagination in its more appreciative and conciliatory moods, not only cherishes the "several beauty" of the created world. By reading the commonplace characters of the vegetable text, "Dwarf cornel, goldthread, and *Maianthemum*," it also discovers the full extent of the relationships between the self and the other, both natural and human.

CHAPTER 7

Tales of a Better Kind

Here are your waters and your watering place.
Drink and be whole again beyond confusion. (379)

1.

The conventional critical view of Frost, simply put, holds that he is not a
visionary poet. A consideration of Frost as an Emersonian poet concludes
typically that "Revelation is engagingly immanent in Frost . . . , but it is
habitually denied. . . . Because revelation . . . does not really come,
Frost's is a poetry of aborted communion" (Porter 20, 88). Another
study summarizes: "In Frost, moments of relationship, of peace and
harmony, are not only rare *gifts* but . . . cannot be expected from nature"; "we see man seeking but only seldom finding harmony between
himself and nature" (Oster 108, 221). Even as sympathetic a reader
as fellow poet Charles Simic finds Frost (like Dickinson and Stevens)
to be both a visionary (since "All truly philosophical poetry is visionary") and an "anti-visionary"—in sum, a "visionary skeptic" who has
"a lover's quarrel with Emerson and his transcendentalism," for whom
"Nature is opaque, inert, mute, and often malevolent. Nature transmits no message. It is a realm of endless ambiguity"; "Nature is oblivious of us"; we live "in a vast, mysterious, perhaps even meaningless
universe" (114–15, 119–20). Or, as Harold Bloom would have it,
Frost's "harsh landscapes" are full only of "the cosmological emptiness into which we have been thrown by the mocking Demiurge"
("Introduction" 5).

Anyone who has ever read Frost with care must agree that his nature can be dark and impassive, and the poet himself willfully "anti-

visionary." One might say that the phrases I have quoted fairly accurately describe the Frost of the fablelike emblem poems and of many of the prototypical emblem poems (though hardly, I would say, of poems like "Hyla Brook" and "Moon Compasses"). Such phrases do not, of course, recognize the Promethean Frost whom I described in the previous chapter. Above all, I would insist, such phrases do not adequately—in fact, do not accurately—describe the author of most of what I have called the heuristic emblem poems, in many ways the culmination of Frost's achievement in the nature lyrics. As a group, these lyrics both complete the structural development of Frost's emblem poems and act out the final, remarkably fulfilling—even visionary—stage of his imaginative effort.

Structurally, three salient traits distinguish these heuristic emblem poems from the three groups considered in the preceding chapters. First, the character of the emblem itself again alters. Only one of these poems ("Take Something Like a Star") originates, in the manner of the fablelike poems, in a generalized or habitual phenomenon. More surprisingly, only two of them ("A Missive Missile" and "The Need of Being Versed in Country Things") grow, as many of the prototypical and meditative emblem poems do, out of a specific, particularized object or scene. Following the example of "Wild Grapes," the great majority of these poems draw their lessons from natural *events* or incidents. The significance of this change in natural emblem seems clear: like Wordsworth's "correspondent breeze" at the beginning of *The Prelude* or Coleridge's "deadly storm" in "Dejection," these natural signs—active happenings rather than static tableaux—are especially well suited to elicit, and to reflect, the fullest activity of the imagination.

Second, these poems, like the meditative poems, do not simply juxtapose natural emblem and natural lesson; they too are processive, dramatizing the movement of the imagination from natural text to a kind of natural wisdom.

Third, in terms of the fictions of these poems, their natural lessons, unlike those of the meditative poems, are arrived at, not discursively, through an interior train of contemplation, but intuitively. In the stories told in these poems, however complicated the process by which the mind moves from sight to insight, it finds that insight in the emblem itself; it does not need to meditate its way to wisdom, but discovers it—hence the term "heuristic"—in the natural event. In a surprising number of these poems, the natural world does not in fact seem oblivious of the human observer, but seems virtually solicitous of his education, willing, even eager to reveal a kind of natural wisdom. In perhaps the acutest case of such natural revelation, a rainbow, "Instead of moving with us as we went / (To keep the pots of gold from being found)," does something "That never yet to other two befell," and willingly allows two friends to find the metaphorical pots of gold.

The combination of these characteristics serves to provide a type of structure and movement well suited to acting out a completed "reading" process: beginning with active perception of a striking incident, moving through error and obstruction toward the heart of the emblem, and finally—notwithstanding the conventional critical view that Frost's "Nature is opaque" and "mute," and "transmits no message"—achieving something which can legitimately be called natural revelation. The dramatic impact of the process, in turn, is well suited to the vision of the heuristic emblem poems: the final stage of the imaginative effort, in which the seer—notwithstanding the accepted view that Frost's is "a poetry of aborted communion"—achieves recognition of himself and his place in a larger order of things.

2.

The makeup of the heuristic emblem poems as a group tells us something about Frost's self-consciousness: at the same time that most of them describe the fullest moments of his vision, a number of them dramatize the dangers inherent in the visionary enterprise. Three of them in particular warn against the potential dangers of excessive anthropocentrism in reading natural emblems. The best known of these caveats, "The Need of Being Versed in Country Things," serves a function roughly analogous to that of "Design": it reads a natural lesson the point of which is the potential uncertainty of natural lessons. The poem presents an interesting contrast to Promethean pieces like "Wild Grapes" and "There Are Roughly Zones." In each of those poems, an apparent natural lesson suggesting the limitations on human desire is cast aside in favor of a transcendent lesson reasserting the primacy of aspiration. "The Need of Being Versed in Country Things," on the contrary, deduces first an apparent lesson which implies the centrality of human concerns, and then a corrective lesson which insists that the heart's desires are not so central after all.

The first descriptive portion of the poem (lines 1–14) paints a somber natural emblem: a burned-out house, no longer occupied by humans, and a deserted barn now inhabited only by birds, which "At broken windows flew out and in." The preliminary, mistaken lesson of this scene, implicitly drawn in the next two lines, sees natural melancholy at the passing of human presence: the birds' "murmur" seems "more like the sigh we sigh / From too much dwelling on what has been." Such excessive "dwelling on" or living in the burned-out shell of the past would obviously be an un-Thoreauvian lesson, however; indeed, as the first poem of "The Hill Wife" group reminds us, it represents an essentially neurotic view of natural solicitude.

The poem, consequently, traces a second movement in its last two stanzas. There, as the poem's perspective broadens, the scene, though emptied of human activity, is perceived as no less hospitable to the phoebes, to life in the broad sense, than it has always been. In these lines personification, ironically, not only assures us that the birds do not weep for the loss of human companions ("they rejoiced in the nest they kept"—always a double-edged verb in Frost). It also suggests that the nonhuman world—not only the "aged" elm, but even the inanimate pump which "flung up an awkward arm" and fence post which "carried a strand of wire" to provide convenient perches—manifests just the sort of solicitude for the phoebes which the phoebes do not manifest for the departed humans. Thus even a scene of human desolation, perceived in a sufficiently broad natural context, is an emblem of continuing vitality (and nonhuman community). That true lesson has been hinted at as early as the poem's opening quatrain, where the submerged metaphor suggests a Thoreauvian kind of springtime renewal out of apparent autumnal death. "The house had gone to bring" a glow to the sky, but the chimney is left standing "Like a pistil after the petals go"—like the reproductive center of the faded flower, bearing the seed of another generation.

As its structure and title imply, however, "The Need of Being Versed in Country Things" is not primarily about natural resilience and regeneration; it uses that lesson chiefly to illustrate a larger concern: the dangers of a too narrowly human perspective—not unlike that parodied in "The Most of It." The poem does not suggest that natural wisdom is inaccessible to the human observer (the true lesson, after all, waits to be read in the scene); but it does chasten what might be called the Blakean tendencies of the imagination and warn us of the dangers (not to mention the emptiness) of finding only our immediate selves in the natural text. The legitimate use of personification here is to represent something like solicitude in the natural world, not for us, but for itself.[1]

The dangers of excessive anthropocentrism are overcome in "The Need of Being Versed"; in "A Missive Missile," however, they come very close to sheer solipsism and the defeat of the central effort to read the external world; the poem, an important one, is a more pessimistic consideration of the relationship between perception and meaning than the better-known "Design." Ironically, the sign to be read here is man-made—"a little pebble wheel" with red markings which has survived from the prehistorical Azilian culture of Western Europe. The opening description tells us little about the physical appearance of the artifact, instead stressing the assumption (of which Emerson would surely approve) that the markings on it are intended to convey meaning to the modern observer, that this stone missile is genuinely missive. "Someone" in that prehistoric culture, the speaker assumes, marked this stone "with red for me,"

> And sent it to me years and years—
> A million years to be precise—
> Across the barrier of ice:
> Two round dots and a ripple streak,
> So vivid as to seem to speak.

The mute stone refuses to speak, however. The poet does not leap to a preliminary, mistaken reading of the artifact; worse than that, his attempts to get its meaning all end in frustration. He considers but finds unsatisfactory the possibilities that the markings may be a record of general human suffering (lines 9–12) or of human sacrifice (13–18). Now, only a third of the way through the poem's movement, the conventional reading process comes to an abrupt end, and the poet begins to read a more general lesson from the very difficulty of reading the artifact in any specific sense—another lesson about the limitations on the reading process itself. The dilemma which he faces, Frost realizes, is the result of the enormous imaginative distance between his own position and that of the emblem's author—a distance which soon comes to seem unbridgeable.

> So almost clear and yet obscure.
> If only anyone were sure
> A motive then was still a motive. . . .
> There is no answer, I'm afraid,
> Across the icy barrier
> For my obscure petitioner.

In the final third of the poem Frost turns his attention from the arti-fact—the text—to the reader. He never considers the possibility that the markings may not in fact constitute a message of any sort; the quasi-Emersonian assumptions about the intention of the emblem remain unchal-lenged. If the communicative intent is not realized, then, the fault must lie in the imaginative opacity of the reader, thwarting intended revelation with his inadequate perception: "Oh, slow uncomprehending me, / Enough to make a spirit moan / Or rustle in a bush or tree." The spirits of the natural world can only lament the failed reading of the emblem, and the likeliest cause of such incomprehension appears again to be, as in "The Need of Being Versed in Country Things," excessive preoccupation with self, an incapacity to break out of an essentially solipsistic perspective.

> The meaning of it is unknown,
> Or else I fear entirely mine,
> All modern, nothing ancient in't,
> Unsatisfying to us each.

If the reader's perception is confined by the narrow round of his own, or his age's, assumptions, even the most skillfully designed text will fail in its mission to communicate.

> Far as we aim our signs to reach,
> Far as we often make them reach,
> Across the soul-from-soul abyss,
> There is an aeon-limit set
> Beyond which they are doomed to miss.

Certainly "A Missive Missile" is an exceptional heuristic emblem poem, partly because of the withering effects of its vast archaeological perspective and that "aeon-limit." But it is surely not just a poem about deciphering prehistoric markings; it is a double warning against imprisonment in a narrow, selfish, or parochial outlook, ultimately verging on solipsism. Revelation or education, in a larger sense, based on the ability to read that most important artifact, the creation, may be frustrated. At the same time, the poem worries about the difficulties inherent in human communication—a process which, in its efforts to bridge "the soul-from-soul abyss," is a central and recurrent concern of the heuristic emblem poems. The artist in us, shaping an artifact or a poem, cries out not only for design but also for communication. If, however intent our aim, however deep our "mortal longing," our signs fail to reach across that abyss, then "Two souls may be too widely met"; perception, communication, poetry may all fail.

Of the heuristic emblem poems which dramatize the obstacles to vision, "A Missive Missile" is not only the most pessimistic; it is also the only one which does not have a dual movement from sight to insight. "Take Something Like a Star" examines the emblem-reading enterprise from the astronomical rather than the archaeological perspective; just as the latter makes communication seem unlikely across eons of time, so the former threatens to make communication unlikely across vast distances—but only in the first movement of "Take Something." The apostrophe to the star in the first descriptive passage is both unusual and ironic: the burden of the opening monologue to the star is, as I suggested in chapter 1, the great difficulty of reading its lesson when the "language" it uses is not a human language. The first movement to natural lesson appears to be thwarted in the second half of the eleventh line: "And it says, 'I burn.'"

In the second movement, the poet again addresses the distant star, again urging it to "Use language we can comprehend." But now, though the natural emblem does not alter—or rather, because it does not alter—the poet begins to understand what it is "saying" to him. In a sudden shift from direct address to the star to third-person commentary on it—a shift which reflects yet another broadening of intellectual perspective—the poet realizes that the star's very refusal to "say something" is itself saying something.

It gives us strangely little aid,
But does tell something in the end.
And steadfast as Keats' Eremite,
Not even stooping from its sphere,
It asks a little of us here.

Not by any human speech, but by the mute testimony of its transhuman steadfastness, the very brightness of its example, the star teaches us something about how to live. If that lesson is predictable— "It asks of us a certain height," a certain disinterestedness in governing our lives—it is so partly because of the poem's long literary genealogy. Both in its emblem and in its lesson, "Take Something Like a Star" is descended not only from Keats's sonnet but also from Bryant's "Hymn to the North Star":

A beauteous type of that unchanging good,
That bright eternal beacon, by whose ray
The voyager of time should shape his heedful way.

Its lesson also recalls Emerson's final assertion in "Monadnoc" that the mountain—"in our astronomy / An opaker star"—by its very height and permanence "Recallest us, / And makest sane" (*Complete Works* 9: 74).

Unlike any of his nineteenth-century forebears, however, Frost has learned the emblem's ethical lesson only after an imaginative struggle in the poem's first movement. In that movement he fails to read the star's lesson—and again the chief obstacle to comprehension is an excessively man-locked point of view (to borrow a term from Stevens)—"Talk Fahrenheit, talk Centigrade." It can scarcely be coincidental that all three of these heuristic emblem poems which comment on the emblem-reading process warn against the dangers of excessive anthropocentrism. They are, in effect, warning against just those Blakean or Promethean tendencies of the mind which the meditative emblem poems celebrate. They are insisting on a return to natural reality; in distinctly different ways all three of them teach a kind of imaginative restraint, perhaps even humility. It is as if, having flexed its muscle and demonstrated its strength in that stage of vision represented by the meditative emblem poems, the imagination now prepares to put that strength to use in reading lessons, not of its own preeminence, but of its place in a larger order.

3.

In the continuing drama of inner and outer weather described in Frost's seasonal poems, we can recognize, despite the remarkable complexities, an overall visionary process which reaches its culmination in the heuristic emblem poems. Not surprisingly, a wintry stage of vision dominates the fablelike poems. Here the poet is for the most part preoccupied with the end of summer ("In Hardwood Groves," "November") and the coming of winter ("Desert Places"); "In Winter in the Woods Alone" fairly well epitomizes this stage of the imaginative cycle. Yet some of the darkest seasonal poems of the fablelike variety are those which deal with spring ("Nothing Gold Can Stay," "The Strong Are Saying Nothing," "Spring Pools")—and see even the moment of natural renewal as foreboding. The prototypical emblem poems show a noticeable transition. Some of these lyrics still describe a bleak, even ominous vision of autumn ("Bereft") and winter ("A Winter Eden"); and a number of them, like projections from the dark springtime poems of the previous group, tend to view summer as loss ("The Oven Bird") or waste (the first three-fourths of "Pod of the Milkweed"). But this dark vision, spanning almost the entire seasonal cycle, begins to moderate in a number of poems. In something like the obverse of the fablelike group, in which some of the darkest poems are spring poems, here some of the more hopeful visions occur at the point in the cycle where we might least expect them—just before or just after winter ("The Cocoon," "Our Singing Strength").

The brightening of the seasonal vision begun in the prototypical emblem poems continues in the meditative poems. An occasional lyric may still be genuinely autumnal ("The Census-Taker") or wintry ("To a Moth Seen in Winter"), but for the most part these seasonal poems move strongly toward a more assertive vision. In what we should by now recognize as a characteristically Frostian twist, this brighter vision tends to be enacted, not in poems of spring or summer, but in poems of winter transformed by the active imagination ("There Are Roughly Zones," "On a Tree Fallen Across the Road"). Finally, in the present group of seasonal poems, the overall progress is completed. Even the rare autumnal vision here is not wholly bleak; the winter moment is, with only a single exception, a moment of transformation; spring is (quite the contrary of spring in the fablelike poems) genuinely Thoreauvian; and even summer becomes, for the first time, the moment of imaginative fulfillment which it normally represents for Stevens.

Of the seven heuristic emblem poems set in autumn or winter, only "My Butterfly" describes an essentially chilling vision. The poem, Frost's first published lyric (1894), reflects its early composition both in its wistful archaic language and in the essentially youthful mood which the language projects—a mood (also to be found in poems like "Ghost House" and "My November Guest") in which the poet of sensibility not only experiences but savors melancholy. Though the poem's final natural lesson is elegiac (and it was originally subtitled "An Elegy"), even here, in the most leaden moment of these seasonal poems, a more heartening natural message lies embedded in the predominant autumnal sorrow.

Despite its early composition, "My Butterfly" is structurally complex. In the course of its long apostrophe to the butterfly—one of several winged creatures, ultimately natural correspondents to the poet's own spirit, which reappear in the heuristic emblem poems—the poem narrates the relationship of poet and butterfly over the course of six or eight months. That narrative describes three distinct periods of time: the early spring, when the poet first saw the butterfly (lines 10–30); a later moment, presumably in the summer, when he again encountered the butterfly (lines 31–42); and, as narrative frame, the present moment in late autumn. Each of these temporal divisions involves its own peculiar failure or triumph of emblem reading.

In the earliest period, the poem stresses the ignorance of both speaker and butterfly. In their springtime joy they are now seen to have been like the schoolboys in Gray's "Eton College" ode; given no natural sign, they could not read the sobering lesson of the transience of such joy, could not know "That fate had made thee"—and by implication the speaker, too—"for the pleasure of the wind." In autumnal retrospect the poet sees their springtime happiness as only a small exception to a world which is scarcely hospitable to such gaiety, in which a jealous Creator, "fearful" of the very freedom of the butterfly, has since "Snatched thee, o'ereager, with ungentle grasp."

The middle or summer stage of the narrative is the most remarkable of the three, foreshadowing some of the surprisingly bold fictions of later heuristic poems. Here an adult awareness of social discord has entered the speaker's experience. "Ah! I remember me / How once conspiracy was rife / Against my life." In his "languor" and dejection caused by such "conspiracy," the poet for the first time finds a natural sign, the butterfly itself. The approach of that sign is heralded by a "Surging . . . breeze" and a sort of natural enchantment ("a gem-flower waved in a wand!"). Then, just when it is most needed, a gesture of natural sympathy and support is given the troubled poet.

> Then when I was distraught
> And could not speak,
> Sidelong, full on my cheek,
> What should that reckless zephyr fling
> But the wild touch of thy dye-dusty wing!

This remarkable moment is recalled in the context of the whole poem chiefly in order to add poignancy to the natural sign—a clear memento mori—of the present autumnal moment.

I found that wing broken today!
For thou art dead, I said,
And the strange birds say.
I found it with the withered leaves
Under the eaves.

However, this contrast of present lifelessness with the recollected comfort of the butterfly's summertime touch, like any such elegiac recollection, inevitably works both ways. At the same time that it makes the present sense of loss more acute, the recollection also serves to provide a bright center to the poem, to take some of the chill off the autumnal sense of destruction. It is embedded between the ignorance of the springtime moment and the elegiac knowledge of the autumnal present, but that recollection of a kind of natural sympathy prevents "My Butterfly" from being a wholly gloomy vision of relationships—with nature, with other people, with a rather petulant Creator.

Except for that kernel of hopeful vision, "My Butterfly" is by far the darkest of all the heuristic emblem poems dealing with the seasonal cycle. Beyond it, these poems uniformly represent an imaginative triumph, a sense of natural blessing. The fact that the majority of them are set in winter only underlines their vision of what Frost elsewhere calls "fellowship."[2] The prototype of the heuristic emblem poems of winter transformation is the remarkable little lyric "Dust of Snow,"[3] which consists of thirty-four words, thirty-two of them monosyllabic. Typically, its natural emblem is not an object but an event: a crow in a tree "Shook down on me / The dust of snow." That action might seem, to other eyes than Frost's, or to the Frost of the fablelike poems, an annoying or even hostile one. But in its present mood the imagination refuses to interpret the incident as an assault by nature. Nor does it, of course, consider the event to be purely random. Instead, Frost sees the crow's action as a friendly, communicative gesture responding to his earlier "rue" and giving "my heart / A change of mood." (The poem's original title, in fact, was "A Favour.") Though the crow's gesture is a modest one, as the achievements in

Frost's vision so often are, it has also been literally salvational; it has "saved some part" of a previously lost winter day.

The same pattern of winter transformation, slightly complicated, occurs in "Looking for a Sunset Bird in Winter." Again the poet, in the midst of winter, learns a lesson akin to Wordsworth's faith that nature never did betray the heart that loved her; but the learning process here is considerably more dramatic, again following the dual movement from emblem to lesson. As the title suggests, the poet, solitary and extra-vagant, is in the midst of a quest,[4] seeking a kind of natural seal on or confirmation of the winter's day, "a sunset bird." The circumstances of that quest—midwinter and approaching dusk— at first seem menacing, as they so often are in Frost: "The west was getting out of gold, / The breath of air had died of cold." But the poet, "shoeing home across the white," suddenly thinks that he sees something: "I thought I saw a bird alight" (which may also be heard as "I thought I saw a bird, a light").

At this point, before we discover the meaning of the apparent phenomenon, Frost recalls another summer moment when, at this same tree, he was granted a natural blessing.

> In summer when I passed the place,
> I had to stop and lift my face;
> A bird with an angelic gift
> Was singing in it sweet and swift.

Both the meter and the language of this stanza (especially "angelic" and "sweet," unusual words in Frost's vocabulary) recall the *Songs of Innocence;* but that fact emphasizes the apparent contrast between the recollected summer moment and the present moment, in which the poet's search for a sunset bird appears to have been in vain. He has been mistaken in thinking that he saw a bird land in the tree; "No bird was singing in it now." Though he ritually circles the tree twice, the poet can find nothing in it but a lone remaining leaf. Natural communication seems to have failed; the first movement ends in the apparent frustration of the speaker's effort to find a sunset bird and its "angelic gift."

But in the very moment of apparent failure the winter transformation begins. The second descriptive passage turns from the central item, the tree, to the broader landscape.

> From my advantage on a hill
> I judged that such a crystal chill
> Was only adding frost to snow
> As gilt to gold that wouldn't show.

Though the singing tree is now bare, it is located on a hill that gives the poet just the "advantage" necessary for insight. As he expands the field of his vision, he begins to see that even the winter cold is not barren, but creative; it adds, with the profligacy of the artist, to the beauty of the snow-covered landscape, golden in the sunset. Now Frost's perception of the scene all but explicitly recognizes the artistry that has painted it.

> A brush had left a crooked stroke
> Of what was either cloud or smoke
> From north to south across the blue;
> A piercing little star was through.

Here, in the unlooked-for star in the darkening sky—a star so modest that it does not "pierce" but only "*was* through"—the poet implicitly finds a natural surrogate for the sunset bird ("a bird, a light") he has been seeking. That quiet, solitary star, the artist's signature in the sense of both autograph and emblem, also makes the poet "stop and lift my face," also bestows on him "an angelic gift" of natural completion and kinship. (Recall that the crow's action in "Dust of Snow" "Has *given* my heart / A change of mood"; many of the heuristic poems involve natural gifts.) The poetic tact here, in the tone as well as the scene presented, is a thoroughly Frostian, and a moving, achievement.

In a related poem of winter transformation, "Afterflakes," the preliminary danger lies not in a frustrated relationship with nature but, as in "Desert Places," in the poet's own internal darknesses. Again the speaker is solitary, out in nature, in midwinter. As in "Design," he suddenly perceives a natural phenomenon which seems to be an aberration from normal experience.

> In the thick of a teeming snowfall
> I saw my shadow on snow.
> I turned and looked back up at the sky,
> Where we still look to ask the why
> Of everything below.

It is no accident that the poem begins with such a schematically vertical perspective, sky above and man "below"; that axis reflects the central question here, one of moral worthiness or the lack of it. The first conclusion which the poet moves to draw, almost instinctively, is a lesson of his own corruption, the darkness which must be in his heart if he casts a dark shadow even in the midst of a snowstorm.

> If I shed such a darkness,
> If the reason was in me,
> That shadow of mine should show in form
> Against the shapeless shadow of storm,
> How swarthy I must be.

This preliminary reading is a rare moment for Frost. Like Coleridge in "The Mad Monk" or Wordsworth at rarer moments (e.g., after the theft of the boat in Book I of *The Prelude*), he senses here a gulf between the normality of nature and the depravity of his soul which seems to be imaged in the natural sign.

But again, as in the previous poem, something makes the poet lift his face and expand his field of vision.

144

I turned and looked back upward.
The whole sky was blue;
And the thick flakes floating at a pause
Were but frost knots on an airy gauze,
With the sun shining through.

In looking back at these "afterflakes," which correspond to the after-thoughts of his imaginative experience, the speaker is doubly reassured. Physically, the presence of the sun means that the shadow he casts, even in this snowstorm, is not abnormal; the human traveler is as natural a part of this scene as the snow which is about to stop falling. Beyond the physical level, the implicit lesson of the poem is quite the opposite of the dark judgment which the poet feared when he saw only part of the natural emblem. The blueness of the sky and "the sun shining through," so much like the star at the end of the preceding poem, suggest that, even in his shadowy world "below," the poet, if he has been judged, has been found worthy of a natural place in a brightening natural scene.

These first three poems of winter transformation are all of a kind—extremely short, almost skeletal in their plots, tremendously compressed in action and implication. They demonstrate the power (and the limitations) of extreme poetic instances, the moment of imaginative peripeteia stripped to its bare essentials. Correspondingly, their lessons are all of an affective character: nature lifts the poet's face or heart or assures him of its kinship or his own worthiness. "The Wood-Pile," another poem of winter transformation, is of a more usual Frostian—less crystalline—sort; its modesty consists not in compression of plot or detail but in apparent ordinariness of incident and tone. Its lesson is also of a more frequent sort: nature seems to endorse a specific ethical virtue. For an understanding of that virtue, and of the imaginative experience by which it is taught, the poem is best read with Thoreau in mind throughout.

Again in this winter setting the poet, if he is to learn anything, must pursue extra-vagance. He is "Out walking in the frozen swamp one gray day," but the poem's drama begins with his decision to wander still farther into the swamp. "I paused and said, 'I will turn back from here. / No, I will go on farther—and we shall see.'" The linkage of the two verbs in that latter sentence is instructive: it is precisely by being open enough to "go on farther" into the depths of the winter woods that "we shall see." Pressing on, the poet soon fulfills the Thoreauvian prescription of achieving physical lostness as a prelude to finding himself in some deeper sense.

> The view was all in lines
> Straight up and down of tall slim trees
> Too much alike to mark or name a place by
> So as to say for certain I was here
> Or somewhere else: I was just far from home.

This is the essential condition for insight in the whole tradition of American nature writing; just as Isaac McCaslin must lose himself in the wilderness in order to see the bear, so the poet here must relinquish control of his course. And just as Isaac McCaslin, the moment he is fully lost, is granted a natural pointer in the form of the bear's tracks, so the poet is immediately granted a natural guide: "A small bird flew before me." The bird soon leads the speaker to the poem's central emblem, the pile of wood.

The wood-pile is a patently human creation, its artful arrangement standing out against the softer order of the wilderness. It is "cut and split / And piled—and measured"; "And not another like it could I see." But though it is man-made, artful, and thus unique, the woodpile is being slowly absorbed back into the wilderness.

> The wood was gray and the bark warping off it
> And the pile somewhat sunken. Clematis
> Had wound strings round and round it like a bundle.

The metaphor and simile of that last line suggest that, as the woodchopper's artful arrangement is collapsing, nature's own artful arrangement is being reasserted; the wood-pile is midway between two states of order, the order of nature which is taking it over (held "on one side" by "a tree / Still growing"), and the human order which is lapsing (held on the other side by "a stake and prop, / These latter about to fall"). It is possible to read this wood-pile returning from art to nature as an emblem of entropy, of the sheer running down and wearing away of all signs of human effort (see Baym 719); or as a sign of "complementarity" between human art and natural disorder (see Rotella 75); but I would read it in still another fashion. If the clematis "winds strings round and round" the wood-pile "like a bundle," surely it is not reducing the wood-pile to sheer chaos; it is ordering and preserving it in a different form (as nature does to human offerings in "The Bear," again). The explicit lesson which the poet draws seems to me clearly to suggest that the gradual disappearance of the wood is not chiefly a loss. It is true that, for all the labor, care, and meticulousness which have gone into the making of the wood-pile, it has apparently been abandoned with no thought of squandered utility. But Frost may well relish such recklessness. For the man who shaped the wood-pile, work must have been something like "play for mortal stakes" (277). Frost reads in it a lesson of the essential profligacy of human creativity—like that of the artist in "Looking for a Sunset Bird in Winter," who adds "gilt to gold that wouldn't show."

> I thought that only
> Someone who lived in turning to fresh tasks
> Could so forget his handiwork on which
> He spent himself, the labor of his ax,
> And leave it there far from a useful fireplace
> To warm the frozen swamp as best it could
> With the slow smokeless burning of decay.

Like "Looking for a Sunset Bird," and like several of the prototypical emblem poems—"Unharvested," "Something for Hope," and "A Young Birch" (following Emerson's "Rhodora")—this poem celebrates a vitality which transcends the narrow material demands of utility. Despite its superficial uselessness and waste the wood-pile does genuinely (if metaphorically) "warm the frozen swamp" with the fervor of the sheer human energy and creativity which it represents. And in doing so, the wood-pile teaches the poet, even in the midst of winter, the crucial lesson which Thoreau reads in the return of spring: the life-giving value of unceasing newness and re-creation, of living always "in turning to fresh tasks." Thoreau also says that "into a perfect work," like the staff made by the artist of Kouroo, "time does not enter" (326). Surely the poem is in one sense an ironic commentary on that faith; but it is also, in another sense, an updated exemplum of that faith. To spend one's labor and one's life in turning to fresh tasks is to be truly alive. The capacity to do so, the poem suggests—for poets, whose work is "measured" no less than that of wood-choppers—is the essential quality of human creativity—and, in quite a different but likewise heartening way, of nature's vitality.

If even winter can so consistently be transformed by the vision of the heuristic emblem poems from a cold and lifeless waste into a realm of natural reassurance and an essentially springtime promise of new vitality, all that remains for Frost's myth of the seasons is to find in summer the full realization of such promise. The central recollections of "My Butterfly" and "Looking for a Sunset Bird in Winter" contain hints of that Stevensian view of summer. "The Quest of the Purple-Fringed," one of the crowning moments in all of Frost's seasonal poems, portrays it directly.

In its structure, its dramatization of the visionary process, and its lesson, "The Quest of the Purple-Fringed" is a relatively simple but classic heuristic emblem poem. It is also no small achievement in control of tone and Frost's peculiar forte, the winning of extraordinary insight in a determinedly modest context. Its textual history indicates that "The Quest of the Purple-Fringed" spans the entirety of the poet's central career. Frost first collected the poem in *A Witness Tree* in 1942, but it had originally been published, in essentially its final form, in *The Independent* forty-one years earlier, and may have been composed as early as 1896 (Thompson, *The Early Years* 223). The chief internal evidences of the poem's early composition are its unusually clear echoes of two of its nineteenth-century precursors, Bryant's "To the Fringed Gentian" (1832) and Emerson's "Woodnotes" (1840).

When Frost first published this poem in 1901, he called it "The Quest of the Orchis." The revised title, referring to the flower by its species rather than its genus, surely represents a homage to Bryant; "the purple-fringed" inevitably reminds a reader of American poetry of Bryant's lyric, itself a classic emblem poem. Both titles, original and revised, direct our attention not only to the flower but to the quest for it—to the imaginative process itself. The word "quest," with its inevitable connotations of medieval romance, invites us to take the search in this poem, despite the muted plot and tone, as an effort of central importance.

The poem begins, once more, with the familiar situation of poet-seer both solitary and extra-vagant, alone in the recesses of the natural world. The object of his search is suggested in the simple opening clause: "I felt the chill of the meadow underfoot, / But the sun overhead." Literally, the question which the poem must answer is simply what time of year it is—whether it is still spring, as the coolness of the earth suggests, or genuinely summer, as the sun's warmth implies. That literal question—where the speaker is in time—like the literal question of where the speaker is in space in "The Wood-Pile," reflects the larger question of his imaginative or spiritual location.

It is the account of the poet's search for a hidden natural sign in the next three stanzas which, as Brower notes (8), clearly recalls Emerson's poem. Like the "forest seer" of "Woodnotes" (who is modeled on Thoreau), the poet here is obviously "A lover true, who knew by heart / Each joy" of the natural world. In whatever hidden depths a flower may grow, such a familiar "would come in the very hour / It opened in its virgin bower."

It seemed as if the breezes brought him,
It seemed as if the sparrows taught him;
As if by secret sight he knew
Where, in far fields, the orchis grew. (*Complete Works* 9: 44)

Seeking just such "far fields," Frost's narrator pushes farther into the swampy fields where the purple-fringed orchis may grow: "I skirted the margin alders for miles and miles / In a sweeping line." But the two metaphors in this sentence, "skirted" and "sweeping," both suggest that the wanderer still carries with him the whiff of domestication. Thus, though the natural world gives the speaker encouraging evidence that this is the proper day for the blooming of the orchis—"The day was the day by every flower that blooms"—it refuses to do more: "I saw no sign."

The only means by which the seeker can willfully pursue natural education is, of course, to purify himself by becoming still more extra-vagant, wandering beyond the last vestiges of human society and control. "Yet further I went to be before the scythe, / For the grass was high." Having done his utmost to escape the taint of human dominion, the narrator can only wait (like Isaac McCaslin) for the intervention of a natural emissary. It comes almost at once: the poet goes on "Till I saw the path where the slender fox had come / And gone panting by." The fox (another echo of "Woodnotes"), implicitly fleeing hunters' dogs, has left *vestigia* which, like the slowly disappearing footprints of Isaac McCaslin's bear, lead the initiate to the natural emblem and lesson he has been seeking.

> Then at last and following him I found—
> In the very hour
> When the color flushed to the petals it must have been—
> The far-sought flower.

The quiet tone of these lines modulates into something close to simple reverence—the connotations of "quest" have not been inappropriate—as Frost describes the orchis, the sign itself.

> There stood the purple spires with no breath of air
> Nor headlong bee
> To disturb their perfect poise the livelong day
> 'Neath the alder tree.

> I only knelt and putting the boughs aside
> Looked, or at most
> Counted them all to the buds in the copse's depth
> That were pale as a ghost.

The almost hushed simplicity of language reflects the perfectly peaceful scene. And the poet's sacramental action—kneeling only to see or count the flowers and buds[5]—is an instructive Thoreauvian contrast to the ravishment of nature in "Nutting" and "Wild Grapes." In Lentricchia's phrase, this is "the purest celebratory moment in Frost's poetry" (86). This poem, from the opening sunshine to the beckoning fox's trail to the orchises themselves, is about a kind of natural grace. That, ultimately, is the lesson of the natural emblem, read in the closing quatrain.

> Then I arose and silently wandered home,
> And I for one
> Said that the fall might come and whirl of leaves,
> For summer was done.

Certainly there are elegiac hints in this poem—not only in the tranquility of the flower's setting, "with no breath of air," and in the buds which are "pale as a ghost," but also in this final look ahead, though the poem is set in June,[6] to the approach of "the fall." That of course is the season of Bryant's fringed gentian and its lesson of how to die. Yet even Bryant's poem is not altogether elegiac; the gentian, looking to the sky which its fragmentary blue reflects, teaches the poet to "look to heaven" with hope even at the moment of death. Death is to be accepted not as an absolute terminus but as one stage in a larger process.

So Frost's poem, in its view of the seasonal process, can accept "the fall" and "whirl of leaves"—not simply because they are part of a larger whole, but because that whole is seen here, as it rarely is in Frost, at its height, at the moment of summer fullness. The speaker began by wondering whether he was in spring or summer, and he has been granted proof that he is at the peak moment of summer; he has been located in the "perfect poise"[7] between chill earth and warm sun, between spring and fall, between growth and decay—the moment when the cup of natural bounty is filled "Up to the brim, and even above the brim." In sharp contrast to "The Oven Bird," "The Quest of the Purple-Fringed" sees the midsummer moment, "the livelong day"—a synecdoche of life itself—as Stevens sees it in "Credences of Summer": this is the "One day" that "enriches a year," redeems the entire cycle. The closing line of Frost's poem—"summer was done"—summarizes the paradox of life itself, what Stevens calls "the barrenness / Of the fertile thing that can attain no more." The moment of imaginative fulfillment, like summer, like the poem itself, is "done"—finished, and destined to be succeeded by a lesser something (a diminished thing), but also accomplished, completed, consummated.

4.

As Frost tells us in "All Revelation," the impulse behind any attempt at vision or apocalypse is the yearning of "Eyes seeking the response of eyes," the paramount struggle of living mind or spirit to evoke a response of other living spirit which is distinct from but fundamentally akin to it. Only in seeking and achieving such a response can the imagination—initially disoriented in space ("The Wood-Pile") or time ("The Quest of the Purple-Fringed")—locate itself in a habitable world. This exertion of "Eyes seeking the response of eyes" is central to all of the heuristic emblem poems. Unlike the Promethean poems, they discover, above all, relationship; their lessons are contextual.[8]

For any U.S. writer, working within the cultural tradition of Hawthorne's tales or "Bartleby the Scrivener" (and, prior to them, Calvin and Adam Smith), the natural world is not the only context in which he or she must struggle to be located. A more worrisome context, which the writer must come to grips with or evade at great cost, is the social. The unpardonable, and highly American, sin of Ethan Brand is, after all, a social sin: to have "lost his hold of the magnetic chain of humanity." Surely there are echoes of Hawthorne's characteristic fear in Frost—who, in an essay, calls it "the fear of Man—the fear that men won't understand us and we shall be cut off from them" (*Selected Prose* 60). It is implicit in the narrator's attitude in "Mending Wall," which sees unnatural barriers between neighbors; more pronounced in "Acquainted with the Night," with its solitary walker on the city's edge; clearer still in the final lines of "A Missive Missile," with its recognition that "Two souls may be too widely met" ever to bridge "the soul-from-soul abyss," try as they may.

Frost's concern in these poems with social or ethical insight is not altogether surprising in view of the American tradition of reading natural wisdom; it is Emerson who insists that nature will teach us lessons not only about self and about "worship," but also about "the moral law" (*Collected Works* 1: 37, 26).[9] There are hints of Frost's concern with human community in a few of the prototypical or even meditative emblem poems ("The Cocoon," "On the Heart's Beginning to Cloud the Mind"); but it becomes central only in the heuristic poems. That concern shapes all six of the remaining heuristic emblem poems which I want to discuss—and in every case Frost gets at that concern by invoking and playing on (or off) a central convention of nineteenth-century American nature writing: the opposition between natural order and social disorder. That convention is central to the Leatherstocking tales, for instance. Cooper likes nothing better than to describe a scene of glorious natural beauty and peace, full of nature's "holy calm"—immediately before or after a battle, massacre, or similar tableau of carnage. The opposition recurs in various poems by Bryant, too, as for instance in "Inscription for the Entrance to a Wood," where the "calm" of the "wild wood" is contrasted with the "guilt and misery," the "sorrows, crimes, and cares," of "the world."

Frost occasionally rings in that conventional opposition fairly straightforwardly. More often (as is true of every convention he invokes), he likes to play *off* the convention—to vary it, complicate it, bend it ironically. (One of the best-known examples of this process occurs in

"Range-Finding," which is not an emblem poem: human activity is characterized, as in Cooper, by war, but Frost clearly relishes the modernist irony of portraying nature, not as a realm of "holy calm" contrasting with human struggle and predation, but as an extension of it.)

Only in "I Will Sing You One-O" does Frost echo that conventional opposition straightforwardly (or almost so). Like "Kitty Hawk," "I Will Sing You One-O" uses extremely short lines—indeed, its iambic or "loose iambic"[10] dimeter is even shorter than the "three-beat phrases" of that poem—to explore manifestly vast questions; but its remarkable vision of cosmic harmony serves ultimately as the bright background for the immediate focus of the poem, the lamentable truth of what man has made of man. "I Will Sing You One-O" begins with an imaginative situation both like and unlike that in most of the other emblem poems. As usual, the poet is solitary and alert ("I lay / Awake"); as often, he finds himself, at night, faced by a kind of winter wilderness, a blizzard which seems almost sinister: "The snow fell deep / With the hiss of spray; / Two winds would meet . . . / And fight in a smother / Of dust and feather." One element of the poet's situation is unusual, however; rather than being outside in the storm, he is inside, in bed; rather than being in the familiar rural setting, he is in a town. That situation, too, suggests the poem's interest in social relationships.

The speaker's immediate problem, as so often in the heuristic poems, is one of disorientation, here again temporal. He lies awake wondering whether it is yet morning, "Wishing the tower / Would name the hour / And tell me whether / To call it day / (Though not yet light)." As in "A Missive Missile" and "The Wood-Pile," the emblem to be read is unusual in being man-made: the awaited striking of the tower clock (and then others) at 1 A.M. Frost assumes from the beginning that the sound is not mere sound. It is at first only an introductory "knock"; but then, "Though strange and muffled" and not yet clear in meaning, "A note unruffled / Of earthly weather," cutting through the tumult of the storm with more than natural clarity; and finally an explicit word: "The tower said 'One!' / And then a steeple."

Soon a whole chorus of bells and chimes explicitly (if metaphorically) speaks to those few human listeners who may be open to inspiration, both literally and figuratively: "They spoke to themselves / And such few people / As winds might rouse / From sleeping warm."

In this outwardly unpromising moment of night and snow and bells chiming across the town, Frost reads a vast, unusually direct, and startlingly monistic annunciation:

In that grave One
They spoke of the sun
And moon and stars,
Saturn and Mars
And Jupiter.
Still more unfettered,
They left the named
And spoke of the lettered,
The sigmas and taus
Of constellations.
They filled their throats
With the furthest bodies
To which man sends his
Speculation,
Beyond which God is . . .

For any modern poet, this is a startling, almost medieval vision of cosmic order and hierarchy: the lone "knock" of the tower clock, echoed by other clocks and bells, expands outward like the ripples from a pebble tossed into a lake, and reaches finally to the very limits of human "speculation," whether that of "yawning lenses" or that of the *mens animi*. That growing wave not only reaches, but includes and unifies, every smallest bit of the entire created universe (even "cosmic motes"), spreading outward as in a Ptolemaic cosmology to the edge of the sphere of the Primum Mobile ("Beyond which God is").

As a result of the perfect order and harmony of "that grave One" which all creation now seems to echo, Frost also reads a lesson of apparent constancy and permanence in even the vastest reaches of whirling bodies.

> In that grave word
> Uttered alone
> The utmost star
> Trembled and stirred,
> Though set so far
> Its whirling frenzies
> Appear like standing
> In one self station. . . .
> It has not changed
> To the eye of man
> On planets over,
> Around, and under
> It in creation . . .

Here, for once, the astronomical perspective gives Frost a sense of the perfection of the created universe—vast but not terrifying, flawlessly ordered, beautifully harmonious, dynamic and self-renewing ("expanding / To be a nova"), yet (again like Keats's star) ever the same—at least as it appears to the human eye "set so far" from its distant reaches. It is an astonishing moment in twentieth-century poetry.

Yet it *is* only a moment—for the poem still has one dependent clause, three short lines, remaining. In that brief clause the poem turns its attention, however fleetingly, to what is really its immediate concern: the one flaw in this vast and perfect order. Juxtaposed against that cosmos, if only at its periphery, are the disunity and discord of the human animal; astronomers have watched the apparently unchanging heavens ever

Since man began
To drag down man
And nation nation.

These closing lines explain why the poem begins against a social backdrop (the town), yet with the poet separated from other human beings,
and why the winds are described as "fighting." Despite the cheerful and
insistently social title—folk songs,[11] after all, are sung in communi-
ties—this is in fact a poem of World War I (first published in 1923).
It comes close to being a vastly expanded version of Wordsworth's
perception in "Lines Written in Early Spring" of "Nature's holy plan"
marred only by "What man has made of man."

"I Will Sing You One-O" thus seems to suggest that the universe
in which people dwell ultimately aims at order and concord. In a number of the heuristic emblem poems, that natural order influences human affairs in a salutary and surprising fashion, even—in some not altogether modest fictions—intervening actively to teach the observer
about his ties with other men and women. In "The Thatch," however, the conventional opposition seems at first to work the other way,
and to make the poem a kind of dark, inverted version of "I Will Sing
You One-O": here human discord spreads outward to taint the peaceful order of the natural world. The narrator's situation at the beginning of the poem is thoroughly bleak: he is "Out alone" at night "in
the winter rain," his wandering motivated not by any desire for natural discovery but by a bitter domestic quarrel which has left him "Intent on giving and taking pain." The visual center of the narrative is
"a certain upper-window light"—the cozy domestic center now made
bitter by the couple's quarrel:

I would not go in till the light went out;
It would not go out till I came in.
Well, we should see which one would win,
We should see which one would be first to yield.

Driven out into the rainy winter night by this bitter struggle of wills, the speaker finds the natural world to be only an inhospitable wilderness, in which he is effectively lost: "The world was a black invisible field," in which he is buffeted by the wind and pelted by the cold rain. (Here, as in "I Will Sing You One-O," winter storms reflect human turmoil.)

But even here lostness has its imaginative uses. Just at this moment of disorientation in the "black invisible field" of the storm, the poet is given a kind of sign, again through the agency of birds:

> the strangest thing: in the thick old thatch,
> Where summer birds had been given hatch,
> Had fed in chorus, and lived to fledge,
> Some still were living in hermitage.

Even in the midst of this wintry storm, the birds are essentially "summer birds," representatives of a fuller and more social season in which they "fed in chorus." Though the exigencies of winter have driven them to live in comparative solitude, that "hermitage" may, paradoxically, teach the speaker something about his relationships.

But that instruction begins only when the wanderer, in his own disarray, brings disarray to the creatures around him, brushing against the low eaves of the cottage and frightening the birds "out of hole after hole, / Into the darkness." The sudden disordered flight of the birds serves as a natural mirror held up to the narrator to make him fully conscious of the human disorder of which he is part. Thinking of the birds' desperate situation—they can neither find "their nest again" in the dark, he fears, "nor find a perch" elsewhere in the storm—he is suddenly filled with sympathy.

> It grieved my soul,
> It started a grief within a grief,
> To think their case was beyond relief—. . .
> They must brood where they fell in mulch and mire,

> Trusting feathers and inward fire
> Till daylight made it safe for a flyer.

In a sense the speaker, too, is forced to brood where he has fallen in mulch and mire, trusting implicitly to the inward fire of natural sympathy and imagination (both aroused by the birds) to remedy his plight. Now that such sympathy and imagination have been awakened, they begin to thaw the speaker's wintry attitude toward his domestic situation.

> My greater grief was by so much reduced
> As I thought of them without nest or roost.
> That was how that grief started to melt.

The closing lines of the poem, bringing us up to the present—in which speaker and wife figure have implicitly left the quarrel far behind them—rather ambiguously describe the cottage which was the scene of this winter transformation.

> They tell me the cottage where we dwelt,
> Its wind-torn thatch goes now unmended;
> Its life of hundreds of years has ended
> By letting the rain I knew outdoors
> In onto the upper chamber floors.

On the one hand, this is another scene (like abandoned houses or wood-piles) of entropy, of human effort and form surviving for some time ("hundreds of years") but ultimately being effaced by ongoing natural processes. Thus it is another suggestion of the opposition between the human and the natural. It is also, however, an image of the breaking down of walls and barriers: "letting the rain in" to the cottage—particularly "onto the upper chamber floors" where the light of the domestic quarrel had burned years before—corresponds to the

central imaginative act of the poem, letting the plight of other creatures into the closed, preoccupied, self-centered mind. Thus, I think,
the human here is not only being destroyed; it is also being softened
and absorbed into the natural order, "healed," as Faulkner puts it in
"The Bear," "into the wilderness' concordant generality" (328).

5.

In terms of their fictions, the best known of the nature lyrics almost
unanimously share a characteristic modesty. Whatever depths of epistemology or psychology Frost may plumb in these poems, they tell
stories of commonplace activities; they remain, for the most part,
unextraordinary—"minimalist" or even "boring," in the words of one
critic (Bell 70). Partly because Frost does normally use unextraordinary
fictions in his nature lyrics, and partly because of the weight of his
reputation as a temperamentally conservative artist, we have largely
failed to see that Frost's usual practice is not his uniform practice, that
the fictions of some of his nature lyrics are anything but commonplace. Upon closer examination, the stories told in a number of the
lyrics we have looked at earlier approach the unlikely, as for instance
in "Design" or "The Most of It." In the remainder of this chapter I
want to examine four heuristic emblem poems containing stories
which are not only not commonplace but, on closer inspection, down-
right unlikely, and to ask the question: what do these unlikely fictions
tell us about Frost's vision and his craftsmanship?

"An Unstamped Letter in Our Rural Letter Box," "The Tuft of
Flowers," "Iris by Night," and "Two Look at Two" all play on the
conventional opposition between natural order and human disorder,
suggesting for the most part that the former can positively influence
the latter. In order to make that remarkable claim, they all tell stories
which are extraordinary if not incredible, containing unlikely natural
events, whether astronomical, zoological, or optical. Finally, they all
arrive at visions of close human ties which are likewise extraordinary,
for any modern writer, let alone a poet as defensive and even cur-

mudgeonly as Frost can sometimes be. If their fictions, in other words, are egregious, their visions might well be called gregious. (My own egregious use of "gregious" may be justified, in part, by Frost's use of the Latin root, *grex*: "Freud made to[o] much of sex as the ruling passion," he writes in *Prose Jottings* [56]. "It is much more likely to be grex or minding each others [*sic*] business.")

"An Unstamped Letter in Our Rural Letter Box," Frost's Christmas poem for 1944, is a strange poem—in its fiction, in its natural lesson, and in its fictive frame (that is, its epistolary form). Yet in all of these respects it looks forward to the other three poems of this group. The poem tells the story of a tramp who sleeps out in a farmer's pasture and leaves a note for him—the poem—the next morning. The protagonist is, predictably, extra-vagant: not only a vagabond, but one who spends the night sleeping in the pasture "freely face to face / All night with universal space." The natural text which the tramp needs to read is an astronomical phenomenon, but again, as in "The Wood-Pile" or "The Quest of the Purple-Fringed," it takes a natural prompter to direct the reader's attention to the text. Here, instead of a bird or a fox, the prompter is a rock. But the poem does not tell us, as we might expect, that the tramp is awakened by turning over onto a rock. Instead, it has the rock intervene actively: "It may have been at two o'clock / That under me a point of rock / Developed in the grass and fern, / And as I woke . . ."

Rocks do not normally "develop" to wake people up. But when the tramp is thus awakened, the natural emblem which he sees is likewise extraordinary.

> The largest firedrop ever formed
> From two stars' having coalesced
> Went streaking molten down the west.

The likeliest explanation of this phenomenon is that these two "stars" are in fact "shooting stars" or meteors, which might, under unusual circumstances, appear to "coalesce." As so often in these four poems, the narrative seeks not to minimize but to stress the rarity of such a phe-nomenon: it is an "undoubted stir / In Heaven's firm-set firmament."

Though he does not explicitly read this unusual emblem, the tramp responds to it in classic Emersonian fashion. The external event inspires a correspondent internal event which results in some kind of revelation: the "tramp astrologer" reports that, seeing this phenom-enon, he "Himself had the equivalent, / Only within."

> Inside the brain
> Two memories that long had lain
> Now quivered toward each other, lipped
> Together, and together slipped;
> And for a moment all was plain
> That men have thought about in vain.

This moment of ostensible vision is an unusual one for Frost: it sounds, in that last couplet, distinctly portentous, yet its precise con-tent is only loosely implied. The external coalescing of two meteors to form a great "firedrop"—presumably modeled on "teardrop"—and the internal "quivering" and "lipping together" of two memories both suggest a kind of emotional union, or reunion, as of lovers. The im-plication would seem to be that the tramp's great insight has some-thing to do with amatory, possibly marital, ties. Now rootless and alone, the vagabond is presumably coming to an understanding of an earlier and more domestic era in his life. Or, to speculate more freely and biographically, the lost and vagabond side of the poet, six years after Elinor Frost's traumatic death, may finally be coming to grips with—or at least fantasizing about coming to grips with—two power-ful memories of their long life together.

Whatever the details of the tramp's insight, which somehow clari-fies "all . . . / That men have thought about in vain," it must have positive implications for his sense of human ties—hence the unusual epistolary form of this poem. The tramp's letter to the farmer, motivated by at least partly fraternal feelings toward his "involuntary host," is designed not merely to recount his own imaginative adventure, but also to recognize that he and the landowner may have shared the gift of the astronomical sign, despite the farmer's distinct lack of extravagance.

'Tis possible you may have seen,
Albeit through a rusty screen,
The same sign Heaven showed your guest. . . .
And it is partly to compel
Myself, *in forma pauperis,*
To say as much I write you this.

The legal phrase suggests not only the tramp's more affluent earlier life but also his faith—a faith which may call into question some of our usual assumptions about Frost's social thinking—that natural lessons can unite men even across economic and social differences.

The more obvious part of the fiction in "The Tuft of Flowers"—in which the speaker again learns a lesson about human ties based on ties with nature—seems unremarkable enough. The gloss in the table of contents of *A Boy's Will* tells us that this poem is (like "An Unstamped Letter") "about fellowship," and it is clear that here—precisely as in Durand's famous painting of Bryant and Cole, *Kindred Spirits* (1849)—the fellowship between men is based on their mutual fellowship with nature. (In Durand's painting, it is not only Bryant and Cole, or poetry and painting, that are kindred spirits, but man and nature as well.) In the two-part movement which we have seen in a number of meditative and heuristic poems, the speaker first describes a basically antagonistic relationship between mower and nature: the mowed field is a "leveled scene," as if in the aftermath of modern warfare; the butterfly is "bewildered" and unable to find its "resting flower," which has been cut down by the mower and is now only "withering on the ground." When people are thus seen as assaulters of nature, they are not surprisingly isolated from each other; the speaker cannot hear the mower or find him "behind an isle of trees," natural isolation reflecting human. On the basis of the preliminary evidence, the speaker first concludes that all people "'must be'" alone, "'Whether they work together or apart.'" Then, seeing an important element of the natural text which he had previously overlooked—the tuft of flowers—the speaker realizes that the mower, like him, loves the natural world. His scythe is now seen, not as assaulting but as "whispering to the ground"; the mowing does not merely "level" the scene but "spares" the crucial tuft of flowers and "bares" or reveals the sustaining brook. Given such additional evidence, the speaker is able to establish contact literally with the butterfly and "the wakening birds around" and metaphorically with the mower, and thus to read the heartening social lesson of the complete text: "'Men work together, . . . / Whether they work together or apart.'" (And the second lesson is expressed in metaphorical dialogue: "I told him from the heart"—rather than monologue—"I said within my heart." This shift to dialogue parallels the epistolary form of "An Unstamped Letter.")

This outer portion of the poem's fiction, interesting and characteristic though it is, contains only commonplace events. But the link between the two readings of the natural text—the conveniently appearing butterfly—is not so mundane. The obvious function of the butterfly is to direct the speaker's attention to the crucial footnote in the natural text, the tuft of flowers, which dramatically alters his reading of the scene. The turning point of the poem, literally and figuratively, is the work of the butterfly: the isolated speaker is about to turn "to toss the grass to dry" when the butterfly "turned first, and led my eye to look / At a tall tuft of flowers beside a brook." In these flowers, the butterfly literally, like the poet metaphorically, "lights upon" "a message from the dawn."

The flowers themselves are described in line 23 as "a leaping tongue of bloom"—a not merely communicative but oracular part of the landscape. Following the next line, the original versions of the poem, from its first publication in 1906 through the *Poems* of 1946, contain another couplet: "I left my place to know them by their name, / Finding them butterfly weed when I came." These lines both show Frost's Thoreauvian penchant for knowing natural phenomena in their particularity and complete the reconciliation of mower and natural world, since the previously displaced insect has now clearly found his "resting flower," butterfly on butterfly weed. Why, then, did Frost choose to excise this couplet in the *Complete Poems* of 1949 and later editions, after having left it through eight published versions? Surely because of the issue of verisimilitude: having the butterfly light on butterfly weed is simply a bit too pat, pushes the fiction a little too hard.

But the toned-down version of 1949 and later years still contains a story which approaches the unlikely: at the crucial imaginative moment, a butterfly appears out of nowhere, shares the poet's disorientation, then—only a stagey whistle and sly wink to the speaker are missing—directs his attention to the flowers which will reverse his reading of the scene. At first glance the butterfly may appear to be derived from a sort of natural experience, but it turns out, of course, to belong to literary tradition. The association of the butterfly with Psyche or the soul, which goes back at least to the Greeks, recurs in English poetic tradition from Spenser ("Muiopotmos") through the romantics (Wordsworth's "To a Butterfly" ["Stay near me—do not take thy flight!"] and Coleridge's "Psyche." The fact that Keats, in his "Ode to Psyche," gives her the form not of a butterfly but of a dove may remind us of the avian messenger which likewise directs the poet's attention to the central emblem in "The Wood-Pile.") Frost's butterfly, like its predecessors, is a carefully crafted element of a literary fiction, intended to objectify the movement of the speaker's mind. Its origin in literary convention suggests that we are moving away from the realm of standard mimesis—in fact, we are moving toward romance. As Northrop Frye reminds us, "romance presents an idealized world. . . . Birds, butterflies (for this is Psyche's world, and Psyche means butterfly), and spirits . . . are . . . naturalized denizens" of that idealized realm (*Anatomy* 151–52). But it is not only romance which the solicitous butterfly suggests. As a Jungian critic has noted, "There are . . . many helpful animals in myths and fairy tales" (von Franz 207).[12] In short, then, though the major part of the narrative in "The Tuft of Flowers" seems to correspond roughly to realistic fiction, the central link, involving the butterfly, resides on the border of verisimilitude and moves us from the realm of realism toward that of romance or myth or fairy tale.

The fiction in a lesser-known poem, "Iris by Night," may well be Frost's most egregious. The poem offers itself more clearly as a quasi-autobiographical account than is usual in Frost. For one thing, it is a first-person narrative—but the speaker seems less the generic poet here than is usual in Frost's first-person narratives, and more nearly the historical Robert Frost, because the companion figure is unmistakably modeled on Edward Thomas, the Welsh poet and critic with whom he developed a uniquely intense friendship in England in 1913–14. (After Thomas was killed in World War I, Frost wrote to his widow: "He was the bravest and best and dearest man you and I have ever known" [*Letters* 216]. He pays homage to Thomas not only in "Iris by Night" and "A Soldier" but also in "To E. T.," where he calls him "brother.") In keeping with the ostensibly historical nature of the story here, the poem's second line—"We two were groping down a Malvern side"—places the remarkable events about to unfold in a particular geographical spot, the area on the border of Herefordshire and Gloucestershire where Frost and Thomas in fact often walked during the summer and fall of 1914. Surely the purpose of such geographical specificity is precisely to anchor the astonishing events of the poem in an actual locale.

Frost might well want to anchor the poem's events in quasi-autobiographical "fact"—indeed, such anchoring must have contributed to Thompson's remarkable suggestion (*The Early Years* 455) that the events described in this poem actually occurred in August 1914—precisely because those events must strike any careful reader as exceedingly unlikely.[13] "Iris by Night" is built on a quadruply remarkable fiction. First, as the two friends return from an evening walk, the poem reports a puzzling astronomical or meteorological phenomenon, "a moment of confusing lights." It is not clear exactly what is happening here—something involving refraction of the moonlight by the wet evening air, presumably. But Frost implicitly makes an extraordinary claim for the significance of such a phenomenon: these "confusing lights" are

> Such as according to belief in Rome
> Were seen of old at Memphis on the heights
> Before the fragments of a former sun
> Could concentrate anew and rise as one.[14]

Both in ancient Egypt and in England in 1914, such phenomena presage the birth of a new order, the "fragments of a former" world "concentrat[ing] anew and ris[ing] as one."

At first the light described in these lines seems unlocalized: "Light was a paste of pigment in our eyes"; the travelers are simply dazzled and blinded by the extraordinary event. But in the following lines the dazzle resolves itself into moonlight: "then there was a moon and then a scene / So watery as to seem submarine." The extraordinary humidity here—the air itself virtually becomes water, "Its airy pressure turned to water weight"—soon brings us again into the realm of ritual, in which the poem remains. In the airy river "we two stood saturated, drowned." But this is a *Tempest*-like "drowning" which is actually a kind of secular baptism, in which the two friends are "drowned" to a former life only to be reborn to a new one, "and rise as one."

If the extraordinary light and the extraordinary humidity of the scene are not pushing the natural fiction here hard enough, Frost soon reports even more astonishing occurrences involving a moon-created (hence imagined?) rainbow. First the rainbow, "like a trellis gate, / A very small moon-made prismatic bow, / Stood closely over us through which to go." This "gate" may remind us of the frost-made breaches in orchard walls, "gaps even two can pass abreast," which also seem to invite close companionship, but it is considerably less likely an opening. If one should in fact see such an archlike rainbow, he would not be able to "go through" it, since any rainbow, formed by a certain angle (42 degrees) between the line of sight and the rays of sunlight, appears to move with the observer. While this phenomenon thus crosses over the borderline of credibility, the final natural occurrence in the poem is still more astonishing. The rainbow gate

> lifted from its dewy pediment
> Its two mote-swimming many-colored ends
> And gathered them together in a ring.
> And we stood in it softly circled round . . .

Physicists know that it is possible, from a mountain top or an airplane, to see a "glory"—a circular rainbow which surrounds one's shadow cast forward or downward on clouds or mists[15]—and the circumstances of moonlight and mist described in "Iris by Night" might well be suitable for such a phenomenon. But the glory must be seen at some distance, surrounding one's *shadow*—not actually encircling the viewer, apparently slightly above the ground. Again we are on—or, it would seem, have just crossed—the borderline between the possible and the impossible. The earlier "moment of confusing lights," the rainbow "trellis gate," and this prismatic ring—all have precisely that effect on a careful reader which constitutes the central part of Todorov's definition of the fantastic: "the text must oblige the reader to consider the world of the characters as a world of living persons and to hesitate between a natural and a supernatural explanation of the events described" (33). Surely such hesitation is exactly what Frost is striving for here. He stresses, not the probability, but the singularity of the climactic phenomenon, the encircling rainbow: it "never yet to other two befell," and—in a tone almost uniquely unrestrained for

Frost—is "A wonder!" Nature, which so often in Frost is jealous of its secrets (as in "For Once, Then, Something"), is no longer so, no longer wants "To keep the pots of gold from being found," but almost explicitly reveals its endorsement of this intense friendship.

The rainbow (its meaning already displaced from that of the original in Genesis) is a central Wordsworthian image of "natural piety," of the covenant between man and nature. Here the arc of concord between man and nature is transformed into a circle enclosing and binding two extraordinary friends, a ring attesting to the marriage of true minds: "we stood in it softly circled round / From all division time or foe can bring / In a relation of elected friends." Thus, in one of the most extraordinary fictions in all of Frost's verse, the natural world essentially conducts a ritual ceremony partaking of both baptism and marriage, and promising that the new life of such a friendship is inviolable, even by the wartime death of one friend. Just as space has been annihilated in "The Tuft of Flowers," so time is annulled here—precisely as so often in romance (Frye, *Secular Scripture* 153).

Again, as in "The Tuft of Flowers," if this poem's fiction might well be called egregious, its vision might well be called gregious, gregarious, or social. Like "An Unstamped Letter" and "The Tuft of Flowers," "Iris by Night" is "about fellowship," here between two particularly close friends rather than two workers. But, of course, the intensest human ties in Frost are consistently the marital ties, those between the poet figure and the wife figure.

Of the many poems which celebrate married love (see Poirier 200–225), none does so with a more egregious fiction than "Two Look at Two." Here husband and wife, like the friends in "Iris by Night," have been moved to evening extra-vagance, but this time natural exploration is stymied by "a tumbled wall / With barbed-wire binding"—the same sort of conventional limit which both separates and unites men in "Mending Wall." At first this wall seems only to separate humans and woods; the lovers sigh, "'This is all, . . . / Goodnight to woods.'" But, just at this limit of natural exploration, extraordinary things start to happen. Though no single one of them is unlikely in itself, the accumulation of events soon (again) stretches the limits of verisimilitude.

First, as they are about to turn back, the lovers see a doe: "A doe from round a spruce stood looking at them / Across the wall, as near the wall as they. / She saw them in their field, they her in hers." This is an archetypal (and privileged) moment in Frost; the human and the animal, each remaining in its own proper "field," are nonetheless able to have a genuine encounter across that wall of demarcation, just as poet and tree do in "Tree at My Window." This encounter is the positive model of the parodic non-encounter in "The Most of It." These lovers, unlike the solitary who "thought he kept the universe alone," are free from the implicit sexual preoccupations of that character and hence able to appreciate a nonhuman (that is, genuine) "original response." The completeness and calm which a couple represents are precisely what reassure the doe here; not only are they still, but (in a scarcely modest fiction) "She seemed to think that, two thus, they were safe." Thus they are as natural a part of this landscape as the deer—"Like some up-ended boulder split in two." The harmonious relationship between the lovers both reflects and nurtures their harmonious relationship with the natural world. Indeed, as the poem's fiction presses at the outer limits of credibility, it threatens, by contrast with "Tree at My Window," to obliterate the dividing line between human and natural and convert the doe into a human maiden out of a romance: "She sighed"—a remarkable verb—"and passed unscared along the wall. / 'This, then, is all. What more is there to ask?'"

If the poem ended here, its fiction would remain clearly within the limits of believability. But we have a final remarkable pairing still to come.

> "What more is there to ask?"
> But no, not yet. A snort to bid them wait.
> A buck from round the spruce stood looking at them
> Across the wall, as near the wall as they.

This second encounter, and the repetition of that last line, remind us of the title of the poem; the tableau here is the ultimate complication and fulfillment of the mirror topos suggested in "Tree at My Window." Just as the man both (in his similarity) reflects and (in his dissimilarity) complements the woman, and just as the buck both reflects and complements the doe, so the human both reflects and complements the natural. This man and woman may also remind us of the couple in "West-Running Brook," who are "'married to each other'" and, at least partly by virtue of that union, "'both . . . married to the brook,'" to the natural source of imaginative sustenance. Thus, in the present encounter,

> Two had seen two, whichever side you spoke from.
> "This *must* be all." It was all. Still they stood,
> A great wave from it going over them . . .

This "wave" is reminiscent of the "drowning" in "Iris by Night"; although a visionary peak rather than literal water, it implicitly cleanses and purifies; it is a sign both of grace ("one unlooked-for favor") and of connectedness by means of love. At such moments of insight, one can at least imagine that, see things "As if," "earth returned their love."

The stylized dance of the man, woman, buck, and doe signifies that we are again, as in "Iris by Night," in the world of ritual, which is preeminently the world imitated by romance (Frye, *Secular Scripture* 55–56). But, if the fictions of these poems are decidedly egregious, we can see now that "gregious" is not quite the right word for their visions. For, as Frye tells us, in the ultimate form of romance "the social setting [is] reduced to the love of individual men and women within an order of nature which has been reconciled to humanity" (*Secular Scripture* 149). The visions of all four of these poems are not exactly "gregious," not visions of a herdlike social order, but rather of close ties between *pairs* of human beings (always the focus of Frost's positive social vision): between tramp and farmer, between worker and worker, between particular friends, between lovers.

Indeed, the most egregious part of the fiction in "Two Look at Two" is precisely the heaping up of pairings: two people, two deer, two males, two females. But such pairings, too, are characteristic of all four poems: friend paired with friend in "Iris by Night"; not just tramp paired with farmer but, implicitly, husband with wife, in "An Unstamped Letter"; not just mower paired with turner but speaker with butterfly and butterfly with butterfly weed in "The Tuft of Flowers." Some of these pairings—of outward phenomenon with the tramp's inward response in "An Unstamped Letter," of speaker with butterfly in "The Tuft of Flowers," of wife with doe and husband with buck in "Two Look at Two"—suggest a kind of Emersonian correspondence between physical fact and spiritual fact, between natural and human. But the significance of most of them is directed not at the relationship with nature but at the relationship between human beings—and such pairings are so often repeated in these poems that they, too, like the pairing of married couple with male and female deer in "Two Look at Two," suggest a combination of mirroring and complementing.

Frost is well aware of the potentially negative implications of the Narcissus and Echo motives. (That these motives are pertinent to such poems is suggested even by verbal and prosodic form at points—e.g., the *a-b-b-a* quatrain in "Tree at My Window," which reflects the mirror motif, or the echoic line "Across the wall, as near the wall as they" [lines 16 and 28] in "Two Look at Two.") As we have seen, in "For Once, Then, Something," the speaker is at least perceived by others as kneeling at the well "Always wrong to the light," so that he can see only his own reflection in the water; in the first part of "The Most of It," the shouter can arouse only "the mocking echo of his own" voice. Such incidents suggest the kind of solipsistic limitations implied in the familiar version of the Narcissus and Echo story (*Metamorphoses* 3: 339–510), in which Narcissus falls in love with his own reflection and pines away because of its inaccessibility.

But, as we saw at the beginning of this chapter, Frost is not likely to fall prey to a simple kind of projection or narcissism or solipsism. More than many of his contemporary poets, Frost is confident that there *is* an other, in various realms of experience; and thus the pairings which we have seen in these poems are never mere reflections, but always, as in "Two Look at Two," reflections-plus-complements or -completions—or, to borrow John Irwin's term, positive "doublings" (61–64, etc.). These pairings are not "mocking echoes" but twinnings—and thus a modern echo of the lesser-known version of the Narcissus story. In this version, told by Pausanias (*Description of Greece*, Book 9, 31.7–9), Narcissus sees in his reflection, which he understands to be his own image, a reminder of his beloved, now dead, twin sister. The pairings in these poems, in other words, suggest that the self, like Pausanias's Narcissus seeing both himself and his sister reflected in the water, finds both similarity and difference in the other. Because of difference, the self is heartened to discover ties with the other, whether wife or friend or fellow worker. But, in the very process of ascertaining ties with the other, the self also discovers similarity, discovers that the other is not *wholly* other, despite differences of sex, economic status, location or time; thus there is also an element of self-discovery in these poems.

It is worth insisting on the fact that Frost's social vision in these four poems (and, in fact, in others like "The Wood-Pile")—at least in the sense of his vision of possible ties between pairs of human beings—is a great deal more positive and assertive than we have generally recognized. I would invert David Porter's remarks quoted at the beginning of this chapter and assert that, because revelation *does* really come in these poems, they are poems of fulfilled communion. The intense ties between human beings here stand in particular contrast to the isolation seen in fablelike poems such as "Beech" and "The Strong Are Saying Nothing," where "Men work alone, their lots plowed far apart."

But the implications of the recurrent "twinning" in these poems may also suggest something beyond the level of social vision. Irwin has noted that echoes of the Narcissus story and other signs of twinning "are part of a Romantic image complex that evokes the narcissistic doubling lying at the heart of artistic creation" (87). In his discussions of Shelley and Hawthorne (86–88, 141, 258–65), Irwin points out that the twin figure is often a version—usually feminine—of the epipsyche, an idealized alter ego which both completes the self and is associated with creativity. Hints of this idea, too, lie beneath the surface of the four poems I am considering. The wife/lover figure who appears in "Two Look at Two" is often associated with poetic inspiration.[16] The friend to whom the speaker is bonded in "Iris by Night," we know, is a fictionalized version of Edward Thomas, the most sympathetic fellow writer whom Frost ever met, a kind of spiritual and intellectual "brother." The tramp figure in "An Unstamped Letter" may represent the unsettled, vagabond side of the poet himself. Even "The Tuft of Flowers" tells us something about the creative process: it is possible to read this poem, as we regularly read "The Oven Bird"—and as John Hollander reads "The Most of It" (19–20) or Sydney Lea reads "Closed for Good" (85ff.)[17]—as a natural parable which images the poetic enterprise. But, while "The Oven Bird," "The Most of It," and "Closed for Good" deal with the burden of poetic belatedness—"what to make of a diminished thing"—"The Tuft of Flowers" suggests something about the other side of the coin, what Keats called the "immortal free-masonry" of genius, the sense of "fellowship" between writers of succeeding generations. Frost elsewhere associates mowing with "making"—the worker in "Mowing" "left the hay to make." So, in "The Tuft of Flowers," the earlier worker, the mower, has created or defined the "leaping tongue of bloom" which speaks to the poet. The poem's opening couplet, then, may be read, like the closing line of "The Oven Bird," as a description of the situation of the modern poet: "I went to turn the grass once after one / Who mowed it in the dew before the sun." If the romantics are fortunate enough to arrive on the scene of a fresh, untouched field, it is the problem of the twentieth-century poet to make something productive in their aftermath, to turn that already mowed grass into hay. (Longfellow, an important precursor of Frost, uses almost precisely the same metaphor to suggest the situation of the mid-nineteenth-century poet in the appropriately named "Aftermath." Or compare Pound's metaphor for the twentieth-century poet's relationship to Whitman: "It was you that broke the new wood, / Now is the time for carving.") Thus any underlying note here about the sense of poetic belatedness is a more positive note than that implied in "The Oven Bird." In "The Tuft of Flowers," making poetry, like making hay, is finally a cooperative enterprise; men work together, whether they work together or apart. Thus again this poem follows Durand's painting in seeing fellow artists as "kindred spirits."

Beyond the significance of any single line or image or poem, the most important question to ask about these four lyrics and their egregious fictions—foreshadowed in poems like "My Butterfly" and "The Wood-Pile"—is this: what does it tell us about Frost as a poet that he does sometimes create such extraordinary, even implausible fictions to embody his vision of intimate ties between pairs of human beings? Regardless of our reactions to them—whether we view them as excessive, as moments in which authorial control slips, or as daring but masterfully managed tours de force—the fictions in all four of these poems, like romance itself, finally suggest something, surely, about the power of desire. Freud calls such desire Eros, in the sense of the totality of "the life instincts"—recall the census-taker's motto: "It must be I want life to go on living"—and writes of "the efforts of Eros to combine organic substances into ever larger unities" (42–43, 61 n). Rosemary Jackson, partly following Freud, suggests that the fantastic is always "a literature of desire, which seeks that which is experienced as absence and loss" (3). Intimate ties may well be experienced—certainly by a man whose life had as many personal tragedies as Frost's—as absence and loss, and desire for such ties may well lead the poet, in compensation, to combine man and man, man and woman, into particularly intense fictional pairs. Indeed, surely that is what happens in these four poems: such desire leads Frost at least momentarily to cast aside some of the restraint with which he normally constructs his fictions, to stretch the boundaries of believability in "An Unstamped Letter," "The Tuft of Flowers," and "Two Look at Two," and to cross them in "Iris by Night." Whether he successfully pulls off his flirtation with incredibility finally depends on the individual reader's response to such fictions; but surely Frost wants to draw our attention both to such fictions and, through them, to the claims he is making for the possible intensity of ties between tramp and farmer, worker and worker, friend and friend, or man and woman. The fact that these stories occasionally cease even apparently to imitate commonplace experience, and move instead into the realm of romance, where fictions imitate ritual or dream, makes Frost, surely, a more remarkable and daring poet than we have generally taken him to be. These poems celebrate genuine, rather than "aborted," communion between humans, a kind of communion actively taught and endorsed—in stories which are far from "minimalist," let alone "boring"—by a nature which is neither a "cosmological emptiness" nor "malevolent," "oblivious of us," "opaque, inert, mute." Frost's social vision in these poems is richer and more assertive than we have recognized, his desire for union is more unrestrained, his narrative strategies more daring, than we have been accustomed to assume.

CHAPTER 8

The Uses of a Tradition

So by craft or art
We can give the part
Wholeness in a sense. (441)

1.

What Frost says of *Walden*—that "it must have had a good deal to do with the making of me"—might equally well be applied to the whole Emersonian and Thoreauvian tradition of reading enlightenment in the natural world. Not only many of the intellectual assumptions, but many of the sensuous details of that tradition contribute, as we have seen, to Frost's poetic achievement. Yet, inevitably, any tradition that helps to shape a poet's work will also in some ways be a limiting condition as well as a source of strength. Frost's roots in the tradition of reading meaning in nature are inevitably responsible for some of the boundaries of his poetic world as well as some of its triumphs.

Structurally, for instance, Frost's relative conservatism, his tendency not to experiment with radical new forms, is undoubtedly related to his "synecdochist" assumptions. After all of the examples considered in the four previous chapters, it should be clear that Frost works a large number of variations on the basic structure of his emblem poems: the descriptive portions of the poems vary from lyric to narrative, from general to specific, from sketchy to detailed; the balance between descriptive portion and translation varies enormously; some poems have a single movement from emblem to lesson, some a dual movement, some a graphic division between, others an intermingling of, the two parts; and the methods of reading the natural lesson vary from explicit meditation to almost direct natural annunciation;

177

from direct statement to gentlest implication; from conceptual deduction to affective reaction. Yet, even granting the full variety of his synecdochic structures, and the twists and turns that Frost works on them especially in the meditative and heuristic poems, one cannot help but be struck by the pervasiveness of the basic structural pattern in a large portion of Frost's lyrics. (Obviously, the narrative-dialogue poems and the masques are another matter.) In a century of prolific structural experimentation—from *Mauberley* and *The Waste Land* to later Yeats and much of Stevens and Williams—Frost's consistency in structuring his nature lyrics is a sharp exception to the general rule.

The essential difference between Frost's characteristic structures and those of his more experimental peers is clearly a function of continuity or discontinuity. From *Mauberley* to the mosaic sections of Stevens's longer poems, the hallmark of twentieth-century poetic structures is, almost without exception, discontinuity—a tendency which of course reflects many of the critical problems of twentieth-century experience (and has thus affected painting as well as poetry). Frost's structures, by contrast, are not only predominantly synecdochic but consistently continuous, even linear; there is never any sharp break, structurally or psychologically, between emblem and lesson in any of Frost's many variations on the synecdochic structure.

As I suggested in chapter 3, Frost's synecdochism also helps to explain his lack of interest in a long poem. (I pass over *A Masque of Reason* and *A Masque of Mercy* as inessential parts of Frost's canon.) One of Emerson's journal entries quoted in that chapter is very nearly a rationale (or a rationalization) for a canon of short poems: "all the laws of nature may be read in the smallest fact. So that the truth speaker may dismiss all solicitude as to the proportion & congruency of the aggregate of his thoughts, so long as he is a faithful reporter of particular impressions." It is hard to conceive of a clearer case in which a poet's roots in a particular tradition—the Emersonian conception of symbol or synecdoche—have been at least partially responsible for a major structural limitation of the poet's accomplishment.

Yet it is also true, as I have suggested, that to read Frost's lyrics only as synecdochic microcosms is to read them only partially. There are at least two senses in which the individual poems are pieces in a comprehensive mosaic. It is possible, first, to read the seasonal lyrics, in a rough parallel to *Walden,* in a sequence that begins with a dark vision of spring and summer, largely in the fablelike and prototypical emblem poems; continues through the unrelieved loss and deathliness of the autumn poems and the bleak winter poems in the same two groups; has its peripeteia in the meditative and heuristic (and some prototypical) poems of winter transformation; rises through the bright spring of the meditative poems, and reaches a climax in "The Quest of the Purple-Fringed." Or, more inclusively, it is possible to read the whole body of Frost's nature lyrics as parts of an overall imaginative drama: from the struggle against the dominance of external fact in most of the fablelike and prototypical poems, through the Promethean conquest of such fact in the meditative poems, to the final reconciliation of imaginative desire and external reality, and the location of the self in various contexts, in the heuristic emblem poems. Thus, despite Frost's lack of a long poem in the usual sense, his nature lyrics might all be said to be parts of an overall work in a stricter sense than is true of the miscellaneous lyrics of most poets. Leaving aside the issue of conscious authorial ordering, the macropoetic unity of Frost's nature lyrics is not unlike the unity of *The Temple,* where Herbert—a kindred spirit of Frost's in several respects—in some sense achieves a long poem, though only three or four of the individual pieces are more than seventy lines long.

Beyond the question of structural limits, Frost has occasionally been charged with a certain narrowness of range—of subject matter, of emotion and tone, and of style. Particularly in the area of subject matter, one effect of the nature-writing tradition seems clear: it has made the variety of Frost's subjects appear narrower than it actually is. Like his regionalism, Frost's natural fictions can be taken naively, so that he appears to be a poet concerned largely with orchises, meadows, oven birds, woods, and snowstorms. Beneath such natural fictions, as we have seen, a close reading of the poems shows a remarkable breadth of intellectual concerns—greater, I would be prepared to argue, than Stevens's. But the range of those underlying concerns is partially disguised by the similarity, and the familiarity, of the natural fictions which Frost uses to talk about them. His interest in epistemological issues of every sort, in poems like "For Once, Then, Something" and "A Passing Glimpse," or in the question of poetic belatedness, in poems like "The Oven Bird," "The Tuft of Flowers," and "The Most of It," is less obvious than Stevens's; his love poems, like "A Late Walk" and "Never Again Would Birds' Song Be the Same," are less obvious than Yeats's; his war poems, like "I Will Sing You One-O," "November," and "Pod of the Milkweed," are less obvious than those of Pound or most other poets of the two world wars. If, like most of his major contemporaries, Frost has made no startling breakthroughs in subject matter, he has nonetheless—as I want to argue shortly—dealt substantially with the central issues of human thought and experience in this century.

In the same way, Frost's ties to the nature-writing tradition have probably minimized the apparent range of the emotions and tones in his verse. Some modes he clearly does not attempt—the confessional, the denunciatory, the hieratic (with the partial exception of "Directive"), the rhapsodic. Otherwise, he has struck probably as wide a range of emotional and tonal chords as most of his contemporaries, but they have sounded less disparate for being filtered through—in a sense, muted by—his nature fictions. Beneath the apparent similarity of those fictions, Frost has been able, in poems like "Desert Places" or "The Strong Are Saying Nothing," to register a sense of desolation at least dimly suggestive of John Berryman's; or, in poems like "Moon Compasses," "The Tuft of Flowers," and "The Quest of the Purple-Fringed," to record an affectionate acceptance which some readers will find no less moving than the more explosive ecstasies of Gerard Manley Hopkins or Dylan Thomas.

The central limit of Frost's poetry, in fact—arguably the single trait that most defines it and distinguishes it from the poetry of others—is its resolutely, almost invariably, restrained tone. Whether we choose to characterize Frost's dominant stylistic chord as "simple" or "common," with Marie Borroff (*Language and the Poet* 6, 29), "vernacular," with Poirier (22, 138, 146), "middle," with Denis Donoghue (171), or "Good Drab," with Auden (342), the fact remains that Frost's manner of speaking in the lyrics has a certain self-enforced restraint; it seldom if ever rises to the musical or incantatory heights which are reached at times, in their very different ways, by the bardic voices of Yeats and Eliot and Stevens. (And when, on rare occasions, Frost *does* try to reach that higher note—I think especially of moments in two poems about Edward Thomas, the last three lines of "A Soldier" and the last ten or twelve lines of "Iris by Night"—he somehow falls short of his most powerful effects.)

What are the causes of this stylistic restraint, even narrowness? A great deal of it, certainly (as Marie Borroff has shown), has to do with vocabulary—and yet Yeats, for one, often shares Frost's penchant for a commonplace diction approximating the normal spoken language. Some of it, also, has to do with syntax, with the shape of Frost's sentences. In the lyrics no less than in the narrative or dialogue pieces (or in the masques), these are intended to reproduce the conversing voice, rather than the chanting bard—as Frost points out in his numerous statements about "the sound of sense," "sentence sounds," the need for a speaking voice in every line of poetry. In addition, some of this tonal restraint issues from Frost's ties to the tradition of American nature writing. With its roots in a substantially pietistic attitude toward the created world, both in the seventeenth and in the early nineteenth centuries, that tradition encourages an anti-Promethean kind of imaginative modesty, and so may encourage a kind of restraint in the speaking voices of its adherents—in Bryant as opposed, say, to Whitman, in Thoreau as opposed to Emerson, in Frost as opposed to Stevens. In this respect, too, Herbert offers an instructive parallel, his voice, too, restrained in part by the imaginative humility of the tradition from which his poetry springs.

And yet, as we saw in chapter 6, Frost is not always anti-Promethean. Tonally, the most remarkable fact about the four groups of poems I have discussed is surely that in the Promethean poems—at the very height of asserting the primacy of human imagination, desire, will, and knowledge over external nature, in poems like "There Are Roughly Zones," "Wild Grapes, " and "On a Tree Fallen Across the Road"—the voice of Frost's lyrics *remains* vernacular, simple, common, middle, and good drab. To compare the tone of the final six lines of the latter poem to an equivalent passage from "The Idea of Order at Key West" is to be fairly well amazed at the way in which Frost succeeds in making his greatest claims by understatement. (The same effect may be seen in comparing "Hyla Brook" or "The Quest of the Purple-Fringed" with "Credences of Summer.") And, at such moments, it seems to me that we arrive at something distinctly more deep-seated than Frost's roots in the emblem-reading tradition or any other intellectual force. Such moments make it clear, surely, that, beyond his theories of "sentence sounds" and his intellectual historical roots, Frost's refusal to raise his poetic voice is a matter of core temperament. There is an unalterable something in Frost's psyche or spirit which, for whatever reasons, simply distrusts and refuses to yield completely to any extraordinary inspiration (Whitman's "divine afflatus") or immoderate release. As Norman Holland and others have hinted, the depths of Frost's psyche must be inhabited by some kind of fears—of acute failure, and hence, perhaps, of the consequences of exuberance?—which Stevens, for instance, simply doesn't feel. And yet, of course, Frost's poetry also proves how much can be accomplished, how much *can* in fact be claimed, without ever going beyond something like poetic understatement.

2.

Throughout the preceding chapters, I have noted ways in which Frost adapts the emblem-reading tradition to his own modernist purposes. It may be useful to attempt a brief summary of a few of those adaptations, and to ponder what they tell us about Frost's habits of mind.

A word, first, about Frost's use of two traditional subclasses of metaphor, apostrophe and personification. Both of these figures, of course, are widely used by nineteenth-century American nature writers—again, the archetype may well be Bryant—to evidence the intimate relationship they feel with the natural world, which is not just seen as human but actually spoken to (Bryant addresses, among many others, both the water fowl and the fringed gentian). In the twentieth century, obviously, we find only rare survivals of straightforward direct address to the natural world. In his early poems, Frost may apostrophize an insect ("My Butterfly," 1894) or a breeze ("To the Thawing Wind," 1913) straightforwardly, in poems which show how directly he comes out of Bryant's tradition. By the time of "Tree at My Window," however (1927), Frost apostrophizes the tree only in playful terms; this is not so much a serious invocation of the tree as a tour de force, a performance designed to show how thoroughly tree and poet can be seen as mirroring each other (whence an opening line like "Tree at my window, window tree"). Or, in "Choose Something Like a Star" (1943), to use its original title, Frost may begin by directly addressing the star (though again with a good deal of wit—e.g., the virtual title "your loftiness"). But this apostrophe is functional in a modernist sense; it is designed to act out the excessive anthropocentrism—"Talk Fahrenheit, talk Centigrade"—which can, in our century, interfere with genuine learning from nature. Frost abandons apostrophe after the first fifteen lines of the poem, the shift to third person ("It gives us strangely little aid, / But does tell something in the end") acting out precisely the broadening of perspective, the overcoming of anthropocentrism, which is necessary if we are to read the sky in our time.

A similar shift from the straightforward to the playful and ironically pointed can be seen in Frost's personification of nature. Again, early poems may personify storms ("Storm Fear") or dead leaves ("Reluctance") fairly straightforwardly. In later poems, Frost continues to personify threatening forces in nature largely without irony—the wind and the rain in "Lodged," the waves in "Once by the Pacific," the "heartless and enormous Outer Black" in "A Loose Mountain"; for him, personification remains a useful way to convey a sense of animism and of menace in the natural world. But even in as early a poem as "The Oven Bird" (published in 1916), we find Frost using personification, too, to make ironic modernist points about the natural world. The oven bird is "a singer" who "knows" how to sing without really singing; three times in the course of the first ten lines, "He says" something. And yet, of course, these tropes are partly ironic—because this "singer" can't really "say" anything; as we see in the famous closing of the poem, he can at best "frame" his "question" "in all but words." For Frost as for Stevens, only human singers can use words. Or, as we saw in chapter 7, Frost may personify the elm tree, pump, and fence post in "The Need of Being Versed in Country Things"— again to make an ironic point: that any solicitude such things "feel" is not for human beings. Thus he succeeds, in effect, in standing personification on its head, using it, not to show the close ties between the human and the natural, but the distance between them.

Again, as we saw in chapter 7, Frost bends, adapts, and plays off the conventional opposition between natural peace and social strife. He may simply complicate that opposition, as he does in "Range-Finding," where human warfare is not opposed but matched by natural predation. He may complicate but still use it, as he does in "The Thatch," where human disorder spreads into and is reflected by nature, as might be said to happen in the scene depicting the slaughter of the pigeons in *The Pioneers*. In Frost's poem, however, the protagonist, seeing that disorder reflected in nature, implicitly learns to resist his own destructive impulses. And, especially in the egregious fictions of "The Tuft of Flowers" and "Iris by Night," Frost may go so far as to imagine natural order influencing and endorsing human order. In such remarkable stories he has, in effect, not so much ironized as intensified the nineteenth-century convention, implicitly claiming that natural order can actively help to shape social order.

Finally, in his use of two fundamental commonplaces of the emblem-reading tradition—those of correspondences generally, and of the particular case of the seasonal myth, or analogies between "outer" and "inner weather"—Frost again both complicates the conventions and uses them. In the locus classicus, "Desert Places," correspondences operate not just conventionally, or positively—that is, the snow-buried ground corresponds to the "blanker whiteness" of the speaker's loss of creative power—but inversely, or negatively—the ultimate measure of the depth of the speaker's "own desert places" is that the "empty spaces / Between stars" can*not* match or serve as emblems for them. Likewise, in the particular case of seasonal correspondences, Frost sometimes uses these traditionally or straightforwardly: autumn corresponds to a feared loss of will or determination ("The Onset"), winter to imaginative hibernation ("Desert Places"), summer to imaginative fulfillment ("The Quest of the Purple-Fringed"). But he is, again, able to do more with the convention—to use spring, with dark irony, as a season in which the imagination feels threatened by the power of external forces ("Spring Pools" or "The Strong Are Saying Nothing") or winter, with considerably brighter irony, as a season in which the imagination is freed from the threat of such forces, either by dominating them ("On a Tree Fallen Across the Road") or by finding a reassuring kind of kinship with them ("Looking for a Sunset Bird in Winter").

In adapting all of these legacies of the emblem-reading tradition, Frost often lights on ironies; he relishes the twist or complication or inversion of a commonplace. But, partly because he does relish such twists, because he takes inordinate pleasure in pulling off such poetic tricks, these ironies strike me as much less dark than those which Harold Bloom finds in Frost.[1] In every one of these cases, in adapting and using a convention Frost succeeds in eating his cake—that is, in complicating, twisting, or ironizing the convention—and having it, too—that is, retaining some of the force of the tradition. However he may modernize or modify such conventions, he does not throw them out. The result, the curious hybrid of such traditions and modernist forces in Frost, is not only a measure of modern displacement from nineteenth-century certainties and comforts, but also, in every case, a carryover of the kinds of ties invoked by the tradition.

It is certainly true, as many critics since Lionel Trilling have pointed out, that Frost regularly qualifies his positive, traditional assertions. But these qualifications run the gamut from very large indeed, as with the last line of "Design," to the moderate, as with the "Unless it was" in "The Most of It," to the very nearly minimal, as with the "As if" in the penultimate line of "Two Look at Two." The whole point of the latter poem, surely, with its elaborate pairings and dance, is to suggest that the human and the natural do, at least in some ways at some times, reflect each other; and the point of many of the other heuristic emblem poems is that, at moments such as those in "Looking for a Sunset Bird in Winter" or "The Quest of the Purple-Fringed," we can feel "as if" earth cares for us, just as we care for it. And, for anyone familiar with modern science, what greater claim is possible? Thus it seems worth insisting that, while contemporary critics may be drawn especially to the ironist side of Frost, readers of all sorts, many of them far from naive, may also legitimately be drawn to a more old-fashioned side of the poet. As Jay Parini puts it, "Frost's poetry stays in the mind, providing comfort and consolation, as well as a coherent sense of the world" (938). Beyond irony, beyond striking visions of darkness, surely this is one of the qualities we most require of any poet—and find, with little sense of discomfort, in Stevens and Eliot and Yeats. Frost, it seems clear, is still suffering from a critical reaction or overreaction against the wise, omniscient, reassuring (sometimes smug) persona which he created for himself in his lifetime. We do not need to return to that pop culture persona to find something more than irony, blackness, "celebrated negativity," or "authentic nihilism" (Bloom, "Introduction" 3) in Frost's poetry. It is true, for instance, that many readers will miss some of the levels of meaning in, some of the complications which lie behind, the last line of "Hyla Brook": "We love the things we love for what they are." But, whether we read that line naively and simplistically or with all of the complications available in the preceding fourteen lines, it remains a powerful line, and may still serve the essential function of poetry, still serve as a vade mecum.

3.

As Frost adapts the tradition of reading the book of nature to his own purposes, he inevitably acquires some limitations, as we saw at the beginning of this chapter. But I am chiefly interested in the positive advantages which Frost gains from being rooted in that tradition, the intellectual resources which it provides him for coming to grips with major problems a century after Emerson. Most of the uses which I want to summarize here involve intellectual or imaginative history, but the first one is a strictly poetic, or even practical, use.

As all of his important critics have agreed, Frost has succeeded in creating a distinct, recognizable, and vital poetic world—the only achievement, in the final analysis, which can claim for any poet our lasting attention. Frost's poetic world is, as any such world must be in order to be distinct and recognizable, at least partly self-referential. We come to understand any one of his lyrics only by reading it in the context of all the others—and by learning to recognize the cumulative meaning, the repeated and varied nuances, of the various elements in it: dark woods, brooks, birches, natural guides, mowing, whiteness, lostness, the seasons of the year, and so on.

Yet Frost's participation in the tradition of reading the vegetable text helps to make his poetic world less thoroughly self-referential than the poetic worlds of most of his important contemporaries—certainly less so than Yeats's or Stevens's, probably less so than Pound's or Eliot's. By constructing them in terms of natural objects, landscapes, and events, and by seeming to report a kind of natural experience, Frost guarantees that his fictions will refer not only to each other, and to a literary tradition, but also to a common external reality—and that simple fact explains in large measure why Frost's poetic world has been accessible to a larger audience than have those of his peers. "Hyla Brook" and "The Quest of the Purple-Fringed" represent imaginatively perceived ideals as surely as "Sailing to Byzantium" and "Byzantium"; and all four poems are self-referential to some extent, fully understood only in terms of other poems by Frost or by Yeats. But, because Frost's poems are not as insistently self-referential—because, unlike Yeats's, they do not seek to leave behind "That . . . country" of ordinary (natural) experience—"Hyla Brook" and "The Quest of the Purple-Fringed" are more easily approached by the common reader.

The fact that Frost's poetic world is significantly mimetic has implications not only for his audience but also for his strategies in dealing with some of the most perplexing intellectual problems of this century. Those problems, like the characteristic structures of modern poetry which reflect them, involve above all discontinuity, disjunction, or fragmentation of various sorts. In such a century of disjunction and dislocation, an intellectual and imaginative tradition which both assumes the existence of some essential bonds and moves forcefully to discover the shape of them might be of considerable use to a poet. Frost's emblem-reading tradition, in fact, helps him to cope with three discontinuities which may be the most crucial of all those confronting a modern writer.

The first of these, to which the mimetic qualities of Frost's fictions point us, is probably the most basic and inescapable of all: the Cartesian. Frost is profoundly aware of the division that may exist between the perceiving mind and its objects, as we have seen not only in chapter 1 but even in the heuristic emblem poems. That awareness pervades the lyrics, both in their philosophical propositions and in their very workings. It informs the basic opposition in some of the fablelike and prototypical emblem poems, between ocean and shore in "Once by the Pacific," between desire and natural process in "Spring Pools," between autumn or winter and "the heart of man" in many of the seasonal poems. The same opposition remains central—only the balance between the terms changes—to most of the meditative emblem poems. It is hard to imagine a clearer statement of Cartesian dualism than the closing assertion of "A Soldier" that "the obstacle that checked / And tripped the body, shot the spirit on / Further than target ever showed or shone." Even in some of the heuristic emblem poems—particularly those which, like "The Need of Being Versed in Country Things," warn against potential dangers in the reading process—Frost stresses his awareness not only of the difference, but also of the distance, between the human and the nonhuman.

Yet all of Frost's lyrics, without exception, speak of a continuous ebb and flow of perception, thought, concern, and action between the human and the natural. Such unremitting interchange is made possible, above all, by the notion of correspondences which Frost ultimately inherits from the seventeenth century by way of Swedenborg and Emerson and which, I have argued in chapter 1, provides a remarkably effective solution to the Cartesian dilemma. If physical facts "correspond to" spiritual facts, then—though the two realms may remain distinct, as they do through the window in "Tree at My Window" or across the wall in "Two Look at Two"—they may provide material for reflection in both of Frost's senses. Because objects are never merely objects, but always signs, materiality and meaning, far from being hopelessly severed, are inextricably linked.

As a result of that kind of philosophical assumption, Frost's poetic vision regularly (though certainly not always) moves to narrow the interval between human observer and nonhuman surroundings, and, under propitious circumstances, to bridge it—though without usurping the autonomy of either pole. Such a movement occurs clearly in prototypical emblem poems like "Mowing," "Hyla Brook," and "Moon Compasses"; in at least one notable meditative poem, "Birches"; and in numerous heuristic poems, like "The Quest of the Purple-Fringed," "The Tuft of Flowers," and "Two Look at Two." Such spanning of the Cartesian gap cannot be accomplished by Promethean idealism, because that approach transcends or conquers one term in the equation (the natural). It can be accomplished only by means of an imaginative recognition and acceptance of, and enthusiasm for, the other—by "sheer morning gladness at the brim." Or, in Frost's own recurrent term, it can be accomplished only by means of love: "the earnest love that laid the swale in rows"; "The mower in the dew had loved them thus"; "We love the things we love for what they are"; "So love will take between the hands a face"; "Love has earth to which she clings"; "Earth's the right place for love"; "As if the earth in one unlooked-for favor / Had made them certain earth returned their love."

Through such love or acceptance of the natural—a distinctly Thoreauvian impulse—Frost often succeeds, like Browne and Milton before him, in reuniting the book of nature and its human reader. What is more, such love—along with its Melvillian inverse, the sheer dread of natural forces which we have seen in chapter 1 and in poems like "Reluctance" and "A Winter Eden"—essentially obviates for Frost the great danger of all idealist approaches, that of solipsism. Such love and such dread both assure the poet of a constant sense of the otherness of the natural world—without which sense any modern writer, however powerful in his assertive moments, lives with the constant danger of being pulled into the black hole of solipsism. Such a danger lurks behind Emerson's idealism;[2] it even causes Stevens to wonder, for a moment, "have I lived a skeleton's life, / As a disbeliever in reality, / A countryman of all the bones in the world?" (*Palm* 396). In one mood Stevens knows that "The greatest poverty is not to live / In a physical world" (262); that is a poverty that Frost, whatever his other meagernesses, never suffers. Whatever desert places may beset him internally or externally, the solipsistic void is not one of them.

In terms of poetic traditions, what Frost has achieved in this balance or reconciliation of the terms of the Cartesian dilemma—by falling neither into materialism nor into idealism or solipsism—is to find a middle way between (to oversimplify greatly) the Wordsworthian and the Blakean extremes.[3] The human is never wholly absorbed and ossified by the natural, as in the Lucy poems; nor, with a few Promethean exceptions, is the natural burned away or washed off by the imagination, as in *A Vision of the Last Judgment* or *Milton*. It is a rare balance in twentieth-century poetry—yet so necessary a balance that even writers as Promethean at other times as Yeats (in "The Circus Animals' Desertion" and "News for the Delphic Oracle") and

Stevens (in "Angel Surrounded by Paysans" and "Not Ideas About the Thing but the Thing Itself") move toward it near the ends of their lives.

One of the traits which make Cartesian dualism the most pernicious in modern thought is that it so readily gives rise to other dualisms. Wordsworth, in many respects the prototypical modern poet, demonstrates, for instance, how the Cartesian dilemma can ramify into a second major problem for romantic and postromantic poets: the problem of time. For Wordsworth the process of aging, the fall into adulthood, is destructive chiefly because it exacerbates the problem of the mind's potential separation from its surroundings; it entails, apparently inevitably, a loosening of the intimate ties with nature which the poet recollects from early childhood.

For many of the major poets who come after Wordsworth, the problems of time—change, loss, decay, impermanence, old age, ultimately death—may not be so clearly and causally related to the question of the mind's ties with external nature. But, whether those problems manifest themselves chiefly in personal terms, as with Shelley, Keats, Tennyson, and Yeats, or chiefly in cultural terms, as with Arnold, Eliot, and Pound, they come to haunt modern poetry almost, at times, obsessively. They are, in essence, the inevitable problems of a purely natural or human faith, the inescapable consequences of the lapse of medieval and Renaissance belief in a power transcending time.

At first glance Frost appears to be a major exception to this modern preoccupation with the problems of time. Where, one might ask, are Frost's poems lamenting the loss of an idealized past, his equivalents to "Tintern Abbey" or "The Wild Swans at Coole"?[4] Particularly in view of his own longevity, where are his poems about growing old? As Auden remarks: "In Frost's poems the nostalgic note is seldom, if ever, struck. When he writes a poem about childhood like 'Wild Grapes,' childhood is not seen as a magical Eden which will all too soon, alas, be lost, but as a school in which the first lessons of adult life are learned" (348). In perhaps the one poem in which he makes a clearly Wordsworthian assertion of the power of memory—"I Could Give All to Time"—Frost still leaves no room for nostalgia in the familiar sense. The despoiler in that poem is not the Wordsworthian source of personal loss, but "Time" in a highly impersonal geological sense. Where is the pathos in "such a planetary change"?

If we look at the question more closely, however, we find that Frost inevitably deals with the modern quandary posed by time—but that he does so in an essentially non-Wordsworthian fashion. (That is why we do not hear the Wordsworthian "nostalgic note" in his poems.) Frost distinctly recognizes temporal discontinuity, for instance, in the restrained but highly charged language of the last stanza of "Reluctance":

> Ah, when to the heart of man
> > Was it ever less than a treason
> To go with the drift of things,
> > To yield with a grace to reason,
> And bow and accept the end
> > Of a love or a season?

Here, unmistakably, is the material of genuine nostalgia or pathos: "the end / Of a love or a season." In all of the autumn poems from "My November Guest" or "The Onset" to "Bereft" or "November," many of which are also set at the end of day, we find, indeed, a longing for that which has slipped away. And the same kind of longing colors other seasonal poems as well: the recollection of spring ("When pear and cherry bloom went down in showers / On sunny days a moment overcast") in a summer poem like "The Oven Bird"; the recollection of bright summertime moments in winter poems from "My Butterfly" to "Looking for a Sunset Bird in Winter."

We discover on closer examination, in other words, that Frost has indeed written a large number of poems which record and regret the loss of earlier times of brightness. If we do not recognize the Wordsworthian "nostalgic note" in such poems, it must be only because Frost's nostalgia is of a different quality from Wordsworth's or Yeats's or Dylan Thomas's.

The key to that difference, again, lies in the nature fictions which Frost uses in his poems about the erosions of time: evening, autumn, or the other seasons of the year. All of those fictions, significantly, involve cycles. By seeing the losses brought about by time in the metaphorical context of the four seasons and similar fictions, Frost is in effect viewing time and mutability in cyclical, rather than linear, terms, at least within the confines of the individual's experience.[5] (And, for whatever reasons, Frost never strikes the Arnoldian note of cultural nostalgia; his geological perspective may involve the destruction of many things by time, but—perhaps because of the sheer scope of such loss—it never moves the poet to nostalgia.) A basically cyclical or periodic view of time within the individual's experience precludes the finality which makes loss so difficult to bear in the Wordsworthian or linear vision of time; any loss is likely to be seen, instead, as temporary, to be followed by renewal or recovery of one sort or another. That pattern is especially clear in poems like "The Onset," "The Cocoon," and "Pod of the Milkweed."

Admittedly, a cyclical view of time also entails some inevitable negative consequences. The new and vital will always run down into the quotidian, as we see in "Nothing Gold Can Stay" and "Spring Pools"; what is usually thought of as fulfillment may turn out to be diminishment ("The Oven Bird"); and even the most genuine and complete fulfillment will always, inevitably, decay ("The Quest of the Purple-Fringed"). But the dynamic balance of an essentially periodic view of time does, in any event, spare Frost the irreversible and unredeemable losses of the Wordsworthian vision.

Furthermore, for Frost, as for Thoreau and for Stevens, a predominantly seasonal or cyclical view of time makes it easier to deal not only with external mutability but also with its Wordsworthian and Coleridgean concomitant, the loss of imaginative power. In winter the imagination may be frozen in weakness and torpor ("too absent-spirited to count"), cowed by the huge blank of completely alien natural fact ("A blanker whiteness of benighted snow / With no expression, nothing to express"). But winter paralysis will presumably be followed, as even Shelley suggests, by the springtime "thawing" or "melting" or stirring of the active mind. Loss, again, tends to be temporary, and to be succeeded by renewal.

All of this is true, I think, of the nature lyrics. But it must also be recognized, if we look at Frost's canon as a whole, that the deepest poems of loss which he might have written—particularly those responding to the seemingly endless series of family tragedies—were not obviated or mitigated by any imaginative tradition, but simply repressed by the poet's profound personal reticence. If Berryman can work the major sequence of the *Dream Songs* largely out of the suicide of his father, what might a confessional Frost have wrought out of the illnesses, physical and mental, and the deaths of his sister, wife, and children? But "a confessional Frost" is, of course, an oxymoron, all but unimaginable. Even when he approaches a family tragedy, as "Home Burial" surely approaches the death of his first child, Frost deflects the poem's focus—whether to sublimated expressions of human helplessness ("'Three foggy mornings and one rainy day / Will rot the best birch fence a man can build'") or to the marital strains which result from the child's death. Here there is no question of being sustained by intellectual traditions.

If we take Wordsworth as our model, the two most obvious and crucial discontinuities besetting modern poetry are the two we have just considered—the Cartesian and the temporal. But Wordsworth's poetry also foreshadows a third kind of disjunction which, growing at least partly out of Cartesian dualism, comes to trouble romantic and postromantic literature: the lack of meaningful ties between human beings. The problem is suggested in Wordsworth not only by the prominence of such solitaries as Lucy, Michael, the leech gatherer, and the poet figure himself, but also by Wordsworth's preoccupation (as he puts it in the "Prospectus" to *The Recluse*) with "the individual Mind that keeps her own / Inviolate retirement."

The removal of the individual from a vital social context stands out as a concern of nineteenth- and twentieth-century American fiction (and, to a lesser but increasing extent, British fiction). More even than fiction, modern poetry is thoroughly dominated by the individual perception or imagination, from all of the romantics (with the single, partial exception of Coleridge), through the Victorians, to Yeats, Eliot (despite his Christianity), and Stevens. Furthermore, despite Wordsworth's theory in *The Prelude* of "Love of Nature Leading to Love of Man," in the long tradition of American nature writing, the love of nature usually necessitates withdrawal from human society. Deerslayer cannot marry Judith Hutter or Mabel Dunham if he is to maintain the purity and intensity of his ties with the wilderness. Bryant, Emerson, and Thoreau must all "leave . . . the world of villages and personalities behind" (Emerson, *Collected Works* 3: 101) and enter the solitude of the woods in order to find "the most sweet and tender, the most innocent and encouraging society" (*Walden* 131). In our own century, Nick Adams must break away from all human companions if he is to enter the waters of "Big Two-Hearted River"; and Isaac McCaslin, reenacting the spiritual celibacy of Natty Bumppo, must give up his worldly wife along with his ancestors' land if he is to remain worthy of the hunt and the wilderness. Yet Frost—of all American nature writers, the one whose reputation might most surely lead us to expect a kind of social atomism in his poetic vision—writes some of his most important poems "about fellowship."

Just as he is well aware of the potential ill effects of Cartesian dualism and of the passage of time, Frost knows the potential separateness of human beings. That fact is inescapable in "A Missive Missile," "I Will Sing You One-O," "The Tuft of Flowers," and others of the nature lyrics. It is if anything clearer still in many of the narrative and dialogue poems with which this study has not dealt—as can be seen in the loneliness of figures like Silas the hired man, the husbands in "The Hill Wife" and "Home Burial," and the protagonist of "An Old Man's Winter Night," or in the neurotic isolation of characters in poems like "A Servant to Servants," "The Fear," and "The Hill Wife."

Furthermore, as we saw in chapter 2, Frost follows Thoreau and the dominant tradition of American nature writing in calling for solitude as a necessary preparation for enlightenment in nature. Except in "Iris by Night" and "Two Look at Two," in all of Frost's nature lyrics such enlightenment is granted only to the solitary wanderer. Yet, as "An Unstamped Letter in Our Rural Letter Box," "The Thatch," and "The Tuft of Flowers" demonstrate, the vision given the solitary wanderer may well be a vision of social ties, a vision which leads him to return to the human community with his sense of "fellowship" strengthened by his solitary excursion.

Recurrently for Frost, that sense of ties between human beings depends on a common relationship with the created world.[6] As "The Tuft of Flowers" makes especially clear, it is love of nature which, in classic Wordsworthian fashion, leads to love of man; one's sense of fellowship with another worker, or of love shared with a woman, is nurtured by the sense of common ties with the vegetable text. This is not, for Frost, merely an attractive myth; it is a logical sequence. The natural world, the valued external reality, provides both a common epistemological basis for knowledge and a common language for communication between people—the latter function illustrated especially by the fiction of "The Telephone." As Eliot suggests in the closing section of *The Waste Land,* individuals are locked in the prisons of selfhood, kept from communicating, precisely by solipsism and the consequent lack of a shared reality. Since the natural world provides a sharable experience in Frost's vision, it may also serve as the basis for discourse and fellowship.

Why is Frost's vision of the possibilities of human ties, at least in certain poems, fuller than that of many other American poets and nature writers? The causes here, presumably, are psychological or biographical. As I suggested at the end of the preceding chapter, one must suspect a kind of compensatory drive, the response of a strong, healthy desire to the grim series of family tragedies which, along with the death of Edward Thomas in World War I, repeatedly broke off Frost's most intimate ties. That same response, one suspects, may also take the form of a correlative obsession with social recognition and reassurance, whether from friends, sycophants, or institutions.

Regardless of the intellectual, imaginative, or psychological reasons for it, Frost's social vision in the heuristic emblem poems represents in some ways the most remarkable of all his achievements in refusing to accept crucial modern discontinuities. Frost achieves his vision of "fellowship" despite being an American, though our culture has historically tended toward acute individualism; despite being an American nature writer, though that tradition has strongly emphasized the need for solitude as a means of apocalyptic preparation; despite being a modern poet, though all of the major poetic traditions since 1798 stress the supremacy of the individual mind; despite, finally, his own ungenerous political theories expressed again and again, not only in conversations and letters but also in many of the "editorial" poems of his last thirty years. It is this side of Frost which has driven a number of intelligent critics to attack his social vision as atomistic or worse. Malcolm Cowley, for instance, in a famous attack in 1944, suggests that "What Frost sets before us is an ideal, not of charity or brotherhood, but of separateness" or "self-centeredness" (346; rpt. 42). Denis Donoghue, more than twenty years later, concludes that Frost is a "Social Darwinist" (181–87). More recently, even as sympathetic a critic as David Bromwich (like Cowley, basing his conclusions substantially on "Two Tramps in Mud Time"), sees Frost as a poet of "charity denied" (220–26). The unsympathetic, ungenerous side of Frost's social vision cannot be wished away—but it is not the only side. At least in "An Unstamped Letter," "The Tuft of Flowers," "Iris by Night," and "Two Look at Two," and in fact in numerous other poems, Frost is capable of celebrating remarkably intense ties between people—though, admittedly, these exist not between groups, or between the individual and a group, but between pairs of human beings. At that level, Frost's social vision is remarkable not just for him but for any twentieth-century American writer.

Thus Frost shows that a poet with a feisty temperament, a genuine relish for imaginative difficulties, and the resources of a centuries-old tradition need not simply or passively accept the great social discontinuity of modern experience any more than the Cartesian or the temporal. Emerson writes that "it is dislocation and detachment from the life of God, that makes things ugly," and that the poet, because he "re-attaches things to nature and the Whole, . . . disposes very easily of the most disagreeable facts" (*Collected Works* 3: 11). Surely Frost would view the desire to "dispose" of any facts, even the most disagreeable, as a fatal kind of self-deception; he neither does so nor wants to do so. Yet he clearly and consistently is concerned with resisting many of the characteristic modern varieties of "dislocation and detachment," with "re-attaching things to nature and the Whole," and, by doing so, fulfilling a major part of the task which Emerson sets for the poet.[7] Using the emblem-reading tradition, modifying it, bending it, playing off it, Frost's nature lyrics move again and again to relocate both the synecdochic emblem and the individual emblem reader in a larger order of being, to show that the emblem—butterfly weed or decaying wood-pile or dried-up brook—is never just an isolated thing, and to help the reader "realize," as Thoreau puts it, "where we are and the infinite extent of our relations" (*Walden* 171). Or, in lines which come close to being a good summary of the ultimate impact of his use of the tradition, Frost suggests in "Kitty Hawk," in a section entitled "The Holiness of Wholeness," that "by craft or art / We can give the part / Wholeness in a sense." The qualifier here, the insistence that any wholeness we achieve is so only "in a sense," may well make this a more characteristic summary of Frost's poetic intent than the famous closing lines of "Directive." And what could be more fitting than that, in various senses—epistemologically, temporally, socially—Frost the synecdochist should, by his craft or art, "give the part / Wholeness"?

Notes

1. *"Assorted Characters"*

1. Quotations from Frost's verse are taken from *The Poetry of Robert Frost,* edited by Edward Connery Lathem. Short passages from poems not identified by title are followed by parenthetical page numbers referring to this edition.
2. Norman Holland suggests that the darker side of Frost's animism, at least, involves the projection of the poet's "dangerous wishes and fears within himself out onto the world around him" (32). Projection is presumably the underlying mechanism of any kind of animism. Whatever its psychological benefits, such a process—unless self-consciousness deflates the animism—clearly involves a poetic benefit: it makes the encounter with nature more dramatic than it would otherwise be.
3. The best general discussions of Frost's Emersonian and Thoreauvian heritage are by Alvan S. Ryan, Reuben Brower (56–74), James M. Cox, and George Monteiro (55–143).
4. See Lawrance Thompson's account in *Robert Frost: The Early Years* (xvi, 11–12, 20–21, 36, 70–71, etc).
5. For an enlightening historical account of the doctrine of correspondences between Herbert's time and Emerson's, see Wasserman.
6. When possible, quotations from Emerson's essays are taken from the currently ongoing Harvard edition of the *Collected Works;* for those essays not yet issued by Harvard, quotations are taken from the Centenary Edition of the *Complete Works.*
7. Of course, there are also moments in which correspondences are considerably less neatly arranged in Frost's practice than they are in Emerson's theory. See, for instance, Yoder's comments (185–86).
8. Frost was apparently concerned lest the playful remark about the tree's "tongues" be taken too seriously. Four years after first publishing the poem, he was still thinking about "deleting the second stanza" for fear that it might "keep the 'head' in the last stanza from ringing as it should" (*Letters to Untermeyer* 208).
9. See Irwin on the impact of Champollion's work in deciphering the Egyptian hieroglyphics on, and metaphorical extensions of the idea of hieroglyphics in, Emerson, Thoreau, Hawthorne, and Melville.
10. For lucid discussions of the historical background of the concept, see Martz (17–18, 54–57, 68–78, 146) and Madsen (113–44).
11. I am reading this passage as commentary simply on the "book of nature"—i.e., taking "printed page" and "bed of world-flowers" to be in apposition. It is certainly possible to take the two phrases as references to two distinct sources of wisdom, which would approximate the seventeenth-century notion of twin books of revelation—the "printed page" of biblical wisdom and the "bed of world-flowers" of natural revelation.

12. For useful summaries of the "book of nature" topos before Emerson, see Madsen (85–144) and Brantley (139–70).
13. On Frost and science, see (among others) Baym, Hiers, Harris, and Abel.
14. For this side of Emerson's geological perspective, see Whicher (150, 171).
15. In an irony characteristic of Frost's relationship with Emerson, the language of "Triple Bronze"—a deeply un-Emersonian poem—echoes Emerson's "Grace." In his poem, Emerson gives thanks for the "defences" of "Example, custom, fear, occasion slow," which have "me against myself defended," saving him from sins he might otherwise have fallen into (*Complete Works* 9: 359).

2. *"Eyes Seeking the Response of Eyes"*

1. The speaker is Meserve, the half-inspired, half-crackpot backwoods preacher in "Snow."
2. The basic image of "eyes seeking the response of eyes" recurs at least twice elsewhere in Frost: in the last two lines quoted from "Snow" as the epigraph to this chapter and in prose remarks about the attempt of infants to make fundamental human contact "by establishing correspondence of eyes with eyes" (*Selected Prose* 60–61).
3. A classic example is Malcolm Cowley's charge that Frost "does not strike far inward into the wilderness of human nature," that "even in his finest lyrics," he "is content to stop outside the woods, either in the thrush-haunted dusk or on a snowy evening" (43, 44). The general idea is echoed by critics as diverse as Isadore Traschen (62–65) and Richard Eberhart (260)—though Eberhart indicates a later reconsideration of this initial judgment.
4. Poirier, however, does not share my view that "The Sound of Trees" and "Into My Own" are genuinely extra-vagant poems; he finds only a "somewhat plaintive promise" to wander in the latter and a kind of "poetic four-flushing" in the prospective nature of both journeys (81, 82).
5. Frost uses the word in exactly its Thoreauvian, etymological sense (though in a comic context) in "A Record Stride." Emerson, too, recognizes the need for a kind of extra-vagance and return: "The daily history of the Intellect," he suggests, "is this alternating of expansions and concentrations. The expansions are the invitations from heaven to try a larger sweep, a higher pitch than we have yet climbed, and to leave all our past for this enlarged scope. Present power, on the other hand, requires concentration on the moment and the thing to be done" (*Complete Works* 12: 58). Frost echoes Emerson's formulation of the idea: "The most exciting movement in nature is not progress, advance, but expansion and contraction. . . . We explore and adventure for a while and then we draw in to consolidate our gains" ("The Poetry of Amy Lowell," *Christian Science Monitor*, May 16, 1925, 8; rpt. in Thompson, *The Years of Triumph* 278).
6. Neurotic repression and the relationship to nature are discussed more fully by Frank Lentricchia (53–54, 59–74) and by Poirier (111–35).
7. Frost quotes the last two quatrains of the poem, including these lines, in his essay "On Emerson" (*Selected Prose* 116).

8. Thompson argues convincingly that Frost wrote the poem to parody a couple of poems by Wade Van Dore (*The Years of Triumph* 360–62). Thompson also reports the original title (361).

9. Camille Paglia examines the implications of "erotic passivity" in Eolian metaphors in Wordsworth (302–3), Coleridge (318–19), and Shelley (378–80). Pursuing sexual implications, one might go so far as to suggest that, in "The Aim Was Song," the poet's holding the wind in his mouth "long enough for north / To be converted into south" and then "blowing it forth" is a rough analogy to germination and birth. If so, Frost's trope both greatly expands the usual Eolian figure and undermines Paglia's assumption that "female" always signifies passivity and "male" domination.

3. Synecdochism

1. A conversation in autumn 1958, reported in *Letters to Untermeyer* (376).

2. The 1915 date for the original statement is assigned by Thompson, in *The Years of Triumph* (485, 693n.23).

3. In "Good Greek," Sergeant also reports Frost as saying: "Imagery and after-imagery are about all there is to poetry. Synecdoche and synecdoche" (147). All three passages from Sergeant are quoted in Thompson, *The Years of Triumph* (693n.23).

4. The idea that nature is synecdochic occurs frequently in Emerson's writing, e.g., in *Nature* (*Collected Works* 1: 27), in "Compensation" (*Collected Works* 2: 59–60), and in the *Journals* (5: 136, 137).

5. The argument about the accuracy of "interval," and Frost's reaction to it, are reported by Thompson in *The Years of Triumph* 539n.28. The dedication of *A Further Range* stresses the dual meaning: "To E. F. for what it may mean to her that beyond the White Mountains were the Green; beyond both were the Rockies, the Sierras, and, in thought, the Andes and the Himalayas—range beyond range even into the realm of government and religion."

6. Many critics have touched on this trait. One commentator, for instance, writing of "Mowing," has noted "the scene's allusive and mythic qualities" (Paton 48). More generally, Robert Penn Warren has discussed Frost's use of "the suggestive-in-the-commonplace" and his technique of "developing images gradually from the literal descriptive level of reference to the symbolic level of reference" (129–30, 135). The trait is related to a central part of John F. Lynen's conception of pastoral in Frost: "Frost, like the writers of old pastoral, draws upon our feeling that the rural world is representative of human life in general. By working from this nodal idea he is able to develop in his poems a very broad range of reference without ever seeming to depart from particular matters of fact. . . . he gives us only the minute particulars of his own immediate experience; yet . . . the things described seem everywhere to point beyond the rural world" (19). Marie Borroff has written about "what may well be Frost's greatest gift: his ability to develop symbolic meaning with cumulative force, seemingly without art or effort, in naturalistically portrayed scene and action"

("'To Earthward'" 30). Finally, William H. Pritchard has noted "the movement from the level of sense to that of spirit," and suggested that "from the very beginning it lay at the heart of Frost's enterprise as poet" (20).

7. This is the subtitle of the original published version of "On the Heart's Beginning to Cloud the Mind."

8. For an interesting account of the manner in which Frost revised the poem to achieve greater compression, see Thompson, *The Years of Triumph* 565n.14.

4. *"Too Absent-Spirited to Count"*

1. What might be called Thoreau's "sacramentalism" in *Walden* comes close to defining the central attitude toward the physical world in American nature writing, a tradition of which Frost is very much part. Thoreau instinctively rejects one extreme attitude, that which would take the physical as adequate in and of itself; this is the attitude which underlies both materialism (attacked in "Economy" and elsewhere) and sensualism (denounced in "Higher Laws"). He is occasionally attracted to the opposite extreme attitude, that which turns away from the physical altogether (as his ascetic tendencies in "Higher Laws" suggest). But, in his most characteristic moments, and throughout the great majority of his writing, Thoreau rejects both extreme attitudes: he treasures the physical more than, say, Emerson, yet insists that it must always lead beyond itself to something more than physical—to ethical or spiritual lessons such as he finds in snakes, bugs, raising beans, or fishing. This double attitude might well be called sacramentalism, particularly in view of Thoreau's summary of the Mucclasse Indians' ceremony known as "the busk": "I have scarcely heard of a truer sacrament, that is, as the dictionary defines it, 'outward and visible sign of an inward and spiritual grace'" (*Walden* 69). Physical objects are always for Thoreau, as for an emblemist, outward and visible signs of inward and spiritual states.

2. It is worth noting the distinction between fablelike poems like "In Hardwood Groves," which imply natural process, and prototypical emblem poems like "Pod of the Milkweed," which expand the poet's original perspective on such process (see chapter 5). The former group of poems, by seeing a particular moment (e.g., the fall of the leaves) as implicitly part of a natural cycle, may invoke such a cycle in its totality; their effect is thus simply to see nature as processive, often in a machinelike way. The latter group of poems also see a particular moment (e.g., the summer's day when scores of butterflies assault the milkweed) as part of a larger cycle; but they implicitly direct our attention, not to the sheer fact of cyclicality, but to *a positive moment elsewhere in that cycle* which, in effect, compensates for the apparent loss or waste of the present moment.

3. Cf. Brower 37.

4. See Poirier's discussion of "Time and the Keeping of Poetry," especially 173–77.

5. Structurally, "Desert Places" and "The Onset" both reside on the border between "fablelike" and "prototypical" emblem poems. Both are nonprocessive,

with fairly general descriptions of habitual occurrences. I have chosen to discuss the former poem in this chapter, because it nicely complements "November," and to discuss "The Onset" in chapter 5, because it fits neatly with some other poems there. But I hasten to point out that, on structural grounds alone, "The Onset" might well be called "fablelike" and "Desert Places" "prototypical"; there is no hard, fast line between the two groups.

6. On the other hand, one might argue that "Sand Dunes"—which I have called a meditative or Promethean poem—is, in its structure and movement, a fablelike poem. If so, it would clearly be the exception to the idea that a nonprocessive poem prevents a triumphant imaginative response to dark circumstances. There, even within the confines of an arguably nonprocessive structure and of the sonnet form, the imagination is able to assert itself against natural assault.

5. *"What to Make of a Diminished Thing"*

1. "Balearic" is the name of the island group off the coast of Spain which includes Majorca and Minorca. In ancient times the natives of these islands were renowned for their skill as wielders of slingshots, the chief weapons they employed as mercenary soldiers. I am indebted to my colleague Thomas T. Mayo, professor of physics at Hampden-Sydney College, for straightening out my understanding of the astronomical phenomena described in this poem.

2. In the early version of the poem ("In White"), the moth is identified specifically as a "miller" moth. "Miller" (or "owlet") moth is a general term for the entire family *Noctuidae,* which includes more than twenty thousand different species. Most seem to be dull brown; some are largely white, but, as far as I know, none are wholly white.

3. The contrast is distinctly enhanced by the revisions which Frost made in the process of composition. See the manuscript version, called "In White," in Thompson, *The Early Years* 582n.25.

4. Interestingly enough, Emerson, too, is intrigued by the transcendental implications of the heal-all (or self-heal), which he takes as a symbol of the self-corrective powers of life—specifically, the ability of universal laws to express themselves in particular details despite our inordinate nearsightedness. He writes in the 1844 "Nature": "All over the wide fields of earth grows the prunella or self-heal. After every foolish day we sleep off the fumes and furies of its [the day's] hours; and though we are always engaged with particulars, and often enslaved to them, we bring with us to every experiment the innate universal laws. These, while they exist in the mind as ideas, stand around us in nature forever embodied, a present sanity to expose and cure the insanity of men" (*Collected Works* 3: 113). Both the emblem and the idea provide an interesting footnote to Frost's sonnet.

5. Thompson argues convincingly (*The Early Years* 383–88) that the specific link between Frost and the traditional argument from design is a passage in William James's *Pragmatism* (1907). James suggests that the traditional argument from design is no longer meaningful to thinkers in the twentieth century, not least

because it might just as easily be used to demonstrate the existence of a "diabolical designer" as of a benevolent providence.

6. As Holland notes of "Once by the Pacific"—and the notion is equally applicable to "Design"—such poems both "call up the kind of thing [Frost] most fears" and "manage that same" fear (32). It is no accident that both poems invoke dark visions in the tightly managed form of the sonnet.

7. "Pod of the Milkweed" was first published as Frost's Christmas poem for 1954; it was presumably written within a year of the end of the Korean conflict.

8. Frost also uses the word to mean something more than just "inhabitant"—to suggest a kind of imprisonment—in an early, lyric version of "The Black Cottage"; "The solitary inmate" of the cottage blesses "The bread of loneliness" (quoted in Thompson, *The Early Years* 592n.2).

9. Meserve learns essentially the same lesson, like Emerson from chickadees, in "Snow," lines 221–32.

10. "Moon Compasses" is all the more remarkable if we read it in its context in *A Further Range*. It comes in the midst of six or eight of the darkest poems of the *Taken Singly* group: "Desert Places," "Leaves Compared with Flowers," "A Leaf-Treader," "On Taking from the Top to Broaden the Base," "They Were Welcome to Their Belief," "The Strong Are Saying Nothing," "Design."

6. The Promethean Frost

1. Or again, in "The Figure a Poem Makes," Frost writes: "The impressions most useful to my purpose seem always those I was unaware of and so made no note of at the time when taken, and the conclusion is come to that like giants we are always hurling experience ahead of us to pave the future with against the day when we may want to strike a line of purpose across it for somewhere" (*Selected Prose* 19). This distancing of the imagination from the "crowding" present, this retrospective use of experience to pave the progress of the mind, is an important part of what Harry Berger has called Frost's strategy of "revision."

2. I would argue that "Sand Dunes," for instance—one of Frost's best poems, and unmistakably Promethean—is genuinely processive: that Frost describes the dunes in the first quatrain, meditates on their meaning in the second and third quatrains, and deduces their significance in the final quatrain. But it would not be unreasonable to see the poem's structure as very nearly nonprocessive (the dunes described in the first two stanzas, then their significance immediately read in the last two)—in which case "Sand Dunes" would have to be classified as a fablelike emblem poem, since its emblem is habitual. In other words, while I believe that processiveness, specifically the meditative pause, consistently accompanies Frost's Promethean impulses, I recognize that that claim is arguable. One might reason that the Promethean impulse is sufficiently powerful that it can express itself not only in an unmistakably meditative poem like "Wild Grapes," whose structure offers a clear invitation to imaginative

uprising, but even in a nonprocessive, fablelike poem, in which natural fact ought, by structural rights, to have the upper hand.

3. Thompson and Winnick report that Frost began the poem "in 1953 after a visit with his friends the Huntington Cairneses at Kittyhawk" (300).

4. Thus man's contemporary, if not his ideal, "relation to nature, his power over it, is through the understanding; as by manure; the economic use of fire, wind, water, and the mariner's needle; steam, coal, chemical agriculture; the repairs of the human body by the dentist and surgeon" (Emerson, *Collected Works* 1: 43).

5. Fifty years earlier, in "The Trial by Existence," Frost himself (like Blake) had apparently equated creation and birth with a kind of fall, into what he calls "The obscuration upon earth." Here, however, he reverses that attitude.

6. See William Doreski's comments on this and several other "wilderness poems": "The 'confrontation with nothingness,'" he suggests, "usually in Frost's poetry stirs at least a response—usually an affirmative one—from the beholder" (30–31). Or again: Frost's "epiphanies occur to spite nature, to fling humanist values in the face of that monumental indifference" (37). I agree with the latter statement in the case of "The Census-Taker" and the other Promethean poems; but, as I suggest in chapter 7, a number of Frost's most important visions occur with the fictive cooperation of the natural world.

7. See, for instance, Thompson (*The Early Years* 579–81n.6; *The Years of Triumph* 300–303) and Poirier (266–67).

8. Compare, for example, the astonishing scene at the end of Part 1 of "The Bear" in which Isaac McCaslin relinquishes rifle, watch, and compass in order to get lost and thus find the bear.

9. Marie Borroff has written about the simplicity of Frost's language perceptively and in substantial detail (*Language and the Poet* 23–41, "Sound Symbolism"). Indeed, she cites "On a Tree Fallen Across the Road"—an extremely Promethean poem—as a good example of Frost's characteristic "speaking voice," which she distinguishes from his rarer "chanting voice" ("Sound Symbolism" 134–35).

10. For differing views on the balance of these two forces in post-Emersonian American poetry, see Bloom (*Ringers* 291–321; *Figures* 67–88) and Yoder (especially chapter 8).

11. Frost's "inner dome of heaven" may also echo "the infinite dome / Of heaven" in "Mont Blanc."

12. See Bacon's comments (especially on 326) on the relationship of "Birches" to "Kitty Hawk."

13. See Hartman, especially 31–69.

14. It is also worth noting that the poem following this one in *A Further Range,* "The Figure in the Doorway," a narrative sequel to it, is about the human ties which may underlie even the most striking apparent isolation. Cf. Thoreau's views on true community in "Solitude" (*Walden* 130–34).

15. See the enlightening discussion of this passage and the vapor image in Hartman (16–18, 39–48); and Bloom's discussion of "the mists of natural imagination" in "Michael" (*Visionary Company* 183).

7. Tales of a Better Kind

1. If we were to read "Come In" as an emblem poem, it would be a dark analogue to "The Need of Being Versed." Again a preliminary reading of the natural emblem is the product of imaginative error; the poet is too quick to impose his own dispirited state of mind on the music of the darkling thrush, which thus sounds to him "Almost like a call to come in / To the dark and lament." But, in the corrective reading of the last stanza, the brighter side of the poet's spirit, led by a correspondingly brighter element of the natural scene—"I was out for stars"—persuades him to turn away from "the pillared dark." Now, from his corrected perspective, the poet concludes that the bird's call has not in fact been a Siren song: "I hadn't been" asked to "come in." Again, one of the poem's points is the danger of reading a too narrowly human meaning— menace no less than solicitude—into a natural emblem.

2. In the gloss to "The Tuft of Flowers" in *A Boy's Will.*

3. Again, as in the case of "Sand Dunes" in the previous chapter, I would argue that "Dust of Snow," though short, is processive—because, even in thirty-four words, the poem unfolds over a period of time: the emblematic event is narrated in simple past tense ("shook"), while the poet's reaction to it is narrated in present perfect ("has given"). But, again, I would not want to insist on the processiveness of the poem; one might, not unreasonably, consider it a prototypical emblem poem, in which case it would belong in the same group of lyrics with "The Cocoon" and "Our Singing Strength"—prototypical emblem poems involving winter or near-winter transformations.

4. I use the word advisedly, since I see this poem as the winter equivalent of "The Quest of the Purple-Fringed."

5. Again in "Rose Pogonias" Frost associates orchises with kneeling in a kind of worship.

6. Thompson reports that Susan Hayes Ward, poetry editor of *The Independent* and one of Frost's few early encouragers, accepted "The Quest of the Orchis" for publication when Frost sent it to her on January 15, 1901, but saved the lines "until she could give them a timely appearance at exactly the right moment in spring when the purple-fringed orchis should be in bloom," finally putting the poem in the June 27 issue (*The Early Years* 270).

7. Again, as so often in Frost, poetic form reflects vision: the "perfect poise" of the long *"a"* and *"c"* lines in the quatrains here against the short *"b"* lines imitates the "perfect poise" of midsummer which the poem celebrates.

8. This is true even of "A Considerable Speck," an all-too-typical example of the "political wit" which becomes more and more prominent in numerous poems of the thirties and forties. On structural grounds, "A Considerable Speck" is unmistakably a heuristic emblem poem, but, in its frivolous plot, sardonic tone, and ostensible point (a very small joke), the poem seems almost a parody of the other members of the group. Even it, however—considering as unpromising an emblem as a microscopic speck on a sheet of paper, and building to the weak literary joke of the closing couplet—enacts the essential drama of these heuristic poems. The poet recognizes that the "speck," which originally seems inanimate, is

in fact "a living mite"; soon realizes that it is possessed of both mind ("Plainly with an intelligence I dealt") and will ("With inclinations it could call its own"); and concludes, just before the anticlimactic final joke: "I have a mind myself and recognize / Mind when I meet with it in any guise." Beneath all the poetic husk of this small and undistinguished satire, in other words, lies the essential imaginative kernel of the heuristic emblem poems as a group: the reaching out of eyes or mind seeking to establish ties of recognition with a living other.

9. Bryant makes the same point in "A Forest Hymn," published eleven years before *Nature*. He too suggests that nature will teach human beings both religious lessons (lines 1–69) and ethical lessons (lines 90–118): "let me often to these solitudes / Retire," he says to the forest, "and in thy presence reassure / My feeble virtue."

10. Frost uses the term in "How Hard It Is to Keep from Being King When It's in You and in the Situation," in "The Figure a Poem Makes" (*Selected Prose* 18), and in numerous talks, as for instance in that at the Bread Loaf School of English, July 4, 1960, reported in Cook (146).

11. "I'll Sing You One-O" (or "One-Ho!"), also known as "Green Grow the Rushes-O," is a Scottish or English folk song.

12. One example which von Franz cites (206) is the helpful fox in Grimm's fairy tale "The Golden Bird"—an example which may remind us of the natural cicerone in "The Quest of the Purple-Fringed," the fox whose path leads the speaker to the orchis.

13. Indeed, the poem's story is so unlikely, and its lesson so insistent, that Poirier has been led to call it "a garden club invocation" (238). On the other hand, Poirier also misstates the plot of the poem, reporting that in it "a rainbow encircles a group, including Frost." The "group," in fact, consists only of the speaker and his friend.

14. The reference in these lines may be to some Latin account ("belief in Rome")—perhaps by Ovid or Plutarch—of the rebirth of Osiris (sometimes associated with the sun), whose body was rent into fourteen pieces and whose reintegration and rebirth heralded the renewal of the natural world. The story of Osiris, including his death, dismemberment, and rebirth, is of course told by Frazer in *The Golden Bough*. (I am indebted to Professor Grover Smith of Duke University for suggesting this line of explanation.) I know of no evidence, however, that Frost had read Frazer; there is no mention of any such reading in Thompson, for instance. The likeliest explanation would seem to be that Frost knew the story directly from some Latin source.

15. See Greenler, 143–46 and Plates 6–7 through 6–10. I'm grateful to Ed Kiess, professor of physics at Hampden-Sydney College, for helping me to understand the puzzling optical phenomena in "Iris by Night." Interestingly enough, Thoreau describes both a "halo of light around my shadow" and an extraordinary phenomenon involving a rainbow, in which he "stood in the very abutment of a rainbow's arch, which filled the lower stratum of the atmosphere, tinging the grass and leaves around, and dazzling me as if I looked through colored crystal" (*Walden* 202).

16. As Frost wrote of his wife a few months before her death, "She has been the unspoken half of everything I ever wrote, and both halves of many a thing from

My November Guest down to the last stanzas of Two Tramps in Mud Time" (*Letters* 450). And see Poirier's comments (63–71) on the relationship between sexual and poetic creativity in Frost.

17. And David Bromwich offers a similar reading of "The Wood-Pile" (17–19), though in his interpretation the latecomer is the reader rather than a belated poet.

8. The Uses of a Tradition

1. Bloom writes that "'Uriel's voice of cherub scorn,' once referred to by Frost as 'Emersonian scorn,' is the essential mode of irony favored throughout Frost's poetry" ("Introduction" 1). I find much irony, but little scorn, Emersonian or otherwise, in Frost's effective poetry.

2. See, for instance, Joseph F. Dougherty's convincing argument.

3. My argument, which deals with poetic practice, parallels Lentricchia's argument concerning esthetic theory: that Frost finds in William James's pragmatism a *"via media"* between the extremes of naturalism and idealism (3–14, 128–30, 152–53, 164–65, etc.).

4. Charles Berger has investigated this question in an essay on beginnings in Frost, suggesting basically that Frost demythologizes origins by recognizing "that all beginnings are fictions" (147). Anticipating my argument at one point, Berger notes that, in "Nothing Gold Can Stay," the fall from Eden is mitigated by the analogy with "dawn go[ing] down to day," which implies a cyclical conception of time.

5. In terms of social history, this cyclical view of time is clearly old-fashioned, and allies Frost with the early nineteenth rather than the twentieth century. Michael O'Malley's study of "how American ideas about time and its authority changed" argues that "In the nineteenth century, time changed from a phenomenon rooted in nature and God to an arbitrary, abstract quantity based in machines, in clocks" (ix). In his first chapter, O'Malley's description of the American view of time before the wide acceptance of clocks is certainly reminiscent of much in Frost's seasonal poems. Almanacs, for instance, placed the individual's life in the framework of astronomical, meteorological, and vegetable cycles (13–19).

6. Poirier, in his discussion of "sexual love and poetic making" (especially 64ff.), basically argues the obverse: that only after he has found reassurance in his relationship with the lover can the poet find meaning in the natural world; "a man alone" as in "The Most of It" "cannot see or hear anything in nature that confirms his existence as human" (71). Clearly, however, the process works the other way around in many of the heuristic emblem poems.

7. Emerson is essentially following Wordsworth, who defines the poet as "carrying every where with him relationship and love" (*Literary Criticism* 52).

Works Cited

A. Primary Works

Blake, William. *The Poetry and Prose of William Blake*. Ed. David V. Erdman. Garden City, N.Y.: Doubleday, 1965.

Browne, Sir Thomas. *Religio Medici. Selected Writings*. Ed. Geoffrey Keynes. Chicago: U of Chicago P, 1968. 1–89.

Cook, Reginald L. *Robert Frost: A Living Voice*. Amherst: U of Massachusetts P, 1974.

Emerson, Ralph Waldo. *The Collected Works of Ralph Waldo Emerson*. Ed. Alfred R. Ferguson et al. 4 vols. Cambridge, Mass.: The Belknap Press of Harvard UP, 1971– .

———. *The Complete Works of Ralph Waldo Emerson*. Ed. Edward Waldo Emerson. Centenary ed. 12 vols. Boston: Houghton Mifflin, 1903–4.

———. *The Early Lectures of Ralph Waldo Emerson*. Ed. Stephen E. Whicher, Robert E. Spiller, and Wallace E. Williams. 3 vols. Cambridge, Mass.: Harvard UP, 1959–72.

———. *The Journals and Miscellaneous Notebooks of Ralph Waldo Emerson*. Ed. William H. Gilman et al. 16 vols. Cambridge, Mass.: The Belknap Press of Harvard UP, 1960–82.

Faulkner, William. "The Bear." *Go Down, Moses*. New York: Random House, 1942.

Freud, Sigmund. *Beyond the Pleasure Principle (Jenseits des Lustprinzips). The Standard Edition of the Complete Psychological Works of Sigmund Freud*. Trans. and ed. James Strachey. London: The Hogarth Press, 1921–23. 18: 7–64.

Frost, Robert. *The Letters of Robert Frost to Louis Untermeyer*. New York: Holt, Rinehart and Winston, 1963.

———. *The Poetry of Robert Frost*. Ed. Edward Connery Lathem. New York: Holt, Rinehart and Winston, 1969.

———. *Prose Jottings of Robert Frost*. Ed. Edward Connery Lathem and Hyde Cox. Lunenburg, Vt.: Northeast-Kingdom Publishers, 1982.

———. *Selected Letters of Robert Frost*. Ed. Lawrance Thompson. New York: Holt, Rinehart and Winston, 1964.

———. *Selected Prose of Robert Frost*. Ed. Hyde Cox and Edward Connery Lathem. Collier Books, New York: Macmillan, 1968.

Lathem, Edward Connery. *Interviews with Robert Frost*. New York: Holt, Rinehart and Winston, 1966.

Quarles, Francis. "To the Reader," preface to *Emblemes. English Seventeenth-Century Verse*. Ed. Louis L. Martz. New York: Norton, 1973. Vol. 1, 223.

Stevens, Wallace. *The Palm at the End of the Mind: Selected Poems and a Play*. Ed. Holly Stevens. New York: Random House, 1972.

Thoreau, Henry David. *The Journals*, in *The Writings of Henry David Thoreau*. 20 vols. Boston: Houghton Mifflin, 1906.

———. *Walden*. Ed. J. Lyndon Shanley. Princeton: Princeton UP, 1971.

———. *A Week on the Concord and Merrimack Rivers*. Ed. Carl F. Hovde et al. Princeton: Princeton UP, 1980.

Wordsworth, William. *Literary Criticism of William Wordsworth*. Ed. Paul M. Zall. (Regents Critics Series) Lincoln: U of Nebraska P, 1966.

B. Secondary Works

Abel, Darrel. "The Instinct of a Bard: Robert Frost on Science, Logic, and Poetic Truth." *Essays in Arts and Sciences* 9 (1980): 59–75.

Auden, W. H. "Robert Frost." *The Dyer's Hand and Other Essays*. New York: Random House, 1962. 337–53.

Bacon, Helen. "Dialogue of Poets: *Mens Animi* at the Renewal of Words." *Massachusetts Review* 19 (1978): 319–34.

Baym, Nina. "An Approach to Robert Frost's Nature Poetry." *American Quarterly* 17 (1965): 713–23.

Bell, Vereen. "Robert Frost and the Nature of Narrative." *New England Review and Bread Loaf Quarterly* 8 (1985): 70–78.

Berger, Charles. "Echoing Eden: Frost and Origins." *Modern Critical Views: Robert Frost*. Ed. Harold Bloom. New York: Chelsea House, 1986. 147–65.

Berger, Harry, Jr. "Poetry as Revision: Interpreting Robert Frost." *Criticism* 10 (1968): 1–22.

Bloom, Harold. *Figures of Capable Imagination*. New York: Seabury P, 1976.

———. "Introduction" to *Modern Critical Views: Robert Frost*. New York: Chelsea House, 1986. 1–7.

———. *The Ringers in the Tower: Studies in Romantic Tradition*. Chicago: U of Chicago P, 1971.

———. *The Visionary Company: A Reading of English Romantic Poetry*. Revised and enlarged ed. Ithaca: Cornell UP, 1971.

Borroff, Marie. *Language and the Poet: Verbal Artistry in Frost, Stevens, and Moore*. Chicago: U of Chicago P, 1979.

———. "Robert Frost: 'To Earthward.'" *Frost: Centennial Essays II*. Ed. Jac Tharpe. Jackson: UP of Mississippi, 1976. 21–39.

———. "Sound Symbolism as Drama in the Poetry of Robert Frost." *PMLA* 107 (1992): 131–44.

Bradford, M. E. "Artists at Home: Frost and Faulkner." *Modern Age* 30 (1986): 274–82.

Brantley, Richard E. *Wordsworth's "Natural Methodism."* New Haven: Yale UP, 1975.

Bromwich, David. *A Choice of Inheritance: Self and Community from Edmund Burke to Robert Frost*. Cambridge: Harvard UP, 1989.

Brower, Reuben A. *The Poetry of Robert Frost: Constellations of Intention*. New York: Oxford UP (Galaxy Books), 1963.

Cowley, Malcolm. "The Case Against Mr. Frost." *The New Republic:* Sept. 11, 1944, 312–13; Sept. 18, 1944, 345–47. Rpt. in *Robert Frost: A Collection of Critical Essays*. Ed. James M. Cox. Englewood Cliffs, N.J.: Prentice-Hall, 1962. 36–45.

Cox, James M. "Robert Frost and the End of the New England Line." *Frost: Centennial Essays*. Ed. Committee on the Frost Centennial of the University of Southern Mississippi. Jackson: UP of Mississippi, 1974. 545–61.

Derrida, Jacques. "Nature, Culture, Writing." *Of Grammatology*. Trans. Gayatri Chakravorty Spivak. Baltimore: Johns Hopkins UP, 1976. 95–316.

Donoghue, Denis. *Connoisseurs of Chaos: Ideas of Order in Modern American Poetry.* New York: Macmillan, 1965.

Doreski, William. "Robert Frost's 'The Census-Taker' and the Problem of Wilderness." *Twentieth Century Literature* 34 (1988): 30–39.

Dougherty, Joseph F. "Emerson and the Loneliness of the Gods." *Texas Studies in Literature and Language* 16 (1974): 65–75.

Eberhart, Richard. "Robert Frost in the Clearing." *Southern Review* 11 (1975): 260–68.

Feidelson, Charles, Jr. *Symbolism and American Literature.* Chicago: U of Chicago P, 1953.

Frye, Northrop. *Anatomy of Criticism: Four Essays.* New York: Atheneum, 1966.

———. *The Secular Scripture: A Study of the Structure of Romance.* Cambridge: Harvard UP, 1976.

Greenler, Robert. *Rainbows, Halos, and Glories.* Cambridge: Cambridge UP, 1980.

Harris, Kathryn Gibbs. "Robert Frost's Early Education in Science." *South Carolina Review* 7 (1974): 13–33.

Hartman, Geoffrey. *Wordsworth's Poetry 1787–1814.* New Haven: Yale UP, 1964.

Hiers, John T. "Robert Frost's Quarrel with Science and Technology." *Georgia Review* 25 (1971): 182–205.

Holland, Norman N. *The Brain of Robert Frost: A Cognitive Approach to Literature.* New York: Routledge, 1988.

Hollander, John. *The Figure of Echo: A Mode of Allusion in Milton and After.* Berkeley: U of California P, 1981.

Irwin, John T. *American Hieroglyphics: The Symbol of the Egyptian Hieroglyphics in the American Renaissance.* Baltimore: Johns Hopkins UP, 1980.

Jackson, Rosemary. *Fantasy: The Literature of Subversion.* London: Methuen, 1981.

Jarrell, Randall. "To the Laodiceans." *Poetry and the Age.* New York: Knopf, 1953. 37–69. Rpt. in *Robert Frost: A Collection of Critical Essays.* Ed. James M. Cox. Englewood Cliffs, N.J.: Prentice-Hall, 1962. 83–104.

Lea, Sydney. "From Sublime to Rigamarole: Relations of Frost to Wordsworth." *Studies in Romanticism* 19 (1980): 83–108.

Lentricchia, Frank. *Robert Frost: Modern Poetics and the Landscapes of Self.* Durham: Duke UP, 1975.

Lynen, John F. *The Pastoral Art of Robert Frost.* New Haven: Yale UP, 1960.

Madsen, William G. *From Shadowy Types to Truth: Studies in Milton's Symbolism.* New Haven: Yale UP, 1968.

Martz, Louis L. *The Paradise Within: Studies in Vaughan, Traherne, and Milton.* New Haven: Yale UP, 1964.

Monteiro, George. *Robert Frost and the New England Renaissance.* Lexington: UP of Kentucky, 1988.

O'Malley, Michael. *Keeping Watch: A History of American Time.* New York: Viking Penguin, 1990.

Oster, Judith. *Toward Robert Frost: The Reader and the Poet.* Athens: U of Georgia P, 1991.

Paglia, Camille. *Sexual Personae: Art and Decadence from Nefertiti to Emily Dickinson.* New Haven: Yale UP, 1990.

Parini, Jay. "Robert Frost." *The Columbia Literary History of the United States.* Ed. Emory Elliott et al. New York: Columbia UP, 1988. 937–46.

Paton, Priscilla M. "Robert Frost: 'The fact is the sweetest dream that labor
    knows.'" *American Literature* 53 (1981): 43–55.

Poirier, Richard. *Robert Frost: The Work of Knowing.* New York: Oxford UP, 1977.

Porter, David. *Emerson and Literary Change.* Cambridge: Harvard UP, 1978.

Pritchard, William H. *Frost: A Literary Life Reconsidered.* New York: Oxford UP,
    1984.

Rotella, Guy. *Reading & Writing Nature: The Poetry of Robert Frost, Wallace
    Stevens, Marianne Moore, and Elizabeth Bishop.* Boston: Northeastern UP, 1991.

Ryan, Alvan S. "Frost and Emerson: Voice and Vision." *Massachusetts Review* 1
    (1959): 5–23.

Sergeant, Elizabeth Shipley. "Robert Frost: A Good Greek out of New England."
    New Republic: 30 Sept. 1925: 144–48.

———. *Robert Frost: The Trial by Existence.* New York: Holt, Rinehart and Winston,
    1960.

Simic, Charles. "Visionaries and Anti-Visionaries." *Denver Quarterly* 24 (1989):
    114–23.

Thompson, Lawrance. *Robert Frost: The Early Years 1874–1915.* New York: Holt,
    Rinehart and Winston, 1966.

———. *Robert Frost: The Years of Triumph 1915–1938.* New York: Holt, Rinehart
    and Winston, 1970.

——— and R. H. Winnick. *Robert Frost: The Later Years 1938–1963.* New York:
    Holt, Rinehart and Winston, 1976.

Todorov, Tzvetan. *The Fantastic: A Structural Approach to a Literary Genre.* Trans.
    Richard Howard. Ithaca: Cornell UP, 1975.

Traschen, Isadore. "Robert Frost: Some Divisions in a Whole Man." *Yale Review* 55
    (1965): 57–70.

Untermeyer, Louis. "Robert Frost" (introduction to poems). *Modern American
    Poetry / Modern British Poetry.* Combined Mid-Century Ed. New York:
    Harcourt, Brace, 1950. 178–82.

von Franz, M[arie]-L[ouise]. "The Process of Individuation." *Man and His Symbols.*
    Ed. Carl G. Jung. New York: Doubleday, 1964. 158–229.

Warren, Robert Penn. "The Themes of Robert Frost." *Selected Essays.* New York:
    Random House, 1958. 118–36.

Wasserman, Earl R. "Nature Moralized: The Divine Analogy in the Eighteenth
    Century." *ELH* 20 (1953): 39–76.

Whicher, Stephen E. *Freedom and Fate: An Inner Life of Ralph Waldo Emerson.* 2nd
    ed. Philadelphia: U of Pennsylvania P, 1971.

Wilbur, Richard. "Poetry and Happiness." *Responses: Prose Pieces: 1953–1976.*
    Harvest Books ed. New York: Harcourt Brace Jovanovich, 1976. 91–114.

Wilde, Oscar. "The Decay of Lying." *The Artist as Critic: Critical Writings of Oscar
    Wilde.* Ed. Richard Ellmann. New York: Random House, 1969. 290–320.

Wyatt, David M. "Frost and the Grammar of Motion." *Southern Review* 16 (1980):
    86–99.

Yoder, R. A. *Emerson and the Orphic Poet in America.* Berkeley: U of California P,
    1978.

Index